# The United States
# and
# World Poverty

# The United States and World Poverty

## and

## World Poverty

by

### E. Boyd Wennergren

### Donald L. Plucknett

### Nigel J. H. Smith

### William L. Furlong

### Joan H. Joshi

Seven Locks Press
Cabin John, MD / Washington, DC

Copyright © 1989 by Seven Locks Press

**Library of Congress Cataloging-in-Publication Data**

The United States and world poverty / by E. Boyd Wennergren . . . [et al.].
    p.    cm.
    Includes bibliographical references.
    ISBN 9-932020-76-3: $10.95
    1. Economic assistance, American—Developing countries. 2 Food supply—
Developing countries. 3. Poor—Developing countries. 4. United States—
Commerce—Developing countries. 5 Developing countries—Commerce—
United States. I. Wennergren, E. Boyd.
HC60.U65   1989
338.9'17301724—dc20                                    89-10757
                                                                            CIP

Manufactured in the United States of America
Typeset by Robert Rand
Figures by New Age Graphics
Printed by McNaughton & Gunn, Inc., Saline, MI

For more information, contact:
    Seven Locks Press
    P.O. Box 27
    Cabin John, MD 20818
    (301) 320-2130

# Contents

# List of Tables and Figures

# Appreciation

*The United States and World Poverty* became a reality because of the commitment and assistance of many people. The authors are grateful for the numerous reviews of both the original version and this manuscript. Special thanks are due to Eileen Fesco of Utah State University for extensive research assistance with the first edition, to Dr. Kelly White and Dr. Ed Overton of the USDA Economic Research Service for their invaluable help in updating the data, and to Dr. Earl Kellogg of the Consortium for International Development for his critical review of chapter 3. Editors Lois Cox and Jane Gold deserve extraordinary commendation for their devotion to clarity and accuracy. Finally, the authors want to acknowledge the financial support of Utah State University and of the Agency for International Development, whose grant under the Biden-Pell development education program provided the initial impetus for the production of this volume.

# Foreword

Hunger and malnutrition are pervasive phenomena in our global village. They are more significant in our global village than they really ought to be. Surely a country with the technological prowess and the political will to send a person to the moon should be able to ensure that its citizens have a nutritionally adequate diet. In low-income developing countries, hunger and malnutrition are far more pervasive and, in some cases, a much more urgent problem for policymakers.

It is easy to be jaded by and to distance ourselves from the television shorts or even the full-length documentaries that appeal to our emotions by showing pictures of dying children and starving mothers. But the issue is of very direct interest to U.S. citizens, and it is so in ways that affect our own welfare and prosperity. Hunger and malnutrition are symptoms of an international economic and political system that has gone awry. In the interdependent world in which we now live, the welfare and prosperity of other countries strongly influence our own economic welfare. It behooves us to use our creativity, energy, and resources to help solve these problems.

*The United States and World Poverty* is about these issues. It is the story, in part, of U.S. efforts to assist people in other countries in their struggle toward economic development. In particular, it is the story of U.S. efforts to contribute to a better-fed world and of the role of international trade and development efforts to address the problem of hunger.

It is common for observers of the international scene to believe that hunger is primarily a production or supply problem that can be solved by national self-sufficiency and the carrying of adequate stocks. Nothing could be further from the truth. Hunger, malnutrition, and even famine are largely the result of poverty and inadequate means to purchase available supplies. No better example can be found than India: despite her recent success in achieving self-sufficiency, hundreds of millions of Indians are still inadequately nourished.

The United States and other developed countries have committed significant resources over the years to strengthen agriculture in developing countries. The motivation behind those programs is not just to produce large supplies of food to feed even larger numbers of people. Instead, agricultural development is the key to alleviating poverty in those countries since the bulk of their poor people can be found in the rural sector. But agricultural development is also critical to alleviating urban poverty. The reduction in food prices that is made possible by increased supplies is equivalent to an increase in real income for all consumers. More important, such an increase in real income rebounds especially to the poor, who spend a larger (and in most cases, a major) share of their available income on food.

Representatives of some important commodity groups in the United States have missed this important linkage. They see only the supply side of such programs and fail to see the equally large if not larger effects on the demand side. Available evidence indicates that strengthening the agriculture of developing countries can lead to increased imports from the United States. It can do that by giving consumers in those countries the means to improve their diets.

By focusing on these interdependencies, *The United States and World Poverty* throws light on one of the important policy issues facing this nation and the world at large, thereby highlighting what a truly interdependent world we live in. For this reason, it should be valuable supplementary reading for students in both political science and economics courses, as well as for those in more general education programs.

G. Edward Schuh, Dean
Hubert H. Humphrey Institute
of Public Affairs
University of Minnesota

# Introduction

This book is an update of an earlier one entitled *Solving World Hunger: The U.S. Stake,* published in 1986. The revisions are primarily found in the numerical data used to demonstrate the nature of the world hunger problem and the role played by the U.S. foreign assistance program. The general problems, issues, and solutions, however, remain essentially the same as analyzed in 1986. Similarly, the need for U.S. participation and for public awareness and support persists and is perhaps even more critical today.

In his 1949 inaugural address, President Harry Truman committed the United States to assist in the development of poorer nations, an endeavor that has come to be known as the Point Four program. With his pronouncement, the United States embarked on a worldwide effort, later supported by other developed nations, to rid the planet of poverty and hunger.

The expanded assistance that has evolved has been both praised and criticized. Some see it as an ethical issue involving basic humanitarian obligations to contribute to both the welfare of the poor and international security. Others call it a wasteful and ineffective squandering of U.S. resources that could be better used at home. Most Americans, though, do not know enough about the program to have an informed opinion.

This book tries to eliminate that information gap. It provides a perspective on issues of world hunger and poverty, and a discussion of why and how the United States participates in solving related problems. As the public gains in understanding of the issues, their informed concern may help generate new solutions and create the needed long-term commitment to eliminate hunger from the planet.

It is worth noting here that one of the most difficult problems facing those who write about international development issues is the choice of a terminology that is neither inaccurate nor pejorative to describe countries other than those known as "Western industrialized" or "Eastern bloc." To refer to India, Burkina Faso, and Colombia as "developing" countries is to suggest there are nations already "developed" when, in fact, all nations are in constant change. Indeed, on some indicators of development—infant mortality is a case in point—the United States is surpassed by so-called developing nations.

The authors of this book have opted for two terms: *less developed countries,* or *LDCs,* and *countries of the Third World,* neither entirely satisfactory. For example, LDCs include such economically diverse nations as Bangladesh with a GNP of $160 in 1986 and Kuwait with a GNP of $13,890. They include countries with such vastly different political and social systems as Cuba and Singapore. The term *Third World,* on the other hand, which some deplore as suggesting "third class," was first used by a French journalist in 1952 to describe nations seeking freedom from their colonial rulers just as commoners—the Third Estate—pursued liberty, equality, and brotherhood with the nobility and clergy during the French Revolution. In this context, the industrialized nations have come to be known as the First World; the Eastern bloc nations, as the Second World. More recently, in an attempt to deal with the diversity noted, some have begun to refer to a Fourth World of nations—those with the lowest growth and fewest resources. (The division of the world into a developed North and a less developed South, while equally inaccurate, is still another categorization and is discussed in chap 5.)

# ONE

# Hunger, Poverty, and Constraints on Development In the Third World

## E. Boyd Wennergren

The world hunger problem is characterized by an imbalance or inadequate distribution of people and food, and has both immediate and long-run features that threaten the welfare of millions. Instances of hunger and malnutrition occur when people are unable to obtain an adequate share of the world's supply of food. The Food and Agriculture Organization (FAO) of the United Nations (UN) estimates that as many as 500 million people suffer from hunger and the effects of malnutrition. The Overseas Development Council (ODC) estimates that in 1980, as many as 400 million people in developing nations lived in absolute poverty. The Hunger Project estimates that 13 to 18 million people die each year from hunger. For the most part, these conditions are chronic. They are a daily fact of life.

Periodically, conditions worsen dramatically and people in famine-affected regions are thrown into a food crisis that subjects them to starvation and the increased threat of immediate death. These short-run crises are usually precipitated by political unrest, drought, or floods that create even greater disequilibrium between food supplies and people. Food crises are part of the anatomy of the world hunger problem, but while they are most often the outgrowth of chronic conditions made worse, they are not the essence of the long-term problem that confronts the less fortunate people of the world. That problem is typified by the insidious advance of malnutrition and hunger into the lives of millions of people, subjecting them to rampant disease, excessive infant mortality, limited life expectancy, and a truly substandard quality of life. (Appendix table 1.1 provides data on some of these basic indicators for about 140 nations.)

The nature of the long-term problem can be illustrated by looking at the differences in per capita supplies of calories (energy) and protein in various regions of the world during 1983–85 (figure 1.1 and appendix table 1.2). The per capita supply of calories in developing nations averaged about 9 percent below the world average. Developed nations averaged about 27 percent above the world average. For developing nations, the general pattern worsened somewhat for protein supply when both vegetable and animal sources were considered. (These data are virtually unchanged from the years 1980–82.) Only African, Far Eastern, Middle Eastern, and Latin American countries were below the world average. Most of the world's less developed countries (LDCs) are contained in these four regions. The poor within wealthy or developed nations are typically not considered to be part of the world hunger problem.

The numbers of malnourished or hungry people in an area are mostly calculated in terms of how many individuals do not receive that area's standard minimum of daily calories needed to support a person's normal growth and/or development. The differences in standards depend on age and sex distributions, the average size of people, work patterns, weather, and other local factors. The requirements are aggregate per capita averages for individual nations; these are compared with the estimated national average per capita availability of calories to determine the adequacy of the diet. Because it is difficult to measure these variables accurately and because averages do not reveal who does and does not receive food, it is clear that calorie and protein data provide only approximate information about the location and numbers of hungry people. There is general agreement, however, that food shortages are most critical in the developing nations of Africa and Asia, and somewhat less so in Latin America and the Middle East.

Food shortages, inadequate food distribution, and other conditions that are often dramatized to focus on the world hunger problem are merely symptomatic expressions of more fundamental causes of world hunger, the principal one of which is poverty. People are chronically hungry and malnourished because they are poor. In LDCs, poverty first limits the ability of people to purchase

**Figure 1.1  Per Capita Food Supply, 1983–85**

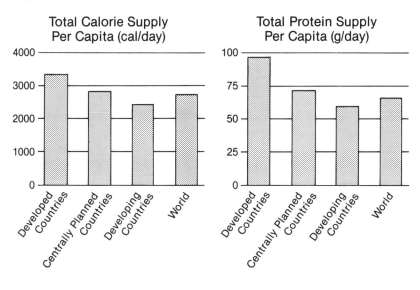

Source: ERS/USDA, Agriculture and Trade Indicators Branch, January 1989.

food. (Poor people have little, if any, money to spend on food.) At the same time, people in LDCs also lack the money and energy to invest in learning and applying production-increasing technology to produce food for their families. The hunger problem is thus a poverty-induced dilemma with two horns: too little money-backed demand (people need food but cannot buy enough) and too little supply. Combine aggregate poverty with unprogressive agriculture; soaring population growth; poor income distribution; and inadequate social, political, and economic systems and policies, and the result is a dilemma of staggering complexity. At its apex, however, is the inability of people to purchase and produce adequate amounts of food.

In simple terms, the widespread presence of poverty in LDCs creates a gap between the demand for food and the capacity of agriculture to supply adequate amounts. If the issues are approached in terms of this gap, the components that determine the supply of and demand for food can be identified and considered along with other complex factors that affect food issues. The potentials for feeding the world's projected population can also be examined in this context.

## DEMAND FOR FOOD

As an economic concept, the demand for food is one of many different needs that people must satisfy with whatever purchasing power they can command. An individual's ability and willingness to pay for food will help define his or her demand (but not need*) for food. Demand implies the ability to buy, whereas need is based on nutritional requirements whether or not money is available for buying food.

Increases in income, however, do not necessarily mean equal increases in the demand for food. Part of any expanded income may be spent on nonfood items. This discriminatory tendency is higher for people with incomes that already exceed the poverty level. When incomes are minimal, most increases will be spent for food. As incomes continue to rise, however, smaller and smaller proportions of the new income are spent on food, and the composition of the diet shifts from staples (e.g., cereals) to nonstaples (e.g., fruit and vegetables).

At a more personalized level, tastes and preferences for specific foods are conditioned by cultural and social traditions as much as or more than by nutritional need. For example, people in Asia want a high proportion of rice in their diet while people in some regions of Africa show an equally strong preference for corn.

Within a nation, then, the total demand for food reflects the sum of demand by individuals and is, in economic terms, a function of population size, per capita income, and learned preferences. These determinants must be clearly understood before existing and projected worldwide demands for food can be calculated, and effective strategies to balance supply and demand put in place.

### Population Trends and Impacts

Today's population and its growth rate make the world hunger problem more urgent that it ever was in the past. Since 1950, the world has experienced an unparalleled explosion in population, from 2.5 billion in 1950 to 5.1 billion in 1988 (figure 1.2). In other

---

*Food need is a normative concept of what requirements would be if all people ate according to some officially defined nutritional statndard. Using this concept, aggregate food is defined by the food consumption per person required to meet the nutrional standard and the number of people to be fed. Demand, in contrast, has economic and personal choice facets.

**Figure 1.2 World Population and Growth, 1950–88**

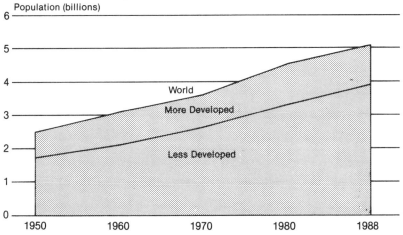

Source: Population Reference Bureau, Inc., "1988 World Population Data Sheet."

words, during those 38 years, more people were added to the population than existed in 1950. At the 1988 growth rate of 1.7 percent annually, however, the 5.1 billion population of 1988 may be expected to double in about 40 years. By comparison, it took the world several million years to reach its present population.

This rapid expansion in numbers of people has had a dramatic impact on the need for food. The nature of that impact can be better understood by looking at population growth patterns in different nations and regions during the period (table 1.1). Several important points are demonstrated by these data.

- Of the 15 most populated nations in the world in 1988, 8 (including China) were LDCs. Moreover, the same 8 LDCs comprised the list in 1985.
- Of the 23 nations having 5 million or more people and the highest population growth rates, 18 were LDCs that had per capita incomes of less than $1,000 per year.
- All of the 26 nations with the slowest population growth rates were developed nations. West Germany, Hungary, and Denmark had negative growth rates in both 1985 and 1988, meaning that their populations were declining.
- Growth rates have declined even in some LDCs, but their overall rates are still much higher than those of developed nations. The average is about 2 percent annually for all

## Table 1.1a  World's Most Populous Nations, 1985 and 1988

|  | Population (millions) | |
|---|---|---|
|  | 1985 | 1988 |
| China | 1042.0 | 1087.0 |
| India | 762.2 | 816.8 |
| USSR | 278.0 | 286.0 |
| United States | 238.9 | 246.1 |
| Indonesia | 168.4 | 177.4 |
| Brazil | 138.4 | 144.4 |
| Japan | 120.8 | 122.7 |
| Nigeria | 91.2 | 111.9 |
| Bangladesh | 101.5 | 109.5 |
| Pakistan | 99.2 | 107.5 |
| Mexico | 79.7 | 83.5 |
| Vietnam | 60.5 | 65.2 |
| Philippines | 56.8 | 63.2 |
| West Germany | 61.0 | 61.2 |
| Italy | 57.4 | 57.3 |
| WORLD | 4846.8 | 5110.8 |

## Table 1.1b  World's Fastest Growing Nations (5 million or more)

|  | 1985 | | 1988 | |
|---|---|---|---|---|
|  | Population (millions) | Annual Growth Rate (percent)* | Population (millions) | Annual Growth Rate (percent)* |
| Kenya | 20.2 | 4.1 | 23.3 | 4.1 |
| Syria | 10.6 | 3.9 | 11.3 | 3.8 |
| Rwanda | 6.3 | 3.6 | 7.1 | 3.7 |
| Zambia | 6.8 | 3.3 | 7.5 | 3.7 |
| Tanzania | 21.7 | 3.5 | 24.3 | 3.6 |
| Zimbabwe | 8.6 | 3.5 | 9.7 | 3.5 |
| Iraq | 15.5 | 3.3 | 17.6 | 3.5 |
| Uganda | 14.7 | 3.5 | 16.4 | 3.4 |
| Saudi Arabia | 11.2 | 3.0 | 14.2 | 3.3 |
| South Yemen | 6.1 | 2.7 | 6.7 | 3.3 |
| Guatemala | 8.0 | 3.5 | 8.7 | 3.2 |
| Algeria | 22.2 | 3.3 | 24.2 | 3.2 |
| Malawi | 7.1 | 3.2 | 7.7 | 3.2 |
| Iran | 45.1 | 3.0 | 51.9 | 3.2 |
| Ghana | 14.3 | 3.2 | 14.4 | 3.1 |
| Ivory Coast | 10.1 | 2.8 | 11.2 | 3.1 |
| Somalia | 6.5 | 2.6 | 8.0 | 3.1 |
| Ethiopia | 36.0 | 2.1 | 48.3 | 3.0 |
| Nigeria | 91.2 | 3.1 | 111.9 | 2.9 |
| Mali | 7.7 | 2.8 | 8.7 | 2.9 |
| Niger | 6.5 | 2.8 | 7.2 | 2.9 |
| Pakistan | 99.2 | 2.7 | 107.5 | 2.9 |
| Burundi | 4.6 | 2.7 | 5.2 | 2.9 |
| WORLD AVERAGE |  | 1.7 |  | 1.7 |

## Table 1.1c World's Slowest Growing Nations (5 million or more)

| | 1985 | | 1988 | |
|---|---|---|---|---|
| | Population (millions) | Annual Growth Rate (percent)* | Population (millions) | Annual Growth Rate (percent)* |
| Hungary | 10.7 | −0.2 | 10.6 | −0.2 |
| West Germany | 61.0 | −0.2 | 61.2 | −0.1 |
| Denmark | 5.1 | −0.1 | 5.1 | −0.1 |
| Austria | 7.5 | 0.0 | 7.6 | 0.0 |
| Italy | 57.4 | 0.1 | 57.3 | 0.0 |
| East Germany | 16.7 | 0.1 | 16.6 | 0.0 |
| Sweden | 8.3 | 0.0 | 8.4 | 0.1 |
| Belgium | 9.9 | 0.1 | 9.9 | 0.1 |
| United Kingdom | 56.4 | 0.1 | 57.1 | 0.2 |
| Bulgaria | 8.9 | 0.2 | 9.0 | 0.2 |
| Czechoslovakia | 15.5 | 0.3 | 15.6 | 0.2 |
| Greece | 10.1 | 0.5 | 10.1 | 0.2 |
| Switzerland | 6.5 | 0.2 | 6.6 | 0.3 |
| France | 55.0 | 0.4 | 55.9 | 0.4 |
| Netherlands | 14.5 | 0.4 | 14.7 | 0.4 |
| Spain | 38.5 | 0.6 | 39.0 | 0.4 |
| Romania | 22.8 | 0.5 | 23.0 | 0.5 |
| Portugal | 10.3 | 0.5 | 10.3 | 0.5 |
| Japan | 120.8 | 0.6 | 122.7 | 0.5 |
| Yugoslavia | 23.1 | 0.7 | 23.6 | 0.6 |
| United States | 238.9 | 0.7 | 246.1 | 0.7 |
| Canada | 25.4 | 0.8 | 26.1 | 0.7 |
| Poland | 37.3 | 1.0 | 38.0 | 0.7 |
| Australia | 15.8 | 0.9 | 16.5 | 0.8 |
| Hong Kong | 5.5 | 1.0 | 5.7 | 0.8 |
| USSR | 278.0 | 1.0 | 286.0 | 1.0 |
| WORLD AVERAGE | | 1.7 | | 1.7 |

*Sources:* Population Reference Bureau, Inc., "1985 World Population Data Sheet" and "1988 World Population Data Sheet."

*Annual population growth rate is the rate of natural increase (birth rate minus death rate) without regard for net migration.

developing nations, while some of the poorest and most populated LDCs have growth rates of up to 4 percent.

- The absolute number of people being added to the world's population continues to go up. Most of this net increase is occurring in the developing world. Population growth in the developed world is approaching zero.
- LDCs now hold about 77 percent of the world's population, and it is predicted that they will have about 85 percent by 2050. Most of this population (55 percent) is in Asia, with

significantly fewer people in Africa, the Middle East, and Latin America.

The immense population growth in developing nations since World War II has resulted from high birth rates combined with drastic reductions in death rates. Vaccination programs and modern medical treatment, though not universally available, have been widespread enough to affect life expectancy significantly. As the disadvantages of rapid population growth have become evident, family planning and other population control programs have been widely initiated, although with varying degrees of success.

Despite efforts to limit population growth, birth rates in developing nations persist at levels well above those that could stabilize their population. Projections to the year 2000 indicate that population will continue to grow at slightly less than 2 percent per year in the developing world. Significant reductions in population growth will be difficult to achieve in these nations for several reasons.

- Just as no one automobile is responsible for the total air pollution in New York City, one person's family size does not create a population problem in Bangladesh. It is the collective effect of individual actions that creates the dilemma. Rarely, however, can an individual be persuaded to see this and to act in the group's interest, especially if such action is not obviously in his or her self-interest. In developing nations, particularly in rural areas, limiting family size is not usually in the best interest of individual families.
- In many societies, decisions about having children and how many to have are unencumbered by government regulations. Only a few nations, such as China, have enacted public policies that have a meaningful influence on population growth. To have effective government intervention, a nation must be organized to implement and enforce incentives to limit family size. For example, a government might not allow free schooling or free medical treatment to more than two children per family as an incentive to restrict family size. Most developing nations, however, do not have the capacity either to create or administer such incentive systems. Then, too, the people in most developing nations still retain a high sense of

individuality, especially in family matters, and they would probably resist a restrictive policy.

- The agrarian nature of LDCs automatically encourages large families. In agrarian societies, children represent productive assets. They provide low-cost labor to the farm and may earn income from nonfarm employment. With the historical (and sometimes persistent) high infant mortality rates, only a large number of live births could ensure an adequate number of living offspring. Further, since most LDCs cannot provide public care for their elderly, having a large number of children is a sort of old-age security system for parents. The pattern is perpetuated when parents in rural and disadvantaged urban families discourage their children from attending school. Time in school limits time for farm or other work and can require money for books and clothes that the parents cannot afford.

Americans who grew up during this nation's rural, agrarian period will readily empathize with this type of value system. It was only after economic development occurred and the role of children was redefined that people in the United States (and in other developed nations as well) found reasons to limit family size voluntarily. A better quality of life replaced subsistence as the family goal. Children then became economic liabilities rather than economic assets. The nation became more urbanized and fewer families worked on farms. To give children educational opportunities and access to a lifestyle thought appropriate, the number of children had to be held in line with family resources if all members were to benefit somewhat equally.

Higher incomes and improved education among rural families in LDCs would promote changes in value systems. Voluntary control of population would then be more likely, based on evidence from around the world. Unfortunately, not enough people in enough LDCs have been exposed to these kinds of changes to produce widespread voluntary reductions in population growth.

As a consequence, extensive efforts at population control through organized planning projects are ongoing in most LDCs, but few of these include a broadening of education and employment opportunities. Instead, population projects generally attempt to encourage family planning both by informing the populace, especially those of childbearing ages, about the ways to achieve birth control and by supplying modern means to do so, such as pills and other contraceptives. More drastic control measures such as vasectomy and sterilization are also offered on a voluntary basis. However, the United States has made "voluntary consent" for these operations a strict requirement of the population control programs it supports.

The effectiveness of these efforts varies among nations, but in at least one important LDC, progress has been slow. In Bangladesh, the world's most densely populated nation, use-rates of birth control measures among married women under 50 years of age were 18.6 percent in 1981 compared with 7.7 percent in 1975. In 1985, the rate rose to 29.8 percent. To stabilize the population in that nation, use-rates would have to reach an estimated 65 percent.

Projections of population growth to the year 2000 reflect the expectation that moderate success with birth control programs will slow somewhat the rate of population growth in most regions of the world (table 1.2). Even so, population will continue to rise significantly. Most of the forecast aggregate improvement is expected to occur in developing nations, where growth rates are projected to fall from the current 2.1 percent to 1.9 percent by the year 2000. Africa will still be the most rapidly growing region, and despite anticipated improvements, many individual nations will continue to experience rising growth rates and significant population pressures.

The problems of population growth cannot be wished away. Even the moderate success of some control programs offers no solution. Unless a better approach is initiated, the areas of the

**Table 1.2    Population Growth Rates of World Regions (percent)**

| Region | 1988 | 1995–2000 (projected) |
|--------|------|-----------------------|
| More Developed | 0.6 | 0.5 |
| Less Developed | 2.1 | 1.9 |
| Africa | 2.8 | 3.0 |
| Latin America | 2.2 | 1.8 |
| East Asia | 1.3 | 1.1 |
| South Asia | 2.1 | 2.1 |
| WORLD | 1.7 | 1.6 |

*Source:* Population Reference Bureau, Inc., "1988 World Population Data Sheet."

world least able to do so will be dealing with the desperate problems of hunger and starvation for the foreseeable future. The impact will likely be felt by all nations.

**Income Trends and Effects**

Despite the ominous food-versus-people problems, general economic improvement has slightly outgained population growth in most of the world (figure 1.3 and appendix table 1.3). For example, from 1971 to 1985, the average growth in per capita gross national product (GNP)* was generally positive for all three country categories shown in figure 1.3. However, the trend has been downward for developing nations. In fact, for the period 1981–85, the growth rate for developing nations was –1.0 percent, negative for the first time and down from a very respectable 3.3 percent achieved in 1971–75.

Growth trends in per capita income between 1971 and 1985 were slowed by the petroleum price increases in the early 1970s. The

*GNP is the value of all goods and services produced in a nation. Economic development is said to occur when GNP per capita rises. It is desirable to have the increased GNP distributed widely among the populace.

**Figure 1.3 Per Capita Growth of GNP, 1971–75 and 1981–85**

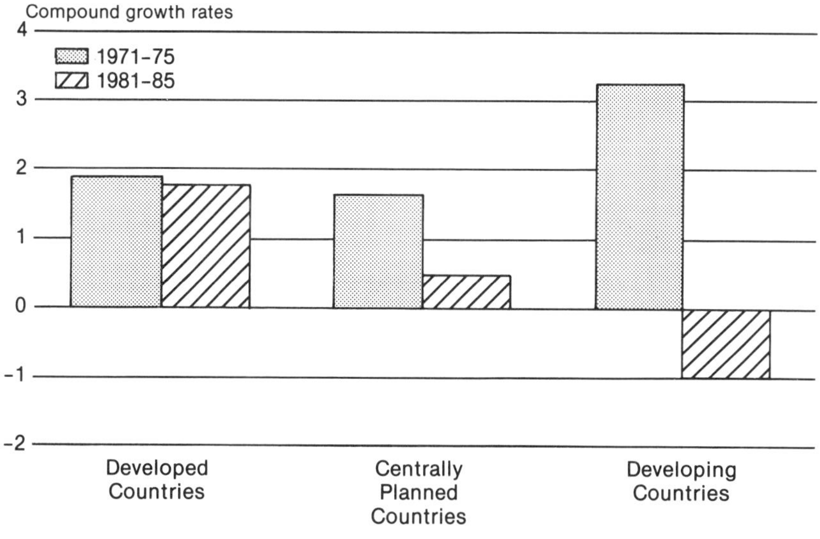

Source: ERS/USDA, Agriculture and Trade Indicators Branch, January 1989.

cumulative impact of these catastrophic events, plus the added difficulties being imposed by the crisis over the mounting external debts of LDCs and the continued high levels of population growth, are at the base of the limited growth in GNP reported for 1981–85. Even now, civil turmoil and extreme weather conditions in some nations are taking their toll on food production and incomes. In nations where the population continues to grow while aggregate income growth is slowed, per capita incomes are likely to continue to fall.

Today, a significant number of nations have per capita GNPs of $300 or less per year. All such nations are in Africa and Asia. Chad and Bangladesh are the two countries most often cited for their low average incomes. Among the nations having per capita GNPs above $300 but below $1,000 annually, most, again, are in Africa and Asia but several are in Latin America. In only one developed nation—Switzerland—does annual individual income equal or exceed the $17,480 average found in the United States (appendix table 1.1). Low or declining income implies less of a market demand (though not of a need) for food.

Economists like to point to improvements in average per capita income (or GNP) as indications of increased consumption and progress in achieving economic development. Such changes, however, do not guarantee that the welfare of all people is improving. The old truism, "the rich get richer and the poor get poorer," still holds. The reason in LDCs is that as development occurs, incomes rise at different rates, which can aggravate existing inequalities. Well into the 1960s, it was being argued that the benefits of general economic improvements would eventually expand to all parts of the economy and "trickle down" even to the poorer segments. Beginning in the late 1960s, however, it became apparent that this process was far from automatic. The poor segments of populations were not participating adequately (if at all) in economic development. Inequalities were, in fact, being enlarged in some LDCs.

Today, achieving a fair income distribution is given attention comparable to that assigned to improving per capita income. In other words, not only is it considered important to increase the size of the economic pie, but its distribution must also be improved. This concern has led the United States to attach special importance to its aid programs that address the "basic human needs" of the "poorest of the poor" and small farmers. (These points are discussed further in chap. 2.)

In most nations, an unregulated distribution of income will favor the already rich. In LDCs, the distortion often is magnified. Most of their populations typically receive a small share of the nation's income (figure 1.4 and appendix table 1.4). Kenya is an example of the distorted distributions of income that can occur in LDCs. In 1969, the 40 percent of the people who had the lowest incomes received only 3.8 percent of the nation's income, while 68 percent of the income went to the 20 percent of the population who had the highest incomes.

Questions about income distribution weigh heavily on issues of overall economic development and a nation's ability to share its wealth equitably among all its people. Studies of these very complicated issues have produced no pronouncements of what distribution of income would be best for each nation. The tendency, however, is to consider "more equal as better."

Many nations, including developing countries, have adopted extensive public policies aimed at redistributing income among their people. Welfare payments, land reform, and graduated income tax systems are techniques that have been used by some developed nations. Developing nations, however, generally lack

**Figure 1.4  Income Distribution in Selected Countries**

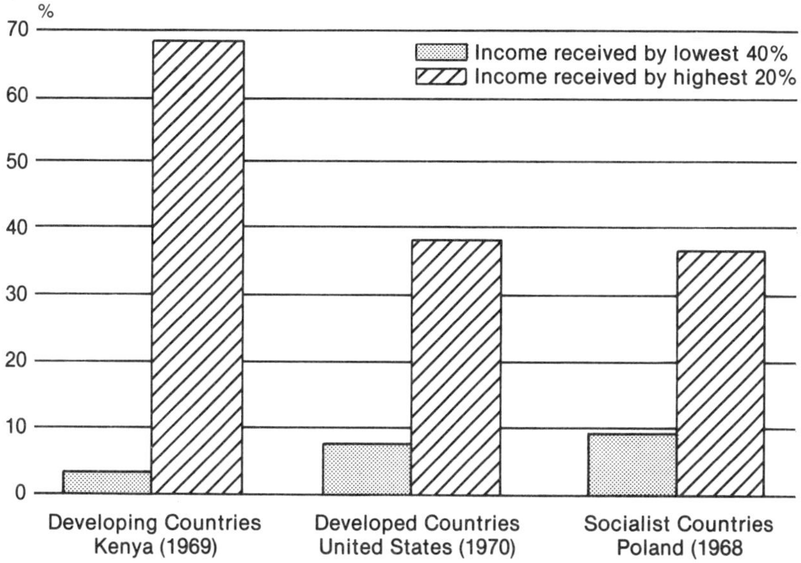

Source: Montek S. Ahluwalia, "Inequality, Poverty, and Development," *Journal of Development Economics* 3 (1976): 340-341.

the administrative structures or resources needed to implement such programs. Instead of trying to redistribute income in the manner of developed nations, they often opt for cheap-food policies. These involve combinations of subsidies and price controls that are supposed to make basic food items available to large segments of the population at a low cost.

Such policies are frequently counterproductive. Artificial control of consumer food prices can increase the amount demanded. At the lower prices, people demand more food and greater supplies are needed. Simultaneously, the low prices penalize the farm producers who then grow less. Resultant food shortfalls may have to be offset by food aid from developed nations. This is one of the great dilemmas facing LDCs. In addition, administering these programs requires both large amounts of budgetary support from the LDC government and an extensive bureaucracy.

Correcting severely distorted distributions of income in LDCs is a complicated but essential step toward overall development success. An approach now gaining support calls for government policies to influence the pattern of development in such a way that low-income producers (located mostly in agriculture and small-scale enterprises in both rural and urban areas) will see improved earning opportunities and simultaneously will receive the resources necessary to take advantage of them. One important focus of this strategy is to create more employment through labor-intensive technologies. When people are productively employed, whether in or out of agriculture, they have income to buy food. The strategy also emphasizes greater reliance on market forces and less on government controls to determine food prices.

**Aggregate Food Demand**

Over time, the combined effects of changes in population and in per capita income determine the magnitude of the demand for food that must be met worldwide. Based on the population trends over the past 35 years and on predicted potentials for improving per capita incomes, the most optimistic estimates place future increases in the demand for food at about 2 percent annually. More pessimistic estimates place it at about 2.5 percent. This is the likely range of food demand that will have to be met just to keep world conditions from deteriorating. General improvements in human well-being will require even higher levels of agricultural output.

Also, demand increases in the poorer nations will exceed the averages suggested above, probably by as much as 1.0 percent to 1.5 percent. This will be due to their population growth rates and possibly to slight income pressures as more of their poor people are able to afford more adequate diets.

Demand levels for food will continue to vary for specific food types. One estimate provided by the U.S. Department of Agriculture (USDA) suggests that between now and the year 2000, the greatest increases in demand will occur for meat and oilseed foods, with lesser increases for milk, cereals, and fibers (appendix table 1.5). Such predictions allow for differences among areas of the world based on their population and income growth rates, plus their diverse preferences for food types. For example, people in Asia and China show a much greater preference for cereals than do those in some other areas of the world. For the 20-year period from 1980 to 2000, estimates of annual percentage increases (not compounded) in demand for food range from 3.2 percent for meat to 1.8 percent for milk and fiber foods.

A possible paradox with respect to the projected changes in demand for food should be clarified. In one sense, a rising demand for food is desirable since it suggests that more food is being consumed, hopefully leading to improved nutrition and diet. But these benefits will be realized only if the primary source of the increase in demand is higher per capita incomes and not population growth. Population growth adds mostly to increased food need, but the ability of people to obtain food improves only with better incomes or expanded farm production opportunities or both. For this reason, a rising population in developing nations is often a strong deterrent to eliminating hunger and starvation if income levels and food production do not also increase. Too often, food output must go up merely to keep pace with more numbers of people. Nations must "run just to stay even."

## SUPPLY OF FOOD

The economic notion of the supply of food, like that of demand, is not commonly understood. Supply is defined by economists as the amount of an item that producers are willing and able to produce and market when they are paid a given price. In general, producers will supply more if assured of high prices and less when prices decline. The actual supply, however, is necessarily determined by biological realities as well as by economic forces and management decisions.

The difficulty for managers and analysts comes when any one of the factors is overemphasized. For example, those who concentrate their attention on the fixed physical factors related to food production often conclude that potentials for improving food output are limited. They argue that few new land frontiers remain to be opened, that the world's best farmland is already being farmed, and that available irrigation water supplies are already being used.

This view of food production ignores the effects of economic forces and human ingenuity. Land and water are undeniably important to food production, but as they become scarce, economic forces create strong incentives to use them more efficiently. History shows us how new technology and management skills have regularly increased production from U.S. land and water resources whenever scarcity became a problem.

## Determinants of Supply

The amount of food supplied by producers is determined by several interrelated factors. Seven of the more important general classes of determinants are discussed here.

**Level of Technology.** Improvements in agricultural technology often permit farmers to overcome production constraints imposed by scarcity of inputs. For example, if land is limited, research may provide new seeds and more potent fertilizers. In some cases, introducing irrigation can increase yields per land unit. If labor is in short supply, new mechanical devices can sometimes be substituted for manpower and can raise output per unit of labor. In such instances, new technology raises the food output from each unit of the scarce input. It is important to remember that technology does not always mean machinery.

Developing nations have a particularly high potential to respond to new technology since their present "ways of doing things" were generally intended to support much smaller populations in centuries past. These traditional production methods were adequate for their time, but they no longer yield high enough outputs. Dramatic increases in production are possible if LDC farmers can be helped to accept and use new methods and inputs that are more appropriate to today's world and needs. Such factors are usually developed by agricultural research systems, while extension service personnel help the farm population understand how best to put them to use.

**Weather.** The influence of weather on food production is especially critical in LDCs since rain-fed (not irrigated) agriculture is common. Crop yields are very often determined by whether the rains arrive when and in the amounts needed. Weather extremes such as excessive rains or drought can devastate agricultural production. Persistently humid environments pose their own set of problems. The Sahel region of Africa typifies how extremely arid conditions can wreck food production expectations. Bangladesh is another example of a nation that in recent years has had its agricultural production ravaged by extreme weather in the form of rains, winds, and tidal waves.

**Natural Resources.** Natural resources are an obviously crucial factor in agriculture. Rich soil combined with sufficient, high-quality water and a moderate climate, which can mean year-round cropping, are the kinds of resources that translate into high agricultural productivity. Developing nations often have an abundance of natural resources. Unfortunately, however, their productivity is too often limited by the level of technology and other indigenous factors, many of which are discussed in the rest of this section.

**Infrastructure.** Aspects of a country's physical and institutional infrastructure that affect farmers include transportation, communications, electricity, roads, and storage facilities. Additionally, land distribution and leasing arrangements (land tenure); means of making credit, seeds, and fertilizer readily available; systems to deliver water for irrigation; and the efficiency of the product-marketing process all affect the profitability of farming and the willingness of farmers to produce food. In LDCs, many essential elements of their infrastructure and institutions have not been constructed or developed. These deficiencies represent the first and most critical needs if agricultural production is to be improved. For example, without adequate roads and efficient forms of transportation, products cannot be moved profitably to a market for sale; without electricity, many aspects of the quality of life, especially in rural areas, are diminished. In many developed nations, infrastructure development was often a critical first step toward today's thriving agriculture. LDCs are finding the same to be true.

**Producer Incentives.** In many ways, LDC farmers are no different from U.S. farmers, even though more of the food they produce is consumed in the home and less is sold in the marketplace. Farmers everywhere try to maximize returns on their efforts and react positively to perceived economic opportunities. Once beyond mere subsistence, they are motivated considerably by the prices paid for their products, by their input costs, and, when evaluating new technology, by any production risks it may entail.

Unfortunately, production incentives for farmers are diminished in most LDCs by market controls and public policies that artificially hold prices in check or otherwise discriminate against agriculture. Many analysts argue that most LDC governments favor urban dwellers. An example is their tendency to maintain low food prices for urban consumers in hopes of improving food and income distribution. These policy-induced low prices do not motivate farmers to produce more. Under valuing food in this way has serious adverse production consequences and inhibits farmers' interests in new agricultural techniques. Rules governing foreign exchange rates, import/export controls, and subsidized input prices are examples of other interventions that can overvalue or undervalue farm products, thus giving farmers misleading economic signals. If the potentials for large increases in agricultural production that exist in LDCs are to be realized, government policies must do a better job in optimizing incentives for producers.

**Political Constraints.** Government stability can dramatically affect agricultural productivity in LDCs. Only in a stable environment can substantial improvement in food output or overall development be initiated and sustained. Unfortunately, developing nations experience a great deal of political unrest, much of which arises from the pressures that accompany widespread poverty. For example, Bolivia has had a reported 150 changes in government since it achieved independence in 1825. Political groups use poor and illiterate people as prime targets for promoting their particular philosophies of social organization and justice. In some nations, it is not uncommon for 15 or more official political parties to exist, with each pursuing its own solutions for the nation's ills. Others that have fewer parties are not, however, immune to public unrest.

Turnovers in government frequently mean that the people at the head of agricultural institutions (such as the ministry of agriculture) and programs also change. National development goals tend to be altered, and continuity (one of any nation's most critical needs) in planning and implementing agricultural and other development strategies can suffer.

**Human Resources.** Agricultural production is critically influenced by both the quantity and quality of a country's human resources. It is people, whether agricultural researchers, farm managers, or laborers, who determine the productivity of land and other resources. Most developing nations do not yet have enough training facilities and qualified teachers to create a highly skilled labor force. In too many of these nations, illiteracy is high, skill levels are low, and public schools are inadequate. (Appendix table 1.1 lists literacy levels for 125 nations.) This situation limits the quality of available labor and hinders the capacity of the labor force to command reasonably good employment options. Studies further suggest that the more education and training farmers have, the more likely they are to adopt new agricultural technologies.

The seven determinants of food supply listed above obviously constitute a mosaic that influences producer decisions in a complex fashion. It is important to realize that only two of the seven are natural or physical endowments. The remaining five can be more readily altered by individual or government initiative. Enlightened management that remedies the constraints associated with these determinants can dramatically affect the food output of LDCs.

## World Food Production

Aggregate growth in the world's food supply since World War II is encouraging. From 1950 to 1985, world agricultural production grew at an average annual rate of 2.5 percent (figure 1.5). On the whole, developing nations fared better than the average with a growth rate of 3.0 percent, although in two regions with rapid population increases—Africa and South Asia—agricultural output grew at only 2.4 percent and 2.7 percent, respectively (appendix table 1.6).

**Figure 1.5  Growth of Agricultural Output, by Major Regions, 1950–85**

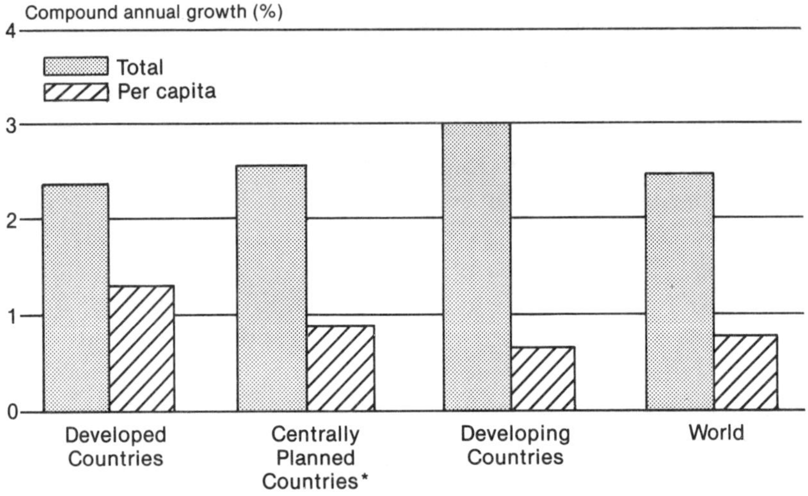

Compound annual growth (%)

*Excludes China

Source: ERS/USDA, Agriculture and Trade Indicators Branch, January 1989.

During the more recent five-year period from 1980 to 1985, the rate of growth in world food output increased to 2.8 percent annually. Again, developing nations did better as their rate of output increased to 3.3 percent. South Asia showed the most dramatic increase in agricultural output for developing nations, with a 3.9 percent rise from 1980 to 1985 compared with only a 2.7 percent rise from 1950 to 1985 (appendix table 1.6).

Much of the improvement in the aggregate food output of LDCs was offset by their increases in population. Growth in per capita output averaged 0.6 percent annually during 1950–85 and increased slightly to 0.7 percent for the recent period. Africa and East Asia registered the least impressive results during 1980–85; per capita output in Africa fell by 0.2 percent annually and in East Asia by 1.4 percent. The present food supply is acutely inadequate in many nations in these regions where population growth is high and where weather and civil unrest have exacerbated the incidence of chronically poor diets.

Despite improvements, some see these overall trends for LDCs as discouraging. But in the face of their rapid population growth rates and wide assortment of production problems, the agricultural production performances of most developing nations can, at a minimum, be called heartening. Two features associated with the output trends are particularly noteworthy. First, the 1950–85 growth in per capita food output was broadly shared among LDC regions and nations, except for Africa and East Asia. Second, most of the increased growth in agricultural output was associated with new technology that produced high yields per unit of input. Of the total world increase in agricultural output, a USDA estimate shows that about 75 percent resulted from greater use of improved technology during 1950–80. The rest came from an expansion of the land area under cultivation. As will be seen later in this chapter (see "General Constraints on Development: Available Natural Resources"), the expansion is progressing very slowly.

**Potentials for Increased Food Production**

The likelihood of boosting the world's output of food in the years ahead is promising for two reasons.

First, the efforts of the past 40 years have provided a diversified base of knowledge and experience on which the LDCs can build. All developing nations have been exposed to development programs. Each better understands the issues it must deal with if agricultural output is to increase. Most of the LDCs have at least some of the necessary programs in place.

Second, in most LDCs, past and ongoing programs have established an initial technological foundation for agriculture. Regrettably, certain nations in Africa and Asia still have extremely deficient in-place technology and agricultural research capabilities. On the positive side, the "green revolution" (which introduced high-yielding varieties of rice and wheat to several areas in the developing world in the 1960s and 1970s), plus continuing progress in agricultural research and the creation of improved institutional capacities, has given many LDCs a noteworthy base of technology and knowledge. This evolution is not yet complete, and research and extension must continue to emphasize finding ways both to eliminate remaining production constraints and to sustain productive agricultural sectors. Even so, it is encouraging that the overall agricultural research base of LDCs is better prepared now than at any time in the past to contribute a strong impetus to future advances in their food outputs.

Toward that end, the LDCs will have to create and implement effective programs and policies that earn broad popular support. The challenge of world hunger is both political and technological. In turn, developed nations must make long-term commitments to promoting a sustained growth of agriculture and other areas of the economy in LDCs. The increases in food production that will defeat hunger and malnutrition among their people must come from within the LDCs. Even if the developed nations produced enough to feed the world (which some feel is now the case), the associated massive transfers of food aid would be impractical and would introduce pressures on domestic markets within LDCs that may be self-defeating over time. Similarly, work opportunities that can help defeat poverty must also come from within the LDCs.

**Some Indicators**

The potentials that exist for increasing domestic agricultural output in LDCs can be illustrated by considering regional disparities in grain yields as they correlate with the relative uses made of fertilizer and irrigation. Research has repeatedly proved that applications of fertilizer most often produce increased yields when combined with access to irrigation systems. The regional disparities detailed below obviously reflect complex developmental issues as well as the relative uses made of fertilizer and irrigation water. Nevertheless, these two inputs are critical to agricultural production and warrant consideration.

In 1986, grain yields in Latin America averaged 79 percent of the world average. In North Africa and the Middle East they were 60 percent (appendix table 1.7). In Subsaharan Africa, grain yields averaged only 41 percent of the world mark. In all three regions, these percentages reflect decreases from estimates for 1979–80.

Similarly, Subsaharan Africa was (and remains) well below the world average in its percentage of cropland area being irrigated (appendix table 1.8). China's progress in expanding its irrigated acreage during this period is significant, as are estimates showing that as of 1985, only 15 percent of the world's cropland was under irrigation. This represents a minimal increase over the 11 percent for the period 1961–65.

Fertilizer use in the three low grain yield regions is also desperately inadequate (appendix table 1.9). In Subsaharan Africa, fertilizer use in 1986 was only 16 percent of the world average and 15 percent of U.S. levels. Latin America applied 47 percent, and North Africa and the Middle East 63 percent, of the world average. China has shown dramatic increases in fertilizer use, consistent with its extended applications of irrigation, and has the highest use per hectare among developing nations. However, the improvements since 1965 have not even dented the enormous need.

Each region has its particular constraints that affect progress in agriculture. One that is fairly universal, however, is the availability of water either from rainfall or irrigation.

The problems in Africa are of special concern since economic progress there has been slow, and projections suggest that the continent's existing major developmental problems will persist for some time. The Subsaharan region looks to an especially bleak future. In general, the delay in activating technological change in most regions of Africa is the result of a number of conditions centered around the limited use of modern agricultural inputs. The qualified personnel and agricultural institutions that are essential to research and extension efforts are still not available. As a consequence, data about major African crops (cassava, millet, yams, etc.) have not been developed by local researchers. Attention to these crops by research groups outside of Africa has been limited since the crops are of much less importance elsewhere. (This was not the case with rice and wheat, the major beneficiaries of the green revolution research that spread across much of Asia.) Africa also has lacked the physical and economic infrastructure to promote progress. In addition, the special environmental problems that characterize most of Africa make water development both difficult and costly.

Strategies to increase food production in individual LDCs must necessarily accommodate the special conditions of each. For example, strategies in a labor-surplus nation like Bangladesh should not initiate programs that would displace labor with machines. A nation like Bolivia, however, which has extensive land areas and less population pressure, may find value in a strategy that does advocate mechanization, at least in some parts of the country.

### General Constraints on Development

Regardless of such special considerations, however, several general constraints must be addressed as part of development strategies in all LDCs if their food production potentials are to be achieved. Many of these constraints are juxtaposed alongside the emerging environmental issues in LDCs, a large number of which are closely associated with agricultural production and water and land usage.

**Focus on Agriculture.** Planners and leaders throughout the developing world need to better understand the basic importance of agriculture to each country's overall economic development. Too often, agriculture is viewed as a tradition-bound sector whose only mission is to produce food. In reality, it is the foundation on which overall development must rest.

In the early stages of a country's development, agriculture provides the pool of labor for the economy. A high concentration of people committed to agricultural production is a common characteristic that distinguishes low-income from developed nations. For example, as of 1980, Chad had 85 percent of its population working in the agricultural sector, Niger had 91 percent, and Nepal had 93 percent. Typically, upwards of 70 percent of the population in the poorer LDCs works in agricultural production. By contrast, the United States and England had 2 percent of their populations employed in agricultural production in 1980, West Germany had 4 percent, and Japan had 12 percent (appendix table 1.1). These percentages do not include people employed in agricultural support industries such as marketing, credit, and processing.

A rise in agricultural production catalyzes adjustments throughout the economy. For example, when farmers produce a food surplus that can be marketed for cash, they can then use their new income to purchase nonagricultural goods and services. Again, as agricultural production becomes more efficient, it requires less labor. Some people can then migrate from rural life to nonagricultural employment and, hopefully, higher incomes. Since much of the new income of poor people is spent on food, these purchases promote more agricultural production while improving nutritional levels. In conjunction with the other changes, relative prices of food will fall, allowing urban as well as rural people to buy food more cheaply. They can then use these savings to upgrade their diets or to buy nonagricultural goods. The lower food prices can also make the country's agricultural products more competitive in world markets. For these reasons, rising agricultural productivity is viewed as the basic engine for overall economic development.

As people leave agriculture to work and live in other sectors of the economy, however, special problems arise. If jobs are not available near home, rural people often seek the perceived excitement and employment possibilities of the "big city." If employment cannot be found in the city, these people must usually accept extremely deprived living conditions. Urban slums and civil disorder are common consequences. Creating employment in nonagricultural sectors must therefore be an important component of the development process that begins with rising agricultural output. (The need to enhance employment options is discussed later in this section.)

It is commonplace in LDCs to acknowledge the value of, but not assign a high priority to, agricultural development in national planning. This counterproductive attitude must be replaced with one that guarantees substantial investments of public funds in agriculture, long-run commitments to agricultural programs, and coordinated efforts to create jobs simultaneously in the nonagricultural sector.

**Development of a Scientific Base and Research/Extension Capability.** Despite substantial progress, large gaps continue to exist between actual and potential crop and animal yields, even in LDCs where farmers have started to adopt new technology. Yields achieved on agricultural experiment stations also continue to outrun those obtained by local farmers by a wide margin.

A prime problem in most LDCs is the absence of a base of scientifically competent people and of institutions with modern research facilities to support the agricultural sector. Research capability is usually very limited due to serious underfinancing by the government, too few properly trained and experienced scientists, and insufficient experiment station facilities. The agricultural research that does occur often does not address the most critical production problems of farmers. Unlike in the United States, LDC governments do not yet have a long-run commitment to support scientific discovery and innovation.

Extension services also are mostly inadequate in LDCs. Operating budgets are often so low that the few agents who are hired have difficulty traveling and maintaining their autos. The training given to LDC extension agents rarely prepares them to give effective help to farmers confronting practical, everyday production problems.

Ongoing scientific research is the key to the long-run success of any agricultural sector. Just because agricultural methods in developing nations are not highly mechanized or sophisticated does not mean the problems are simple. For example, LDCs have an extremely high incidence of plant diseases and damaging pests that reduce crop output. Doing effective battle against these hazards requires reliable research, which can only come from competent scientists. The special problems of each nation must be diagnosed and solved on site. Scientific assistance may have to come first from scientists in the developed world, but, ultimately, local scientific capability is essential. A similarly vigorous, long-term commitment is needed for the creation of an effectively trained and adequately supported extension system.

The case for expending public funds to develop an effective research/extension capability is well documented. Studies of investments in specific, research-oriented projects in LDCs have demonstrated a fairly consistent trend of high rates of return that range from 25 percent to as high as 100 percent annually.

**Improved Human Skills and Education.** A high-quality scientific capability cannot evolve unless advanced educational opportunities are made available to large segments of the population. Competent universities are needed to train students in the sciences and arts of agriculture. Such schools would not only support agricultural research and extension systems, but they would also provide personnel for the government offices where national policies are set and where millions of dollars of public funds and development assistance from donor nations are managed each year.

Besides strengthening higher education, there is a pressing need to eliminate illiteracy among, and provide job skills for, the general public. Illiteracy rates typically are high in LDCs (appendix table 1.1). In Bangladesh, for example, adult literacy is 26 percent, and only 6 percent of the country's students of proper ages were enrolled in high school in 1982. Early "dropout" from primary schools is common. Without skills basic to the job market, a person's options are narrowed and his or her capacity to earn income is extremely limited.

Many elements of a nation's development process are curtailed by an unskilled labor supply. Progress in both industrial and agricultural systems suffers. There is evidence that it is the better-educated rural people who most readily adopt new ways of doing things. In the history of the United States, for example, agricultural education, especially among rural youth via 4-H and Future Farmers programs, had important impacts on agricultural progress.

Perhaps more than on any other factor, the future of the developing world depends on the education and training of its people. Only people can make land produce more crops and industries produce more goods. Investments that provide LDC residents with both basic and technical skills will greatly improve the potentials for increasing outputs of agriculture and of all goods and services in these economies.

**Government Interventions and Economic Incentives.** Farmers in developing nations are no less economically rational than those in developed nations. Farmers invest their money, plant their crops, and adopt new production techniques when they believe such actions are in their best interest. What they believe depends largely on what they have learned from the marketplace. That is where farmers find out how much they will be paid for the products they sell and how much they must pay for the inputs they buy. If intelligent decisions are to be made, the market's messages must accurately reflect the public's valuation of scarce products, services, and resources in the economy.

A nation's government has a key role in maintaining the kind of economic environment that gives accurate information to farmers. Governments can do things to improve agricultural market efficiency that individual farmers cannot do. This may include providing roads and other forms of infrastructure, guarding against market imperfections such as monopolies, supplying price and market outlook information, standardizing the system of weights and measures for all products, and establishing grades and standards for food products and farm inputs marketed in the system. Governments also secure a nation's framework of law and order, legitimizing the rights of ownership and creating the proper climate within which people can invest capital and exchange goods. Education, research, transportation, and communication are other services government should rightly provide, along with protecting consumers and producers from unscrupulous exploitation.

As developing nations modernize, their farmers become increasingly dependent on nonlocalized support systems to assist in production and marketing. Furthermore, the farmers need help in learning how to gather, process, and use increasingly complex information as it becomes available.

These types of interventions, plus public policies concerned with prices and other economic factors, are some of the government actions that affect incentives for farmers. Unfortunately, governments do not always clearly recognize their own roles nor the importance of encouraging investments that will enhance market efficiency for agricultural commodities. On the contrary, because they often distrust the marketplace and the private sector, they create government agencies (which often prove ineffective and unprofitable) to carry out many functions. Likewise, government policies that fix prices at low levels to favor urban consumers inadvertently penalize farmers. Ironically, these types of counterproductive actions usually occur in nations where agriculture is poorly developed, where population growth is soaring, where expanded food production is most needed, and where the capacity to manage a government-controlled economy is least satisfactory.

The policy issues in developing nations are extremely complicated and can only be inadequately addressed in this limited explanation. If efforts to increase the world's food supply are to be successful, however, they clearly must rest upon a proper framework of public policy in each LDC. Those policies will have to be designed, installed, and monitored with the goal of sustaining an economic environment that provides production incentives to farmers.

**Adequate Employment Options.** Production efficiency must also be a goal in nonagricultural areas, and the creation of jobs and employment in those enterprises deserves a high priority in the development strategy. It is highly unlikely that agriculture in LDCs will be able to absorb and employ the entire increase in the rural labor force as population continues to rise. In the long run, solutions to the plight of the rural poor in LDCs must come largely from outside of agriculture. Expansion of nonagricultural employment for rural households usually occurs first in small-scale, rural industries of the cottage or handloom types and in small consumer-goods industries. Service industries also commonly provide important job options outside of agriculture.

Employment opportunities can be helped to expand efficiently if governments commit resources to programs that teach rural and slum-dwelling people the technical skills needed by employers. Whenever poverty is so rampant and jobs so needed as in LDCs, governments must encourage employment in all sectors of the economy. Failure to do so will work against a successful development strategy even if agricultural production initially improves.

**Available Natural Resources.** Major importance must be attached to developing land and water resources and to combating the vagaries of weather. Estimates vary and are probably imprecise, but they suggest that the world contains about 2,500 million hectares (1 hectare equals 2.7 acres) of potentially arable land that could ultimately be put under cultivation (appendix table 1.10). Only about 1,476 million hectares were cultivated in 1985, which means the potential land area under cultivation could be expanded by as much as about 70 percent. Among LDCs, such lands are extensive in the humid and subhumid parts of Latin America and Africa, but reserves in the Mediterranean area and in most of Asia (except Indonesia) are very limited. China has apparently reached the limits of its arable land, and a number of other nations are also approaching this point. However, the rate of developing new lands has been slow.

The impediments to developing the remaining lands for cultivation are both physical and economic. Much of the land is currently used for livestock, located in marginal climatic zones, or situated in tropical areas poorly suited to production of major grain and other crops. Animal, crop, and human diseases also discourage people from settling and developing lands in tropical and subtropical regions. Production risks are high for these lands, and efforts to develop them will be quite costly. Future food needs may, however, redefine the current structure of costs and returns and render development of more of these cultivable lands economically feasible. The FAO estimates that 10 to 15 percent of the unused arable land in 1980 might be cultivated by 2000.

The surface and subsurface water resources with which to expand irrigated agriculture are considered extensive, but inventories are sketchy. Much of the world's surface irrigation water has been or is being developed, but further expansion is possible if certain obstacles can be overcome. In many areas, development of rivers for surface irrigation requires intercountry cooperation. In some cases, political and territorial disputes among nations curtail progress.

Use potentials for subsurface water are high, even though extensive development in some microregions has already caused water tables to recede. A major constraint is not knowing how much water exists in individual underground aquifers and how to sustain their specific recharging processes. The requisite water management skills and information are especially deficient in most LDCs, and their water policies and pricing strategies do not lead to efficient water use. Many of these deficiencies probably can be corrected, however, and water availability should not generally constitute a serious limitation to expanding food production, at least for the rest of this century. But as with land, the cost of developing water resources tends to rise as development proceeds, and the effort becomes technically more difficult.

Weather is always an unpredictable factor for any nation attempting to increase food production. Prolonged droughts, major floods, and irregular rain patterns can cripple agricultural production, sometimes for extended periods, despite the best efforts of government and individuals. Fortunately, weather extremes tend to be localized, so while one area of one nation suffers, others do not. (Subsaharan Africa is an exception.) The inevitability of weather fluctuations emphasizes the need for countries, and especially LDCs, to activate programs and policies that will produce increasing amounts of food and provide a reasonable level of food security.

**Continued Donor Support.** Developed nations must continue to provide LDCs with development assistance if food production is to be improved in the next decade. Per capita agricultural and industrial output in most LDCs are not far enough above subsistence levels to permit a significant mobilization of domestic savings. Their own people thus can rarely invest much in developmental programming. LDCs do surprisingly well, even now, in providing local resources for development efforts, but they are too poor to shoulder the total burden. Developed nations will have to continue their investment commitments (for food and money) until the LDCs become productive enough to satisfy their own needs.

Since World War II, several nations such as Taiwan and South Korea have made significant progress toward developed status. But a prolonged struggle with all or some of the seven noted food production constraints lies ahead for most LDCs. As will become apparent in later chapters, developed nations that provide the necessary development assistance at this time are benefiting and will likely continue to benefit from their efforts beyond a purely humanitarian satisfaction.

## SUMMARY COMMENTS

Strategies to end hunger and malnutrition for much of the world's populace must successfully cope with burgeoning population. Rising population adds to the need for food but does little to create the wherewithal that people can use to purchase or produce that food. It is obvious that population growth since 1950 has nullified some of the impressive gains in the worldwide production of food made during the same period. Potentials for population control are restricted by the desire for large families that is inherent in highly agrarian societies. Expanding access to formal education and skill training, which will augment earning capacity, constitutes one potentially effective control strategy. But such an effort will take time and far more emphasis than is now apparent in most LDCs.

For the present, the accent is generally on increasing the supplies of food in LDCs by promoting their own production capabilities. Even this approach, however, presents serious obstacles. LDC farmers must be convinced to replace old technologies and methods (which they have found adequate for decades) with modern means that have considerably greater output potentials but are unfamiliar and mistrusted. Change of this type comes slowly and demands persistent persuasion. Also, a way must be found to ensure that the poor people in each LDC have the jobs and money they need if they are to benefit from higher food output. On the plus side, most developing nations have accumulated two to three decades of self-governing experience and have put many elements of an effective development strategy into place. With enlightened help from developed nations, the LDCs have a good chance of increasing their food production and of simultaneously mounting attacks on poverty (by improving job options and incomes) and population growth. Only such a multi-factored effort is likely to produce the desired results.

The tragedies in Ethiopia and the Sudan in the 1980s brought the realities of extreme developmental failures into vivid focus. Such emergencies often indicate both internal strife and neglect in developing a healthy agriculture. Similar patterns in other LDCs with strong population pressures could make these situations commonplace in 20 or 30 years and could place increased demands on the United States and other donor nations. The response to these crises by the United States, other donor nations, and large numbers of people acting independently has been impressive. Past emergencies have witnessed a similar U.S. response. Since 1964, the United States has assisted victims of more than 750 disasters in 128 countries. These disasters killed more than 2 million people and ravaged another 750 million. The United States alone provided $2.4 billion in official relief funds to help the victims.

History thus suggests that this nation and its people will always try to respond to the world's food emergencies. The big question is whether we could continue to respond should the emergencies become more frequent and extensive. Our wisest course, therefore, is to provide development assistance now since it offers the hope of avoiding future food crises by attacking the longer-term problems. Through continued development assistance, the United States can substantially increase the innate productive capacity of LDCs and help them defeat the threat of an ever malignant spread of chronic hunger and malnutrition.

# TWO

# The History and Nature Of U.S. Foreign Assistance

## E. Boyd Wennergren

The configuration of U.S. foreign assistance has been evolving since the 1940s. U.S. aid to other nations began principally as assistance that could be described as economic, technical, or developmental.Its goal was to improve the economic welfare of people living in less-developed or war-devastated countries.

The rise of cold war pressures in the 1950s added a new dimension: pursuit of political objectives in the form of what today is known as security assistance. Since then, the United States has expanded its assistance programs to include nations judged important to its foreign policy strategy. Under that cloak, such nations as Iran, Vietnam, Israel, and Egypt have been recipients of substantial packages of U.S. aid.

In the 1980s, U.S. foreign assistance has encompassed a composite of technical, economic, and military aid. The aid categorized as economic furthers development objectives in poor nations as well as security interests in diverse parts of the world.

To provide a more complete picture of the nature and scope of the U.S. effort, this chapter will first deal with an overall description of foreign assistance. The prime focus will,however, be on the economic aid given to combat world hunger and to promote U.S. security interests abroad.

## ORIGIN OF U.S. FOREIGN ASSISTANCE

The genesis of U.S. foreign assistance came in 1939 when passage of Public Law (P.L.) 355 gave U.S. legislative concurrence with the 1937 Buenos Aires Convention. Participants in that convention had agreed to closer cultural and economic ties among nations throughout the American hemisphere. The 1939 law provided for more scientific and cultural exchanges between the United States and other nations of the continent. From this initiative, the Institute of Inter-American Affairs (IIAF) was established in 1942. It formally recognized the need for attention to rural problems and set into motion the concept of *servicio* (service) to agriculture. Discussions within the IIAF and the State Department led to creation of the U.S. Interdepartmental Committee on Scientific and Cultural Affairs. This committee, chaired by the assistant secretary of state for economic affairs, included representatives from several departments of government. The most active participants were from the Departments of Health and Agriculture. The committee was the first forum to consider rural problems in Latin America and ways that U.S. government agencies could help solve them.

Efforts by these groups in the mid-1940s provided both the aegis and the impetus for agricultural and rural development assistance to Latin America. Numerous agricultural research and health programs were initiated. By the 1950s, the "Servicio Agricola," sponsored by the IIAF, was operating throughout much of Latin America and was acknowledged as the primary U.S. foreign economic assistance effort in health and agricultural extension. A similarly widespread program n agricultural research had been put in place by the Interdepartmental Committee.

The ground-breaking philosophies, concepts, and program ideas generated by these early efforts provided he intellectual background for subsequent U.S. technical assistance outside of Latin America. The case or U.S. aid to all of the developing nations was formulated in the 1940s, and when the Marshall Plan assistance to Europe in 1947 showed early evidence of success, the stage was set for formalizing the commitment of the United States to humanitarian causes. President Truman did so in his 1949 inaugural address when he said:

> Fourth, we must embark on a bold new program for making the benefits of our scientific advances and industrial progress available for the improvement and growth of underdeveloped areas.

More than half the people of the world are living in conditions approaching misery. Their food is inadequate. They are victims of disease. Their economic life is primitive and stagnant. Their poverty is a handicap and a threat both to them and to more prosperous areas.

For the first time in history humanity possesses the knowledge and the skill to relieve the suffering of these people.

The United States is preeminent among nations in the development of industrial and scientific techniques. The material resources which we can afford to use for the assistance of other peoples are limited. But our imponderable resources in technical knowledge are constantly growing and are inexhaustible.

I believe that we should make available to peace-loving peoples the benefits of our store of technical knowledge in order to help them realize their aspirations for a better life. And, in cooperation with other nations, we should foster capital investment in areas needing development.

With this, President Truman set in motion the Point Four program, the nation's first peacetime development assistance effort. The most obvious catalyst for the president's pronouncement had been the deliberations and positions on development assistance that grew out of P.L. 355. In fact, it is noteworthy that President Truman made no reference to military aid or to the concept of security assistance. His intent was to assist LDCs to improve their well-being primarily through the use of U.S. technical knowledge and, to a lesser extent, U.S. capital investments.

Prior to the Point Four program, however, the idea of security assistance had been born with the U.S. Mutual Assistance Program in 1947. Most of that aid went to Greece and Turkey and was designed to contain Soviet expansion after World War II. That concept was to evolve and expand in the years that followed through the Mutual Security Program (1951), the Security Supporting Assistance (1971), and, finally, the Economic Support Fund (1978).

It was probably inevitable in the atmosphere of the cold war following World War II that U.S. development and security assistance programs would become interrelated under the umbrella of

U.S. foreign policy. In 1953, a commission headed by Nelson Rockefeller made such a recommendation. Development- and security-type aid efforts were subsequently accorded the joint roles of fostering economic and political stability and assisting the emergence of democratic societies throughout the world. Initially, emphasis was on nations in need of reconstruction after the war. Later, as the size of the program increased, the focus of U.S. economic assistance shifted from reconstruction to security concerns. Development aid to LDCs, as proclaimed by President Truman, was incorporated into the administrative structure, and as the years have gone by, the objectives of development and security assistance have occasionally been intermingled, despite some effort to keep them separate. However, the criteria for fund allocation have been defined over time (see "Classes of Assistance" below) and are generally followed.

The United States has now become a preeminent donor nation in terms of total assistance offered to others. As a major world power, it has tremendous potential for doing either good or harm by its actions and policies. People in the developing world do not vote in America's elections, but their lives are often significantly influenced by what happens here. Every administration since 1949 has supported foreign assistance as an essential part of this nation's commitment abroad. Still, the programs have been controversial and have generally suffered a lack of public support.

## JUSTIFICATIONS FOR
## U.S. DEVELOPMENTAL ASSISTANCE

The justifications for LDC assistance that were valid in 1949 remain so today and have been strengthened by intervening events. As the world has changed, nations have become more interdependent, and the need for action has intensified. The rationale for the U.S. commitment to help has several dimensions ranging from humanitarian concern to self-interest (furthering our own developmental and political priorities).

### Humanitarian Responsibility

A sense of humanitarianism was the primary motive of the United States in 1949. Most Americans readily embrace the moral and ethical responsibilities inherent in President Truman's original statement. The critical world need for food (discussed in chap. 1) is evidenced by misery and deprivation among many of the world's inhabitants. Certainly, the right to food is fundamental. Discussions of such issues as individual freedom, human dignity, and social justice are pointless until the poor are adequately fed and clothed. The humanitarian basis of our economic and developmental assistance is deeply rooted in our national values, which are embraced just as strongly today by the general public as they were in 1949.

**Economic Benefits**

While the economic interests of the United States may not have been considered important as objectives or justifications for U.S. assistance in 1949, it has since become clear that these interests are enhanced by U.S. efforts to help developing nations. Global economic aid is not simply a sharing of the resources and wealth of this nation. Economic interdependence has grown, and the United States is as influenced by external events as is any other nation. This country depends on world markets to maintain its own strong economy. Much of its export trade, especially of agricultural products, is with LDCs. Furthermore, successful economic development in these nations can make them more active trading partners with the United States, as increased incomes in the hands of their citizens foster rising demands for imported goods and services. The economies of all nations are much more likely to thrive when the purchasing power of today's poor is improved and the mutually beneficial process of extensive international trade is encouraged. In the long run, an improved global economy and increased world food production will benefit large portions of the world's populace. A more reliable global food supply would lessen pressures to increase food prices and would be advantageous to U.S. consumers as well as those of other countries.

**National Security and International Stability**

The forces that threaten international stability and the security of the United States will be discussed in chapter 5, along with the role enhanced food availability may play in controlling them.
of the more explosive factors in the world today is the frustr
desire of rapidly rising numbers of poor people to improve

standard of living. As the presidential Commission on World Hunger observed in its 1980 report:

> The developing nations now actively involved in interna-
> tional affairs are resolutely determined to move into the
> modern world and secure its benefits for themselves. But
> as the aspirations and expectations of the developing world
> grow, poverty within it remains prevalent and con-
> spicuous—with hunger as its quintessential symptom. As a
> result, hunger has been internationalized and turned into
> a continuing global political issue, transformed from a
> low-profile moral imperative into a divisive and disruptive
> factor in international relations.

Beyond its impact on international relations, political in-stability within the LDCs also retards their economic improve-ment. Hunger can create a discontent that contributes to unstable political processes and often to changes in national leadership, both of which limit the continuity of and commit-ment to development. Civil unrest has repeatedly disrupted development programs in these nations. Hungry people, unless made pathetic by starvation, are difficult to rule, no matter what the form of government.

### Administrative Structure Supporting U.S. Assistance
The U.S. assistance effort is administered by the U.S. Agency for International Development (USAID). The agency's ad-ministrator is appointed by the president and reports to the secretary of state. Funding for the agency and its programs comes directly from Congress via USAID's annual budget request, which Congress reviews and may alter. Ultimately, it is Congress that approves or rejects USAID's money requests and its general program directions.

Today's USAID is the product of considerable evolution since 1949. The administrative structure and operational procedures have changed periodically, and e name itself was last changed in 1961.USAID has an extensive organizational structure with its headquarters in Washington, D.C., and branches in the nations where U.S. assistance programs operate. In Washington, the agency has three bureaus that oversee development programming in Africa, Asia/Near East, nd Latin America (figure 2.1). An additional support structure provides guidance to all regional bureaus. For example, professionals in the Bureau for Science and Technology work with the regional bureaus to mobilize USAID technical competence, to provide advice on improving scientific competence in LDCs, and to manage centrally funded projects that operate in countries involving more than one regional bureau.

The USAID programs in each developing nation are administered by a mission director. Normally, mission directors are career USAID employees who have progressed through the USAID system to leadership positions on the basis of merit. Occasionally they are political appointees. The rest of each in-country organization varies depending on the size and nature of the program. The mission usually comprises a deputy director, a controller, a program officer, and an administrative officer. The expertise of heads of divisions will reflect the types of programs being implemented, such as agriculture and food, population and health, and rural development. Division heads and other USAID personnel are normally responsible for supervising one or more active projects. All permanent personnel of USAID hold appointments in the U.S. civil or foreign service. Many of the secretarial and other in-country support staff of each mission are recruited from the local populace. Americans working in USAID missions normally are assigned for two years but often extend for an additional two-year tour. These relatively short assignments can adversely influence program continuity, and the "memory" of the mission can suffer.

In the 1980s, USAID has annually employed over 3,000 technical and professional people (figure 2.2 and appendix table 2.1). Many of those in the work force have both advanced university training in a variety of specialties and prior foreign experience, often with the Peace Corps. However, relatively few have agricultural backgrounds and training. Since 1980 only about 7 percent of the USAID professional work force have been agricultural specialists, but about 75 percent of these were posted abroad. In 1982, 7.5 percent (250 personnel) were agricultural specialists. The small number of such specialists in the permanent labor force is a concern for an agency that stresses agricultural and rural development programs.

**Figure 2.1  Organization of the Agency for International Development (AID)**

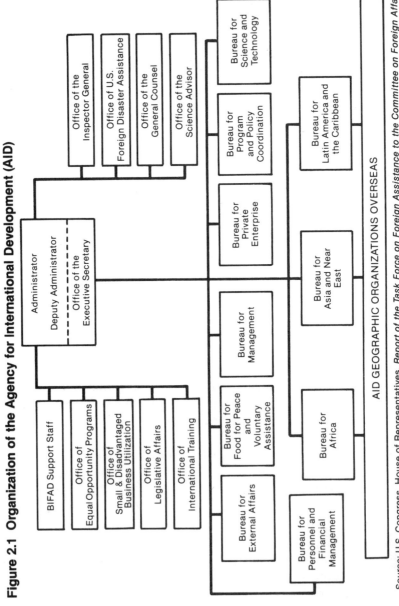

Source: U.S. Congress, House of Representatives, *Report of the Task Force on Foreign Assistance to the Committee on Foreign Affairs,* Washington, D.C.: U.S. GPO, February 1989, 182.

**Figure 2.2  Agricultural Officers in the USAID Work Force\***

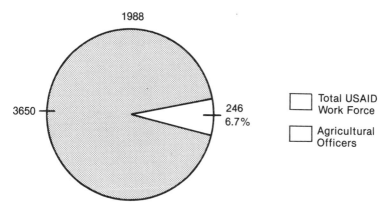

1988

3650 ⊢

246
6.7%

☐ Total USAID
　Work Force

☐ Agricultural
　Officers

\*Excludes overseas complement, positions requested from reserve, and International
Development Intern positions.

Source: BIFAD, *Budget Recommendations: 1985* (Washington, D.C.: USAID, February, 1984),
53; USAID Office of Personnel, 1989.

## ELEMENTS OF THE USAID PROGRAM

**Legal Basis**

Development assistance programs administered by USAID are
authorized under the Foreign Assistance Act of 1961, which is
amended from time to time to accommodate changing world conditions and program needs. The agency also cooperates with the
Departments of Agriculture and State to implement the Agricultural
Trade Development and Assistance Act of 1954—more popularly
known as P.L. 480, or Food for Peace. Under P.L. 480, surplus
agricultural products are distributed free or under concessional
loans to nations that qualify based on need. Low interest rates and
long repayment periods characterize these loans. Then either the
products are sold in the LDC and the funds used to finance development programs within the country, or the products are distributed
as wages to the poorer segments of society in exchange for work on
local development projects. These work projects mostly involve
construction of infrastructure items such as canals, farm-to-market
roads, and culverts and waterways.

A variation to this arrangement, started in the late 1970s, forgives
loan repayment for any LDC that implements policies and procedures that USAID considers vital to the country's development.

Emergency food shipments such as those made to Ethiopia in the 1980s are also authorized under P.L. 480 or can come from disaster relief funds.

P.L. 480 was initiated during a period when agricultural surpluses were a major problem in the United States, but the disposal philosophy still persists. Wheat, corn, cotton, and dairy products have been the commodities most important in P.L. 480 programs. The availability of these crops may cease if domestic U.S. agricultural policy is changed to reduce or eliminate their traditionally surplus status. The drought of 1988 and the U.S. production limitation programs may already have affected these surpluses significantly: according to the Worldwatch Institute, in 1989 the United States will consume more grain than it produces. Further, world grain carryover stocks are at their lowest in more than a decade.

### Classes of Developing Nations

Nations classified by the World Bank as "developing" include four groups that differ widely in income, wealth, and development problems and prospects (see appendix table 1.1). The first group contains the industrial market economies and the high-income oil exporters, including some members of the Organization of Petroleum Exporting Countries (OPEC). Despite their often high per capita incomes, many still retain problem areas characteristic of developing nations, such as low levels of literacy and life expectancy, and a high proportion of their population engaged in agriculture. Obviously, these countries neither need nor receive a concessional type of economic assistance. Instead, they seek a stable and prosperous market for their oil exports and a favorable international environment in which to develop and invest their surplus financial assets.

The second group, referred to by the World Bank as upper middle-income economies, includes newly industrialized countries, several of which have "graduated" from U.S. assistance. These nations have living standards and levels of development comparable to what some developed nations had a short time ago. Their needs for concessional economic assistance are minimal, but they sometimes require specific support to ensure continued progress. For the most part, a strong international economy is their best insurance for sustained development.

The third group comprises the lower middle-income nations, which report per capita incomes roughly between $460 and $1,600. These nations have made some economic progress in recent years but still suffer from widespread poverty. They are usually dependent on a narrow range of exports—usually from agriculture or minerals, which show wide price fluctuations in world markets—for foreign exchange. Having confronted but not always solved many of the traditional development issues, these midlevel nations are still in search of progress, and they continue to require foreign assistance.

Finally, there is the large group of low-income countries in which per capita annual incomes generally are under $460. These nations contain many of the world's worst manifestations of human, social, and economic underdevelopment. They therefore face the most unfavorable economic prospects for the future. Large segments of their populations live at or below the barest biological subsistence levels, and mortality rates are generally high, particularly among infants. They lack basic physical, educational, and social infrastructure, and their involvement in the international economic community of nations is slight. The bulk of future U.S. concessional economic assistance must be directed toward these countries if their people are to make progress.

**Classes of Assistance**

U.S. foreign assistance is composed of two general classes: development and security. Development assistance is given to LDCs friendly to the United States who are judged to have development potential. For the most part, these are nations with problems of extensive poverty, and aid is given on the basis of need to foster economic development. Security aid, on the other hand, is designed to promote development specifically in nations deemed important to the foreign policy and security interests of the United States.

Within each class, major subcategories are commonly identified for administrative/budgetary purposes, as follows:

I. Development Assistance
   A. Bilateral (direct U.S. assistance to another nation)
      1. USAID-administered development assistance. This assistance is primarily used to fund projects designed to

support economic growth and alleviate the causes of poverty in LDCs.

2. P.L. 480. Under this law, U.S. agricultural commodities are provided to countries in the form of loans or grants to support the development and relief efforts of governments, the World Food Program and private voluntary organizations, and long-term concessional sales agreements with recipient nations.

3. Other assistance related to development (includes Peace Corps, narcotics control, migration and refugee assistance, etc.).

B. Multilateral (U.S. aid combined with that from other donor nations). This assistance is passed mostly through multilateral development banks (MDBs) and funds to provide credit for needy nations at concessional interest rates. U.S. funds are combined with those of other donor nations and provide capital markets to enhance the supply and use of credit by these countries.

II. Security Assistance (all bilateral)

A. Military. This category includes grants from Foreign Military Sales (FMS) Credit and the Military Assistance Program. The primary purpose of these programs is to enhance the security of friendly countries via financial aid for military equipment and support. A third subcategory is International Military Education and Training of students from recipient nations in American military methods as well as in the operation and maintenance of U.S. military equipment.

B. Economic Support Fund (ESF). This is the most flexible form of U.S. assistance. It is unencumbered by most of the guidelines imposed on other assistance in terms of the countries that may receive money or the form in which the money is made available. ESF assistance can be justified for political, strategic, or economic reasons, or for any combination of these. It may take the form of a highly concessional loan or grant or of a development project. But it may not be used for defense programs.

Administrative responsibility for foreign assistance lies with either USAID or the Department of State. USAID has jurisdiction over all economic and development resources, including the ESF. Multilateral assistance is controlled by the various multinational boards that direct groups operating the individual institutions being supported, with USAID performing mostly a monitoring function. The Department of State administers all military assistance, as well as other programs related to peacekeeping and migration, and any activities that do not include primarily economic objectives.

**Development Assistance.** As noted above, development assistance includes two broad categories, bilateral and multilateral, that define the jurisdiction and form of administration.

1) **Bilateral assistance.** The bilateral development assistance funds managed by USAID, together with food aid, constitute the main funds directly assignable by USAID to satisfy development objectives and thereby confront the issues of world hunger. Of course, in the daily management of assistance efforts, development assistance programs often feel the pressures of political realities and broader foreign policy interests. Intermingling of objectives can and does occur, and at times nondevelopment interests can override traditional development activities.

Other kinds of bilateral assistance are earmarked by Congress for specific uses, several of which do, incidentally, contribute to the war on hunger. Administratively, these appropriations are mostly monitored rather than managed by USAID. Included are such programs as the Peace Corps and the Inter-American Foundation. Bilateral funds for nondevelopment purposes, such as narcotics control and migration and refugee aid, are under the jurisdiction of the Department of State.

The following budget items, appropriated for 1989 and listed under bilateral assistance, represents 31 percent of the total U.S. foreign assistance of $14,829,299 million:

|  | *$ Millions* |
|---|---|
| USAID-Administered Development Assistance: |  |
| Functional development | 1,243.0 |
| Development Fund for Africa | 500.0 |
| Southern Africa Development Coordination Conference | 50.0 |
| American schools and hospitals abroad | 35.0 |

| | |
|---|---:|
| International disaster assistance | 25.0 |
| Housing Guarantee Borrowing Authority | 30.0 |
| Humanitarian Transport Relief | 3.0 |
| Foreign Service retirement | 40.5 |
| Operating expenses (USAID) | 418.0 |
| Inspector General's operating expenses | 28.5 |
| Central American Reconciliation Assistance | 36.3 |
| Total | $2,409.3 |

| | |
|---|---:|
| P.L. 480 (food aid) | $1,481.9 |

Other Assistance Related to Development:

| | |
|---|---:|
| Trade and development programs | 25.0 |
| International narcotics control | 101.0 |
| Inter-American Foundation1 | 6.6 |
| African Development Foundation | 8.0 |
| Peace Corps1 | 53.5 |
| Migration and refugee assistance | 362.0 |
| Emergency refugee and migration fund | 50.0 |
| Peacekeeping operations | 31.7 |
| Antiterrorism assistance | 9.8 |
| Total | $ 757.6 |

| | |
|---|---:|
| TOTAL | $4,648.8 |

2) **Multilateral assistance.** U.S. multilateral support is channeled through several international banks and development funds whose primary purpose is to serve the needs of developing nations. The United States was instrumental in establishing most MDBs and has traditionally viewed continued participation in their activities as complementing its bilateral assistance program. These institutions are supported by many donor nations and are governed by multinational boards. Donor nation representatives supervise budgetary requests as well as program priorities and performances. The United States contributes to 10 such institutions, including the developmentally oriented agencies in the UN family.

In 1989, U.S. participation in multilateral aid accounted for 10 percent of the nation's total foreign assistance and was allocated among MDBs and agencies as follows:

|  | *$ Millions* |
|---|---|
| World Bank | 50.0 |
| International Finance Corporation | 4.9 |
| International Development Association | 995.0 |
| Asian Development Fund | 152.4 |
| African Development Fund | 105.0 |
| African Development Bank (ADB) | 7.3 |
| International organizations and programs | 226.1 |
| Total | $1,540.7 |

The average U.S. share of MDB assistance is about 25 percent, ranging from near 41 percent for the Inter-American Development Bank (IDB) (although none was appropriated in 1989) to about 6 percent for the ADB. The U.S. share has declined in recent years as the cost of supporting these institutions has become more equitably and widely spread among developed nations. The United States does not act alone in assisting these institutions. For example, the World Bank receives funds from as many as 75 nations.

In contrast to the political orientation of portions of the U.S. bilateral foreign assistance, the help funneled through MDBs tends to be focused more toward the particular development needs of recipient LDCs. For example, the ADB reportedly provides 90 percent of its loans to countries with per capita GNPs under $400. Also, in 1978, the IDB established guidelines that allocate 50 percent of its lending portfolio directly to the poorest groups in borrowing nations. Aid to LDCs through multilateral institutions has consistently emphasized the development of agriculture, industry, physical infrastructure, and, to a lesser extent, social programs. The provision of credit for agriculture and for foreign imports to support development has been important.

The United States further promotes its interests by funding assistance efforts through agencies of the UN. Historically, these agencies have been seen by the United States as offering LDCs a viable and attractive assistance alternative to the controlled or targeted aid from Soviet bloc nations. Within the UN system, the United Nations Development Program (UNDP) is a major instrument for delivering multilateral technical assistance to the developing world. The World Health Organization has a long-standing history of promoting health services and international health standards. The FAO, the World Food Program, and the World Food Council have been instrumental in drawing attention to the world hunger problem and in providing initiatives for finding solutions. The Food Security Scheme, the FAO Global Information and Early Warning System, and the International Fertilizer Scheme are examples of valuable initiatives activated by these UN agencies. The FAO's data collection, analysis, and dissemination service is used by a broad clientele in development and international agricultural trade.

**Security Assistance.** Security assistance funds are all managed bilaterally and frequently merge development objectives with the political and foreign policy interests of the United States. Some see such a merger as a logical way to administer U.S. support so that it preserves this country's independence, helps it fulfill its role as a world leader, and facilitates the collective security interest of peace-seeking nations. For the purposes of this analysis, both military and economic aid are considered under security assistance.

The economic side of security assistance has been designated as the Economic Support Fund. Nations receiving ESF monies must qualify in terms of their developmental needs *and* their strategic importance. Owing to the development use made of these funds, they are managed by USAID. ESF monies are used to help promote economic development and political stability in regions where the United States has particular foreign policy interests and has decided that economic assistance can help secure peace. For example, among the major recipients of ESF support since 1946 have been South Korea, Vietnam, Israel, Turkey, and Egypt, a list that well reflects the world's political trouble spots during the post–World War II era. Almost all of the aid to these nations was categorized as security assistance. On the other hand, it is not uncommon for LDCs to receive a combination of monies from the ESF and development assistance funds. For example, Somalia and Thailand, both LDC recipients of development assistance, have also received ESF support based on foreign policy priorities of the United States. (See appendix table 2.2 for a breakdown of classes of assistance received by all nations from 1946 to 1987.)

The bulk of security assistance money—in 1989 about 62 percent—has been allocated for military aid. It should be noted that the military portions of security assistance represent only a part of the total of U.S. military commitments abroad since

Department of Defense expenditures are separate budget items. The total 1989 allocations to security assistance amounted to 58 percent of the United States' total foreign assistance and were divided as follows:

|  | *$ Millions* |
|---|---|
| Economic Support Fund (ESF) | 3,258.5 |
| Military Assistance Program | 467.0 |
| Foreign Military Sales (FMS) Credit | 4,272.8 |
| Guaranteed FMS loans | 594.0 |
| International Military Education and Training | 47.4 |
| Total | $8,639.7 |

**Development Program Priorities**

Despite the periodic intermingling of foreign policy and development objectives under the aegis of foreign assistance, U.S. development assistance to LDCs (as opposed to security assistance) is sustained in large part by concerns for the poor and a desire to see the world's least privileged benefit from U.S. help. Congress exercises a strong influence over development assistance and has periodically established mandates to guide the program. For example, in the 1970s, Congress decreed an overall concern for the "poorest of the poor" and the small farmers in the developing world as a way to direct U.S. development assistance toward the most needy groups in LDCs. Giving poor people access to basic human needs (food, shelter, education, and health care) was set as the "new direction" for USAID assistance. Since then, the role of women in development and the rights of minorities to participate in development programs also have been stressed to help broaden the distribution of the fruits of development. Specific women-in-development training is considered a priority in USAID programming, especially in the areas of agriculture; private enterprise development, including small and microscale enterprise; and natural resource management and environment.

The recognition given to the role of women in developing nations has gained considerable momentum in recent years. The new emphasis is an attempt to correct a critical oversight of prior development programming, which failed to take into account the fact that women play well-defined roles in determining the economic progress of families, particularly in rural areas. Their roles vary among cultures, but in addition to being mothers, women clearly are important in determining the productivity of agriculture in LDCs. For example, in Bolivia, rural women occupy important places in the marketing of agricultural products. They also work in the fields and participate in major farming decisions such as whether to invest family resources in new agricultural technologies like fertilizer and improved seeds. In Bangladesh, women are not involved in marketing or field work outside of the home, but they manage and directly control the production derived from crops and animals that are located on or very near the family homestead. Furthermore, they are responsible for the post-harvest processing of crops and the storage of food, a task of great importance in a climate with high temperatures and humidity.

Past development programs have erroneously directed their efforts to change agriculture almost entirely at influencing male attitudes, thereby overlooking the critical inputs made by women. Giving more attention to the impact of women on agricultural production is seen as an important factor in raising the effectiveness of USAID-supported programs designed to improve the welfare of rural families.

Congress has strongly opposed development programming that caters to the interests of an entrenched elite or favors higher-income groups in LDCs. Strict adherence to such constraints can limit flexibility and may not always promote the most efficient development of the country. The intent of Congress, however, has been clear and has had a meaningful effect on USAID programs in LDCs. The most recent congressional mandates have sought private sector participation in the development process by encouraging more reliance on the marketplace and on free enterprise in LDCs.

In general, USAID development assistance falls into five categories: agriculture and food; population, nutrition, and health; rural development; energy; and public administration and policy. Each has a wide range of subcategories and a great diversity of individual projects. In the early years of USAID, the focus was on capital-intensive projects such as irrigation, roads, communications, and rural electrification. While these kinds of projects are not neglected where needed, emphasis has recently shifted to supporting projects with social and human development dimensions. Institution building, agricultural research and extension, family planning, nutrition and health, policy dialogue, and more involvement of the private sector and market forces are the issues presently being stressed. Environmental issues in LDCs are now a high-priority concern of USAID in all its programming. Further, development professionals, arguing that some projects in the past ignored the negative long-term impact of measures that may have produced positive short-term results, are becoming increasingly concerned with ensuring that development progress is sustainable.

Historically, the directions proposed by Congress and adopted by USAID have not always found widespread support among developmentalists outside the agency. Of particular note is the earlier focus on small-sized farms as the primary recipient group for development assistance in agriculture. Many found this approach ethically admirable but not always developmentally sound. Such farmers are not always the most responsive group of agricultural producers in an LDC. The small farms lack resources and production options and are therefore less capable than medium and larger farms of adopting new technology or adjusting to the changing needs of a progressive agriculture. On the other hand, the recent focus on human resources and agricultural research/extension development and the increased importance assigned to economic policy and the marketplace have the support of most students of development.

A program as diversified as the one USAID is asked to administer and implement offers many potentials for dispute on both philosophical and practical grounds. Two examples may help orient the reader to the kinds of concerns that surface from time to time.

On a philosophical base, the presence of USAID within the jurisdiction of the State Department is said to make its programs too susceptible to being a tool of foreign policy instead of being concentrated on development issues and the world hunger problem. Although the agency is charged with keeping development and food assistance apart from security assistance, the opportunities and temptations to view both in the same light are heightened by the existing bureaucratic structure. Despite the best of intentions, non-developmental issues can supersede and even displace development concerns in decisions about programs, especially since some classes of U.S. economic aid are already legitimately viewed as a tool of foreign policy. In fact, subportions of Section 620 of the Foreign Assistance Act establish non-developmental preconditions, which, if violated, obligate by law the withdrawal of U.S. development assistance.

Fortunately, the United States has never taken advantage of its food production prominence (in wheat, for example) to organize formal cartel-type arrangements with other producing nations to enhance its economic advantage, as did the petroleum-producing OPEC nations. Such an action would signal an official decision to use food as an overt weapon in foreign diplomacy.

But nonsecurity assistance still can be used to influence political outcomes. In fact, there is considerable evidence that in-country development programs are sometimes altered by non-developmental objectives. For example, development assistance was withheld from Chile because of human rights violations by that government in 1977. In Bolivia, development assistance has been diverted from traditional food production projects to those concerned with substituting other crops for coca or eradicating the crop. (Coca leaves are used in cocaine production, and much of the Bolivian supply reportedly enters the U.S. illegal drug market.)

Another example of concern about U.S. economic assistance, at a more practical level, is USAID's Food Aid Program. Two criticisms are often heard. First, by providing food aid that is sold in developing nations to finance local development projects, the program can increase the supply of the commodities involved and lower their in-country prices. However, while food is thus made available to large segments of the populace, the reduction in prices diminishes production incentives for the country's farmers. Second, food aid can alter existing food systems and create a preference for imported foods over those produced locally. For example, the introduction of U.S.-milled flour under P.L. 480 has led consumers in some LDCs to prefer it to locally produced flour. As a consequence, the demand for local flour is reduced and domestic producers suffer.

Extensive use of food aid is seen by some as a likely signal that food shortages and not poverty persist as the central theme in the U.S. strategy for achieving economic development. Food aid, however, probably serves best during emergencies and as a stop-gap measure at especially critical periods in the development process. Food aid has provided special and direct benefits to very poor segments of the population in many LDCs as support for Food for

Work projects. People are paid in food for their labor on projects such as road and canal construction and maintenance. For most, those supported by these food-aided programs are destitute and without other means of support.

During 1988 and 1989, the implementation of U.S. foreign assistance has been the subject of study by a number of groups, including developmentalists acting in a private capacity, universities, a congressional committee, and staff of USAID itself. Their reports, which recommend substantial change in both the direction and the organization of the entire program, are under review by appropriate authorities in the executive and legislative branches.

**Funding Support**

Total U.S. support for all classes of development and security assistance programs in 1989 was $14.8 billion, the same as it was in 1984 (figure 2.3 and appendix table 2.3). Assistance classified by USAID as "economic" (including the ESF)* amounted to 64 percent of the total, up from 56 percent in 1984. From the $9.4 billion assigned to economic assistance, bilateral development assistance amounted to $4.6 billion, which included $2.4 billion administered

---

As is evidenced in appendix tables 2.3 and 2.4, USAID classifies all aid other than military assistance as "economic."

### Figure 2.3 U.S. Foreign Cooperative Program Obligations, 1968–89

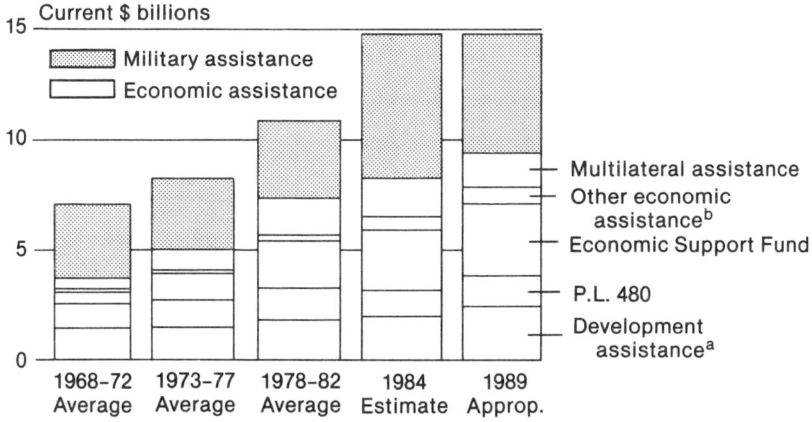

Notes and sources: See appendix table 2.3.

**Figure 2.4  Composition of U.S. Economic Foreign Cooperative Program Obligations, 1968–89**

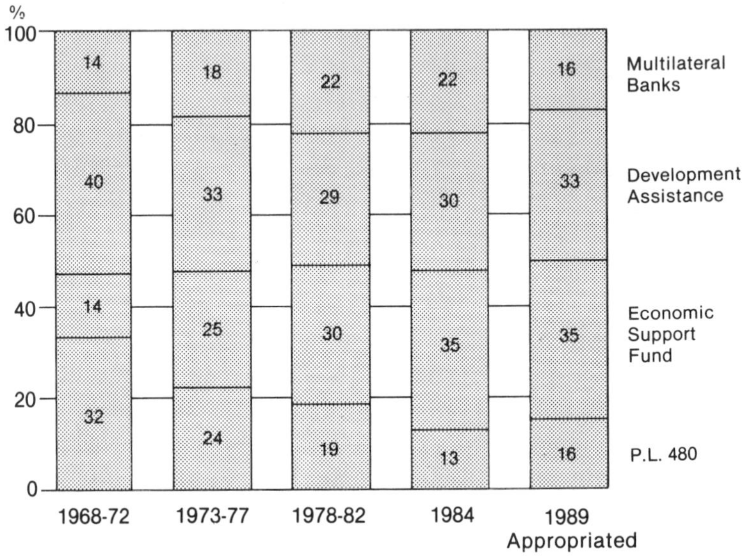

by USAID, $1.5 billion for food aid, and $0.7 billion in assistance administered outside USAID. This represented 49 percent of all economic assistance and 31 percent of the total 1989 appropriation, percentages that are somewhat higher than those for 1984. Multilateral assistance amounted to $1.5 billion, or 16 percent of all economic assistance and 10 percent of the total 1989 appropriation. The ESF, administered as part of security assistance, was allocated $3.3 billion, or 35 percent of all economic asssistance and 23 percent of all aid.

Expenditures from 1968–72 (average) to 1989 show that monies from the ESF have increasingly replaced those for development assistance (figure 2.4 and appendix table 2.3). During that period, development assistance administered by USAID declined from 40 percent to 33 percent of all aid classified as economic, and P.L. 480 funds fell from 32 percent to 16 percent. Conversely, support through the ESF rose from 14 percent to 35 percent of all economic aid.

Measured in current dollars, U.S. appropriations for economic assistance have been increasing consistently. Since 1968–72, total economic assistance has risen 154 percent. The greatest gains have come in aid from the ESF, which has increased more than sixfold. USAID-administered development assistance for the developing world has risen by 113 percent for the approximate 20-year period, while P.L. 480 allocations have increased 25 percent.

### Recipients of U.S. Foreign Assistance

Since 1946, about 150 nations have received some kind of U.S. bilateral foreign assistance. Over 110 nations received American aid in 1987. Most are in Asia and Africa. Fewer nations in the Middle East now receive aid, while support for Latin American nations has been reduced considerably in recent years. Nations in Central America and the Caribbean are receiving more attention, but the amounts of money are small when compared with those given other regions.

**How Much and For What?** From 1946 to 1987, estimates show that the United States has spread $328 billion in bilateral assistance of all kinds around the world. Of that total, $204 billion (62 percent) has been for all types of economic assistance defined by USAID; the rest has been for military purposes (figure 2.5 and appendix table 2.4). Of the total aid, 20 percent went to USAID-administered development assistance while 16 percent was for the ESF. P.L. 480 received 12 percent, and all other economic programs received 14 percent. Trends since 1968–72, however, have favored security assistance.

Regionally, the largest amount of U.S. bilateral foreign aid money has gone to the Middle East and South Asia ($115 billion), of which 53 percent was for economic assistance (figure 2.6 and appendix table 2.5). East Asia received about $69 billion, with 43 percent going for economic assistance. Far less has been distributed to nations in Africa and Latin America. European countries have received about 14 percent of the U.S. assistance dollars since 1946, most of it immediately following World War II.

**Which Nations?** Among individual nations, Israel with $37.9 billion, Vietnam with $23.4 billion (discontinued since before 1980), and Egypt with $23.1 billion top the list of all recipients since 1946 (appendix table 2.2). This aid has mostly been for security assistance (either military or from the ESF). South Korea and Turkey have also received large amounts—also mostly as security assistance. Except for several European nations aided in the aftermath of World War II, the major recipients of development

### Figure 2.5  Distribution of Total U.S. Foreign Assistance, by Type, 1946–87 and 1984–87

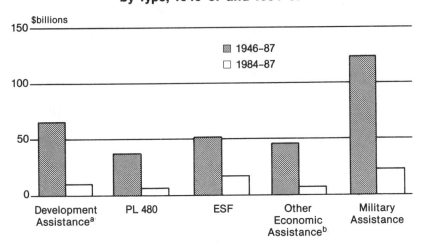

Source: USAID, *U.S. Overseas Loans and Grants* (Washington, D.C.: 1987)
   a) USAID—administered assistance.
   b) Assistance related to development administered by agencies other than USAID.

assistance over the years have been India, Pakistan, Indonesia, Turkey, Bangladesh, and Brazil. Today, Egypt and Israel are the most highly aided nations, although they receive only security assistance and some P.L. 480 shipments to support the Camp David Middle East peace initiatives.

**Recent Trends.** The allocations of bilateral foreign assistance since 1946 reflect the worldwide political and developmental pressures experienced over this period but do not show current conditions. The more recent trends reflect other pressures (figure 2.5 and appendix table 2.4). For 1984–87, military aid still claimed the largest single allocation, with 35.8 percent of the $64.9 billion total. The ESF received 26.5 percent and development assistance 16.0 percent. This reversal of priorities from the 1946–83 pattern illustrates the growing importance of the ESF, which increased by about 10 percent at the expense of both military and development aid.

The rankings of recipient nations for 1984–87 have also changed from those during 1946–87. There is surprising continuity in the list of nations receiving aid in the two periods, however, especially for those receiving the larger amounts (table 2.1). Among the top 10, Israel still heads the list in 1984–87, along with Egypt and

**Figure 2.6 Distribution of Total U.S. Foreign Assistance, by Region, 1948–87**

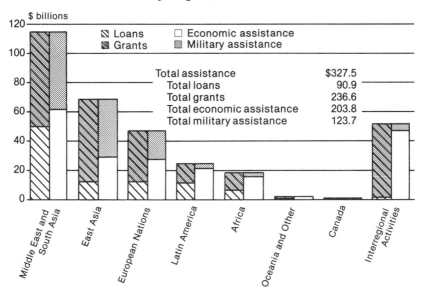

Source: USAID, *U.S. Overseas Loans and Grants* (Washington, D.C.: 1987).

Turkey. Vietnam, France, the United Kingdom, and Taiwan have been replaced by Honduras, Spain, El Salvador, and the Philippines. Of the 30 top recipients for 1946–87, 16 remain in 1984–87. Most of the changes occurred in the last 10 places on the list. Some of the more dramatic shifts in aid patterns have been toward nations in Africa, but the dollar amounts have been nowhere near those allocated to the high-ranking recipients.

**Need Versus Assistance.** Since early in the program, U.S. assistance has involved objectives beyond just economic development. To illustrate this attention to noneconomic development objectives, the per capita GNP figures for individual nations (as indicated on appendix table 1.1) can be compared with the amount of U.S. foreign assistance each nation has received (table 2.1). (GNP is a measure of average individual incomes—the lower the ranking, the poorer the nation.)

Overall, there is very little correlation between the amounts of total foreign assistance received by individual nations for the period 1984–87 and their per capita GNP in 1986. For example, Egypt and Israel, the recipients of the most aid, ranked 53rd and 92nd, respectively, in GNP per capita among 120 nations. In fact,

### Table 2.1    Top 30 Countries Receiving U.S. Foreign Assistance, 1984-87

| GNP Rank* | Foreign Assistance Rank | Country | Amount ($ millions) |
|---|---|---|---|
| 92 | 1 | Israel | 12,581.1 |
| 53 | 2 | Eqypt | 9,795.8 |
| 64 | 3 | Turkey | 3,072.0 |
| 28 | 4 | Pakistan | 2,606.7 |
| 56 | 5 | El Salvador | 2,001.5 |
| 89 | 6 | Greece | 1,779.0 |
| 44 | 7 | Philippines | 1,343.2 |
| 102 | 8 | Spain | 1,339.6 |
| 52 | 9 | Honduras | 925.5 |
| 26 | 10 | Sudan | 834.8 |
| 5 | 11 | Bangladesh | 774.2 |
| 70 | 12 | Costa Rica | 758.6 |
| 20 | 13 | India | 758.2 |
| 81 | 14 | Portugal | 692.3 |
| 71 | 15 | Jordan | 660.0 |
| 85 | 16 | South Korea | 630.2 |
| 45 | 17 | Morocco | 574.1 |
| 42 | 18 | Indonesia | 571.9 |
| 58 | 19 | Jamaica | 507.8 |
| 55 | 20 | Thailand | 499.4 |
| 60 | 21 | Guatemala | 443.1 |
| 49 | 22 | Dominican Republic | 431.2 |
| 65 | 23 | Tunisia | 416.2 |
| 63 | 24 | Peru | 385.9 |
| 18 | 25 | Somalia | 383.3 |
| 23 | 26 | Kenya | 337.7 |
| 46 | 27 | Bolivia | 287.4 |
| 27 | 28 | Haiti | 285.8 |
| 7 | 29 | Zaire | 271.0 |
| 40 | 30 | Liberia | 269.8 |

*Poorest nations begin with numbers 1, 2, 3, etc.

Sources: USAID, *U.S. Overseas Loans and Grants* (Washington, D.C.: 1987); World Bank, *World Development Report 1988.*

among the 30 largest recipients of U.S. foreign assistance, only 8 (Bangladesh, Zaire, Somalia, India, Kenya, Sudan, Haiti, and Pakistan) were also listed among the 38 poorest nations. At the other extreme, Ethiopia, with the lowest GNP, ranked 34th on the U.S. foreign assistance list. Of the 10 poorest nations, only Bangladesh and Zaire were among the 30 nations receiving the greatest aid.

Of the 114 nations that received foreign assistance from the United States between 1984 and 1987 (appendix table 2.6), the world's 38 poorest nations received only 13 percent of the total U.S. assistance. The 34 lower middle-income economies received 37 percent of the aid, the 24 upper middle-income economies received 25 percent, and the 23 richest nations received 2 percent. The 20 countries without GNP rankings were given 1 percent, while the remaining 22 percent was spent on regional and interregional activities, most prominently in Latin America and Africa.

Much of the explanation for these relationships is found in the high proportion of security assistance given to some of the nations with higher incomes (appendix table 2.6). For example, 53 percent of Israel's assistance was military aid and 47 percent ESF. Similarly, 52 percent of Egypt's aid was military assistance. Overall, there is a strong tendency for certain nations to appear as major recipients for all classes of aid and for the amounts they receive to be unrelated to their income rankings.

**Economic Support Fund.** An example of these relationships is seen in the allocation of ESF assistance for the period 1984–87. Generally, recipients of these monies reflect foreign policy interests of the United States, not all of which are military. Israel, Egypt, and Pakistan head the list of ESF recipients (table 2.2). Of the top 30 nations receiving this aid, only 8 were also ranked among the 38 poorest nations.

The regional allocations of security assistance closely follow regional instances of political and military stress (appendix table 2.7). In the 1970s Asia (Vietnam) occupied U.S. attention, but since 1975 (and especially in 1977) the Middle East (Egypt and Israel) has received a large portion of the security assistance support; between 1975 and 1986, the amount spent on security assistance to Egypt and Israel was 71 percent more than that spent on USAID-administered development assistance for the rest of the developing nations. Since 1981, Latin America, particularly Central America and the Caribbean, has had its security assistance increased. In fact, since 1981 the increases in security assistance to *all* regions of the world have increased significantly.

**P.L. 480.** About two-thirds of the nations receiving the most substantial blocks of P.L. 480 aid are also among the largest recipients of ESF aid (table 2.3). Rankings of nations receiving food aid tend to reflect more accurately their levels of development needs and interests, but the list does not conform closely to their per capita GNP rankings. Of the 30 highest-ranking recipients of

### Table 2.2    Top 30 Countries Receiving Economic Support Fund (ESF) Assistance, 1984-87

| GNP Rank* | ESF Rank | Country | Amount ($millions) |
|---|---|---|---|
| 92 | 1 | Israel | 5,958.5 |
| 53 | 2 | Egypt | 3,806.9 |
| 28 | 3 | Pakistan | 914.8 |
| 56 | 4 | El Salvador | 868.6 |
| 44 | 5 | Philippines | 725.4 |
| 70 | 6 | Costa Rica | 568.1 |
| 64 | 7 | Turkey | 533.1 |
| 52 | 8 | Honduras | 388.5 |
| 71 | 9 | Jordan | 326.4 |
| 81 | 10 | Portugal | 261.4 |
| 26 | 11 | Sudan | 244.0 |
| 58 | 12 | Jamaica | 220.5 |
| 60 | 13 | Guatemala | 180.8 |
| 49 | 14 | Dominican Republic | 169.2 |
| 40 | 15 | Liberia | 121.7 |
| 18 | 16 | Somalia | 104.1 |
| 47 | 17 | Zimbabwe | 96.1 |
| 24 | 18 | Zambia | 91.5 |
| 103 | 19 | Ireland | 85.0 |
| 23 | 20 | Kenya | 75.4 |
| 73 | 21 | Lebanon | 75.2 |
| 90 | 22 | Oman | 69.6 |
| 27 | 23 | Haiti | 67.4 |
| 33 | 24 | Senegal | 64.5 |
| 83 | 25 | Panama | 63.2 |
| 65 | 26 | Tunisia | 61.3 |
| ** | 27 | Cyprus | 59.4 |
| ** | 28 | Grenada | 58.1 |
| 7 | 29 | Zaire | 55.0 |
| 45 | 30 | Morocco | 48.6 |

*Sources:* See table 2.1.
*Poorest nations begin with numbers 1, 2, 3, etc.
**Data not available.

food aid, 15 are also among the world's 38 poorest nations; however, 3 have GNPs in excess of $1,000 annually, which places them in the upper level of the lower middle-income nations.

One reason for such phenomena may be that P.L. 480 funds can be used for other than just food grants and emergencies. As indicated earlier, food aid can be provided as loans, and (in selected cases) when economic policy reforms occur consistent

## Table 2.3   Top 30 Countries Receiving P.L. 480 Assistance, 1984-87

| GNP Rank* | P.L. 480 Rank | Country | Amount ($millions) |
|---|---|---|---|
| 53 | 1 | Egypt | 897.9 |
| 5 | 2 | Bangladesh | 468.5 |
| 20 | 3 | India | 423.7 |
| 26 | 4 | Sudan | 330.7 |
| 28 | 5 | Pakistan | 323.8 |
| 45 | 6 | Morocco | 234.8 |
| 56 | 7 | El Salvador | 215.1 |
| 1 | 8 | Ethiopia | 181.1 |
| 42 | 9 | Indonesia | 157.1 |
| 44 | 10 | Philippines | 150.9 |
| 63 | 11 | Peru | 144.2 |
| 58 | 12 | Jamaica | 138.4 |
| 31 | 13 | Sri Lanka | 133.8 |
| 49 | 14 | Dominican Republic | 120.4 |
| 18 | 16 | Somalia | 120.4 |
| 46 | 15 | Bolivia | 106.1 |
| 60 | 17 | Guatemala | 96.6 |
| 27 | 18 | Haiti | 95.7 |
| 10 | 19 | Mozambique | 84.6 |
| 30 | 20 | Ghana | 83.3 |
| 7 | 21 | Zaire | 82.7 |
| 70 | 22 | Costa Rica | 81.7 |
| 52 | 23 | Honduras | 77.3 |
| 23 | 24 | Kenya | 70.2 |
| 65 | 25 | Tunisia | 65.4 |
| 33 | 26 | Senegal | 51.5 |
| 3 | 27 | Burkina Faso | 46.4 |
| 43 | 28 | North Yemen | 45.0 |
| 40 | 29 | Liberia | 44.7 |
| 24 | 30 | Zambia | 41.0 |

*Sources:* See table 2.1.
*Poorest nations begin with numbers 1, 2, 3, etc.

with development objectives, the initial loan can be forgiven. This flexibility permits P.L. 480 assistance to be adjusted to better meet local conditions and to provide policy-change incentives for any nation that qualifies for U.S. help.

**USAID-Administered Development Assistance.** The major recipients of development assistance administered by USAID do not include Egypt or Israel (table 2.4). The largest recipient during 1984–87 was El Salvador, followed by India and Bangladesh. Of the

## Table 2.4    Top 30 Countries Receiving Development Assistance, 1984-87

| GNP Rank* | Devel. Assist. Rank | Country | Amount ($millions) |
|---|---|---|---|
| 56 | 1 | El Salvador | 351.6 |
| 20 | 2 | India | 333.5 |
| 5 | 3 | Bangladesh | 304.5 |
| 42 | 4 | Indonesia | 300.1 |
| 63 | 5 | Peru | 191.7 |
| 52 | 6 | Honduras | 173.4 |
| 44 | 7 | Philippines | 145.9 |
| 26 | 8 | Sudan | 144.1 |
| 60 | 9 | Guatemala | 142.7 |
| 31 | 10 | Sri Lanka | 131.4 |
| 46 | 11 | Bolivia | 123.1 |
| 58 | 12 | Jamaica | 111.0 |
| 27 | 13 | Haiti | 110.8 |
| 49 | 14 | Dominican Republic | 107.8 |
| 43 | 15 | North Yemen | 104.7 |
| 55 | 16 | Thailand | 102.6 |
| 33 | 17 | Senegal | 99.8 |
| 28 | 18 | Pakistan | 99.1 |
| 66 | 19 | Ecuador | 98.9 |
| 23 | 20 | Kenya | 97.4 |
| 59 | 21 | Cameroon | 92.7 |
| 16 | 22 | Niger | 87.9 |
| 7 | 23 | Zaire | 87.0 |
| 45 | 24 | Morocco | 80.7 |
| 18 | 25 | Somalia | 77.6 |
| 70 | 26 | Costa Rica | 72.9 |
| 83 | 27 | Panama | 67.2 |
| 4 | 28 | Nepal | 65.4 |
| 40 | 29 | Liberia | 57.9 |
| 6 | 30 | Malawi | 54.8 |

*Sources:* See table 2.1.
*Poorest nations begin with numbers 1, 2, 3, etc.

top 30 nations receiving development assistance, 13 were also among the 38 nations with the lowest per capita GNP rankings whereas only 4 had per capita GNPs of more than $1,000 annually. This distribution is similar to that for P.L. 480 assistance.

Any analysis of U.S. economic assistance reveals the often-made point that development and foreign policy goals are intermingled. This mixing has become ingrained over time and reflects the expressed intent of the United States to help its friends. The absence of consistent correlations between the food needs of and the aid given to individual nations may deserve additional attention, however, since a closer relationship might imply a more direct impact on the world hunger problem.

Much of the present world need for foreign assistance is centered in Africa, and it has gained a stronger focus in recent years. During the 1960s and into the 1970s, primary attention was given to Asia and Latin America. Now, in the 1980s and beyond, Africa is likely to receive more and more funds, and future summaries of U.S. aid allocations will reflect this change in area priorities. There are limits, however, to how quickly and to what extent the change can be made. Despite their poverty and needs, poor nations are not always capable of absorbing large amounts of aid. Program progress and the use made of external assistance is often most effective if the process is based on previously established in-country capability. Some of the more important preconditions for effective use of assistance funds include improving the training and work skills of the people, updating outdated government institutions, and revising ineffective public policies. Injecting huge amounts of assistance into the economy of ill-prepared poor nations can be wasteful. Gradual buildups of programs and aid dollars have generally proved the most productive.

**Grants Versus Loans**

Bilateral assistance is provided as both grants and loans to developing nations. Grants are gifts and are generally based both on need and on a nation having only a limited ability to qualify for commercial credit. Consequently, bilateral grants tend to go to poorer nations. But the history is mixed. All ESF monies are given as grants. Loans for other classes of assistance are always made at concessional rates of interest (which range from 2 percent to 4 percent annually) and incorporate long repayment periods of up to 40 years. Loans usually provide a grace period of 5 to 10 years, during which time repayment of principal is delayed but interest obligations must be met.

Since 1946, about 72 percent of all U.S. bilateral aid has been disbursed as grants (figure 2.6 and appendix table 2.5). Most of the assistance given to European nations following World War II was in the form of grants. Overall, grants have been most commonly made to nations of Oceania, East Asia, and Africa. Although recent trends show an increasing emphasis on grants following a greater reliance on loans during parts of the 1960s and 1970s—for 1984–87 alone, grants represented 76 percent of all U.S. aid—loans still continue to be important to U.S. foreign assistance.

Nations obtaining loans are expected to repay them, and the history has been fairly good (appendix table 2.8). Since 1946, the United States has loaned about $90.9 billion to other nations, with some of the total going to developed nations after World War II. As of 1987, $54.4 billion have been repaid as principal and interest. The data do not separate principal and interest repayments, so it is difficult to estimate the proportion of principal repaid. Most loans to developed nations have been repaid with interest. USAID policy decrees that LDCs must remain current on their repayment of outstanding loans or other assistance will be discontinued. Even though this policy sometimes causes stress for money-short LDCs, it has generally been followed.

### Problems of Debt Management in Developing Nations

Besides getting financial assistance from donor nations such as the United States, developing nations also borrow from private banks, and private investment flows into these nations in response to private-sector initiatives. The relative importance of various sources of financing depends largely on the development progress of the nation. The more developed the LDC, the greater its creditworthiness and capacity to command commercial financing. For example, in 1982, 93 percent of the capital inflow into lower-income LDCs came from donor assistance plus loans, and only about 7 percent was from private sources. For middle-income, non oil-exporting LDCs, about 65 percent of the inflowing capital came from private investments and 35 percent from donor assistance and loans.

The collective LDC debt for development assistance is owed to a large number of donor nations. In 1981, 26 percent of that debt was owed to OPEC nations, 6 percent to Socialist bloc nations, and 68 percent to other nations, including the United States.

The medium- and long-term debts of developing nations (figure 2.7) increased from $69.4 billion in 1970 to $548 billion in 1982. In 1987, the debt approximated $900 billion. Donor-related debt

**Figure 2.7 Outstanding Debt of Developing Nations, 1970–87**

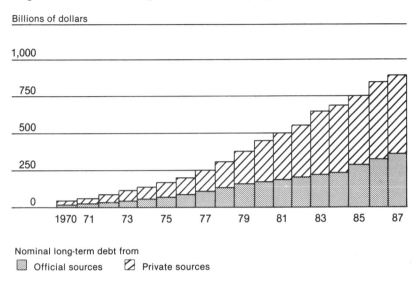

Billions of dollars

Nominal long-term debt from
▨ Official sources  ▨ Private sources

Source: World Bank, *World Development Report 1988* (New York: Oxford University Press).

represented about 36 percent of the 1987 total; the rest was privately held. The average interest rate on new loans, both public and private, rose from 6.3 percent in 1970 to 8.9 percent in 1980 but declined to about 7.0 percent in 1986. LDC interest payments on medium- and long-term debts amounted to about $47.8 billion in 1986.

Debt payments represent a significant hurdle for developing nations as they continue to strive for economic progress and independence. Exports (foreign exchange) are the resource most relied upon to service these debts, but most developing nations have limited export capabilities. Their merchandise imports traditionally exceed exports, creating a negative balance of payments. In 1982, the composite net negative balance of trade for LDCs was about $118 billion, declining to $21.3 billion in 1986. The continuing adverse balance of payments, coupled with the rising total external debt of developing nations, has created a condition that is reaching a critical stage worldwide. It not only threatens the economic welfare of individual nations, but also could significantly affect the world's economic structure.

## U.S. CAPACITY TO SUPPORT ECONOMIC ASSISTANCE

Opponents of U.S. economic assistance often argue that too much money is provided for these programs, money that they say could be used more productively at home. They also suggest that the United States is carrying too much of the burden of assisting poor nations and that other developed nations should be encouraged to do more.

In reality, foreign assistance represents less than 1 percent of this nation's total budget. Programs related strictly to development efforts account for much less, especially if ESF totals are excluded. Cutting all types of economic and development assistance by as much as one-half would have only a miniscule impact on the funds available to apply either to domestic programs or to the national debt. In contrast, those same reductions would decimate an effort that has far-reaching importance to the United States and the future of the world.

This nation's capacity to assist poorer nations is not, however, adequately expressed as a percentage of the national budget. A more valid comparison would consider national overall wealth, or GNP. Since 1949, total U.S. expenditures for economic assistance have been rising, but so has the nation's GNP. In 1982, foreign assistance represented 0.27 percent of the GNP of the United States (table 2.5). About this same proportion has persisted since the early 1970s. In the 1960s the percentage was consistently around 0.53. In 1986, it dropped to 0.23.

The 1986 figure places the United States 17th among the 18 major non-Communist nations that offer substantial economic assistance to LDCs. Only Austria gave a smaller proportion of its GNP than did the United States, whereas Norway and the Netherlands gave slightly more than 1.0 percent.

The United States does, however, still lead all nations in total aid provided, followed by Japan, France, and West Germany, although Japan is expected to take the lead in 1989. The $9.6 billion in economic aid supplied in 1986 include ESF monies associated with security assistance. Still, the contributions from other nations have been increasing relative to those of the United States (figure 2.8). Since 1970, U.S. contributions as a proportion of economic aid from all nations in the Organization for Economic Cooperation and Development (OECD) and OPEC consistently declined from

### Table 2.5   Net Official Economic Assistance from DAC* Countries to Developing Countries and Multilateral Agencies, 1970-86

| Net Disbursements | 1970 | | 1980 | | 1982 | | 1986 | |
|---|---|---|---|---|---|---|---|---|
| Countries | $bil. | As % GNP | $bil. | As % GNP | $bil. | As % GNP | $bil. | As % GNP |
| Norway | ** | 0.32 | 0.5 | 0.87 | 0.6 | 1.03 | 0.8 | 1.20 |
| Netherlands | 0.2 | 0.61 | 1.6 | 0.97 | 1.5 | 1.07 | 1.7 | 1.01 |
| Denmark | 0.1 | 0.38 | 0.5 | 0.74 | 0.4 | 0.77 | 0.7 | 0.89 |
| Sweden | 0.1 | 0.38 | 1.0 | 0.78 | 1.0 | 1.02 | 1.1 | 0.85 |
| France | 1.0 | 0.66 | 4.2 | 0.63 | 4.0 | 0.74 | 5.1 | 0.72 |
| Belgium | 0.1 | 0.46 | 0.6 | 0.50 | 0.5 | 0.58 | 0.5 | 0.49 |
| Canada | 0.3 | 0.41 | 1.1 | 0.43 | 1.2 | 0.41 | 1.7 | 0.48 |
| Australia | 0.2 | 0.59 | 0.7 | 0.48 | 0.9 | 0.56 | 0.8 | 0.47 |
| Finland | ** | 0.06 | 0.1 | 0.22 | 0.1 | 0.29 | 0.3 | 0.45 |
| West Germany | 0.6 | 0.32 | 3.6 | 0.44 | 3.2 | 0.48 | 3.8 | 0.43 |
| Italy | 0.1 | 0.16 | 0.7 | 0.15 | 0.8 | 0.20 | 2.4 | 0.40 |
| United Kingdom | 0.5 | 0.41 | 1.9 | 0.35 | 1.8 | 0.37 | 1.8 | 0.32 |
| Switzerland | ** | 0.15 | 0.3 | 0.24 | 0.3 | 0.25 | 0.4 | 0.30 |
| New Zealand | ** | 0.23 | 0.1 | 0.33 | 0.1 | 0.28 | 0.1 | 0.30 |
| Japan | 0.4 | 0.23 | 3.4 | 0.32 | 3.0 | 0.28 | 5.6 | 0.29 |
| Ireland | ** | 0.0 | ** | 0.16 | ** | 0.27 | 0.1 | 0.28 |
| United States | 3.2 | 0.32 | 7.1 | 0.27 | 8.2 | 0.27 | 9.6 | 0.23 |
| Austria | ** | 0.07 | 0.2 | 0.23 | 0.2 | 0.36 | 0.2 | 0.21 |
| TOTAL DAC COUNTRIES | 7.0 | | 27.6 | | 27.8 | | 36.7 | |

*Source:* World Bank, *World Development Report 1988*, Errata.
  *Development Assistance Committee of the Organization for Economic Cooperation and Development.
**Less than $50 million.

a high of 38 percent to a low of about 15 percent in 1979. Subsequent increases pushed U.S. aid to about 28 percent of the world total in 1985. However, the 1986 estimate drops to 23 percent—the approximate level of 1982. These overall trends indicate a weakening of the U.S. commitment to fund foreign assistance, especially economic aid.

A comparison of economic assistance funds appropriated in 1989 with major classes of personal expenditures by Americans in 1986 reflects an implied value system that sheds light on the relative importance given in the United States to helping the world's poor. The $9.4 billion assigned to official economic assistance in 1989 is

**Figure 2.8  U.S. Share of World Development Assistance, 1970–86**

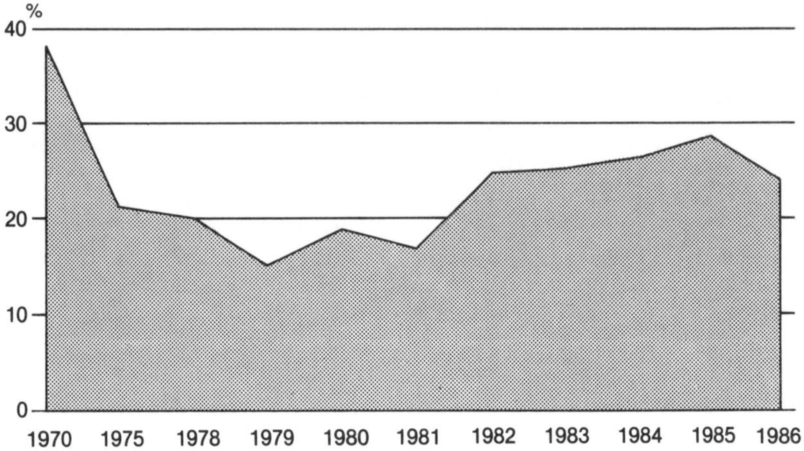

Source: World Bank, *World Development Report 1985* and *1988*.

Note: Fluctuations in U.S. share registered after 1978 reflect timing of recording by DAC of
U.S. contributions to multilateral agencies.

almost $1 billion below what Americans spent on admissions to
movies and theaters in 1986 ($10.3 billion), is just over one-quarter
of what they spent that year on tobacco products ($34.2 billion),
and is less than one-sixth of what they spent on alcoholic beverages
($59 billion).

**Participation by Other Nations**

The 18 nations listed in table 2.5, which constitute the Development Assistance Committee (DAC) of the OECD, are only part of
a much more extensive group of nations and agencies that provide
economic assistance to the developing world. In addition, several
oil-exporting nations of OPEC (such as Saudi Arabia and Kuwait)
provide assistance, as do about 10 nations from the Socialist bloc.
For example, about 35 nations representing these three groups,
plus 10 international (mostly multilateral) agencies, maintain
economic assistance programs in Bangladesh. Although the size of
the commitment to Bangladesh, in both number of nations and
amount of assistance, is not typical of that found in most LDCs, all
LDCs commonly have several donors simultaneously extending
economic assistance.

Most donor nations provide assistance that is directed toward the broad areas of agricultural and rural needs; population planning; energy; physical infrastructure development such as roads, communications, and irrigation needs; industrial development; and a wide variety of education and training programs. Within these general areas, donors may choose some focus, but it is not uncommon for individual nations to have considerable diversity in their portfolio of assistance projects. Donors normally fund projects that fit their particular developmental philosophy, their perspective of development constraints within the LDC, or the availability of excess commodities or food. For example, much of Canada's assistance is given as food aid (wheat), while Sweden has emphasized training efforts.

The tendency of donors not to specialize makes coordination difficult for LDC officials. The problems re further heightened when most donors choose to pursue independent relationships with the host country. Without collaborative planning among donors, the LDCs must try to coordinate diverse, multiple-donor activities. This places stress on the capacities of both individuals and institutions within the LDC government.

In most donor nations, foreign assistance decisions re not shaped by issues of security and politics to the extent found with the United States. Russia and some Socialist bloc nations are the exceptions. Most OECD nations do not utilize a concept akin to security assistance. Instead, they mainly view their aid as developmental without strong political dimensions, although some use their assistance to promote trade and foreign markets for their domestic production.

## Private Support for Development Assistance

In addition to government support, development assistance benefits from extensive private voluntary contributions. Voluntary assistance comes from all 18 of the DAC nations (appendix table 2.9). In 1975, about $1.9 billion was donated from all DAC nations; this amount increased to an estimated $2.9 billion in 1985. Individuals and groups in the United States contributed $1.5 billion in 1985, or 53 percent of the total. West Germany and the United Kingdom were next in total private help. Norway had the highest per capita contributions ($12.54). The United States per capita aid of $6.32 was seventh among all DAC nations, somewhat in contrast to its next-to-last-place ranking when official development assistance is looked at as a percentage of GNP.

**Benefits to U.S. Firms**

There is an implicit assumption by many Americans that the money provided by the United States for economic assistance constitutes an outflow of resources that returns no benefits to the nation. In the next chapter, the impacts of this assistance on U.S. international trade will be discussed. But even more direct benefits than expanded trade relationships accrue to U.S. business and industry from the expenditure of assistance dollars.

A large portion of the support given to LDCs is in dollars or U.S. credits that must be spent for goods and services needed to implement development programs and projects in the LDCs. Machinery, supplies, and personal services are among the types of items normally bought. Assistance agreements between the United States and LDCs specify that such goods and services, when purchased with U.S. dollars for use on development assistance (and to some extent ESF) projects, must have their "source and origin" in the United States. The only exception is if the goods and services are available from the LDC manufacturers or suppliers. Multilateral aid is not regulated in this manner, but portions of that money are also spent in the United States.

Estimates vary, but usually around 70 percent of the regulated funds are ultimately spent on goods and services produced by U.S. suppliers. These expenditures are made in both the public and private sectors. For 1983, reports show that $681 million was spent in the private sector (figure 2.9). During the past 12 years, more than 5,000 U.S. manufacturers and suppliers received USAID-supported orders worth more than $9 billion.

This process is seen by some as a paradox in U.S. foreign assistance. On the one hand, it provides a realistic justification to Congress and the American tax-payer for use of U.S. resources abroad. On the other hand, it clouds the generosity associated with economic assistance by introducing a self-serving dimension that limits the independence of LDCs.

Both positions can have merit based on whether grant or loan funds are involved. It seems reasonable to attach conditions to grant funds and expect them to be used to purchase U.S, goods and services. If a nation is using loan funds that carry a legal responsibility

**Figure 2.9  USAID-Financed Purchases from the Private Sector**

Estimated $ millions

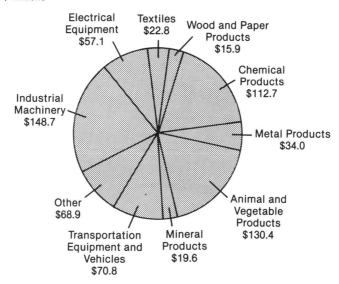

to repay, however, then it may reasonably claim a right to shop for the best deal. Yet the fact that loans are tendered at highly concessional interest rates tempers this argument in some views.

Before condemning U.S. policy too vigorously, it should be noted that this nation's position is less stringent than that of many other donor nations. For example, Japan and the Socialist nations place source and origin restrictions on all their assistance. Most other donor nations, especially the larger ones with important industrial capacities, attach similar restrictions to use of their aid.

## IMPLEMENTATION OF U.S. DEVELOPMENT ASSISTANCE

The administrative structure of USAID exists principally to manage the agency's programming and approval process for projects and programs in LDCs financed by the United States. The agency's procedures require close collaboration and cooperation with the host nation. All projects proposed by USAID personnel for a developing nation require the approval of that nation's government as well as the concurrence of appropriate USAID offices in

Washington. The process is deliberate and perhaps unduly cautious. It is not uncommon for two years to pass between the time a project is conceived either within the USAID mission or by the host country government and the time a contractor is selected and project implementation begins in the LDC. Such a time lapse reflects the fact that a project must meet about 75 statutory requirements before it receives final approval. In fact, a recent internal task force found that the USAID program has been lost in a maze of 75 listed priorities for economic development as well as 288 different congressionally mandated reporting requirements. (Appendix table 2.10 gives a few of the key steps in the process.)

USAID makes extensive use of outside help in implementing projects. Contractors are selected by the agency and the host country through a bidding process. Respondents generally come from the private business sector, from private voluntary organizations specializing in development, or from the U.S. university system. Other U.S. governmental agencies with a needed expertise (e.g., the USDA) can be selected without the bidding procedure. The process has fostered an extensive cadre of private firms interested solely in providing services needed in a wide range of development activities. The firms' specialties range from engineering and construction to population planning. USAID project officers located in the LDCs continually monitor projects to ensure progress and compliance with contract requirements.

### Role of U.S. Universities

The U.S. system of higher education has become a particularly important source of contractual help to U.S. development assistance programs. When the United States embarked on its initial Point Four program in 1949, the U.S. university system was the first group to which the government turned for contracting assistance. By the end of 1952, eight universities had been given responsibilities for agricultural and rural development programs in the following nations:

- Iraq—University of Arizona
- Panama—University of Arkansas
- Philippines—Cornell University
- India—University of Illinois
- Colombia—Michigan State University
- Ethiopia—Oklahoma State University

- Brazil—Purdue University
- Iran—Utah State University

This was a new experience for both the government and the universities. Few universities had previously operated either teaching or research programs in a foreign nation. They found that technical assistance activities far from the home campus posed many unexpected complications. Out of those early efforts has evolved a system of cooperation that continues to improve as it solves successive operational problems.

Involvement of the university system is critical to U.S. development efforts abroad since the system probably houses the greatest concentration of skilled scientific talent in the world. The land-grant universities have a special potential to help LDCs because of both their past record in promoting the rise of a highly productive agriculture in the United States and the agrarian nature of most developing nations. Clearly, with science and agricultural technology at the base of progress in the developing world, universities have an important part to play.

**Problems for Universities and States**

Universities that have placed their faculty and expertise abroad have reaped both problems and benefits. For the most part, the negative issues have centered around the disincentives associated with university commitments abroad, College deans and department heads have a primary responsibility to implement domestic research, teaching, and extension programs. Foreign involvement adds another dimension that must be balanced with the others. Faculty are usually assigned for at least two years to foreign projects, which means ongoing state programs are disrupted and faculty replacements must be found. The manager of a foreign program usually requests the university's most experienced and capable faculty members. These are the people who probably are considered indispensable to an urgent state program, the needs of which are exerting substantial immediate pressures on university administrators. Withdrawal of key faculty to serve abroad may bring strong objections from local producers or other interest groups who argue that their problems have a more legitimate claim on university faculty.

Individually, faculty members must assess the impact of their going abroad on present research or teaching positions. Family relocation and adjustment considerations also influence individual decisions. Family safety, health, and education concerns as well as social relationships within school, church, and the extended family are other important factors.

Consider, too, that a 10-year program requiring five separate agricultural specialists (if each specialist serves only 2 years) means that 25 faculty members will be required to fulfill the entire contract. If the program is in a non-English-speaking nation, the need for language competence presents an added difficulty. The composite of university and faculty issues, the number of faculty involved, and the timing of USAID contract and university needs often mean that technical people cannot be delivered abroad precisely when wanted. Also, all too often, a university finds it difficult to provide qualified replacements for each position over the full life of the contract.

The issues are complicated and their resolution a frustrating process, but the need for participation by university faculty is so critical that university and USAID officials have spent much time establishing a functional relationship. In 1975, Congress enacted Title XII to the Foreign Assistance Act of 1961. The intention was to help strengthen foreign program capabilities in universities and colleges and to enlist fuller and more effective use of their faculty.

About 140 U.S. universities are eligible under this strengthening program to participate in USAID-funded foreign projects. Authority given under Title XII is exercised through USAID, assisted by a seven-member, presidentially appointed Board for International Food and Agricultural Development (BIFAD). This promotion of university/USAID collaboration is helping to make more qualified faculty available for developmental programs abroad.

In 1988, 62 universities had long-term contracts with USAID that were located in 57 developing nations worldwide. The value of these contracts was $582 million. The average life of a project was five to six years, which is typical of USAID projects, although the funding authority of the agency is for only one year at a time.

### Benefits to Universities and States

Despite the difficulties, the university system places hundreds of faculty abroad annually (many with private firms or private voluntary organizations) to participate in the U.S. development assistance effort. The experience of the past 35 years has demonstrated advantages to states and universities alike.

The first is the obvious impact on the quality of education. Faculty with foreign experience bring new perspectives to their classes, are able to improve departmental curriculum, and can stimulate student awareness of world conditions.

Second, an overseas commitment by a university brings more foreign students to the campus, which adds another cultural dimension to the university and the surrounding community. The number of these students nationwide is impressive. For example, during the 1987–88 school year, 356,190 foreign students were registered in 2,552 U.S. universities. They represented almost every nation of the world, but 82 percent were from nations in Africa, Asia, Latin America, and the Middle East.

Third, valuable interchanges of knowledge occur between the university and the host country. For example, while most of the agricultural crops in the United States were growing here before 1949, few are indigenous. Some of the reverse technology flows from LDCs have therefore produced important improvements, such as higher yields and disease resistance, in U.S. crops and animals. This topic is explored in detail in chapter 4.

Finally, there is an economic benefit to each state. Faculty salaries abroad, along with transportation and household shipping costs, supplies, and equipment, are just a few of the contract items purchased with USAID funding. A substantial share of this money is spent or saved within the state, thereby promoting economic activity. Universities are also paid for indirect costs associated with the contracts. In addition, students from abroad spend important amounts of money on goods and services within the state while pursuing their education. During 1987–88, foreign students spent an estimated $2.2 billion in the United States for maintenance, which did not include tuition, fees, books, travel, or dependent costs. Only about 2 percent of these students were supported directly by the U.S. government whereas about 65 percent were entirely supported by family and personal resources.

## SUMMARY COMMENTS

Clearly, the United States has an extensive capacity to assist with development needs abroad and a high level of willingness to do so. The historical evidence shows impressive total assistance, despite some softening of "real" support in recent years. The overall effort has been partly clouded by the introduction of politically motivated security assistance, which has not always proven successful. For example, security assistance to Iran and Vietnam did not produce the desired long-term results. Criticism leveled against development assistance may often be the outgrowth of its being confused with security assistance. Because of this intermingling, the American public has not always been able to evaluate purely developmental efforts separately from those that are politicized and more controversial.

The issues inherent in the intermingling of development and political objectives have often been debated. In fact, past discussions at one time led to a recommendation that a new institutional structure be devised to separate much of the development assistance administratively from security-related aid. The responsible development agency was to be placed directly under the president's jurisdiction. However, the recommendation has never been implemented.

A related concern to the American people, whose taxes support development efforts abroad, is whether past and present aid has been effectively used. Is progress being made at a reasonable rate?

Obviously, world hunger and poverty remain severe problems, with exceedingly complicated issues still to be confronted. Yet since 1970, food output in LDCs has risen enough so that some improvements in per capita welfare have been achieved overall. Certainly, this progress would not have been possible without assistance from donor nations. In addition, a base has been established that should make future assistance even more productive. More is known about the development process, and the LDCs have acquired administrative experience. Part of the learning phase has been completed, and as distressing as world hunger and poverty are today, the situation could be much worse. The world is better off now than it might have been had the needs of the poor nations been ignored these past four decades.

Both successes and failures can be found among individual projects and national programs. Mistakes have been made, and projects have failed or been less effective than they should have been. Poor project planning and implementation are apparent. Developing nations have not always met their obligations in terms of being cooperative and initiating national policies to foment development. Domestic politics in LDCs have not always been stable, and administrative procedures have permitted graft and power seekers to influence efficiency adversely. The U.S. support and programming focus has changed as perceptions of the nation's interests have varied. Population growth has continued relentlessly. In far too many developing nations, domestic political problems, national security issues, and industrial development strategies have attracted much more attention than have efforts to relieve the poor and invest in agriculture and people. Drought in large parts of Africa and periodic flooding in other parts of the world such as Bangladesh have complicated the picture even more by creating atrocious conditions that defy immediate solution.

The required development process is highly dynamic. It involves all gradients of natural, social, political, and cultural variations as they exist in 70 or more widely diverse nations. Even under ideal conditions, its pursuit represents a Herculean task.

Perhaps the greatest flaw to date in U.S. development assistance efforts has been impatience. As Americans, we have come to expect too much too fast. Development is a complicated process, and processes often require extensive gestation periods. Yet the tax-paying public and those in Congress who approve development budgets expect a continuing recitation of success stories if support is to be sustained. It is not unreasonable to ask for accountability and demonstrated progress for USAID efforts. But if too much value is placed on immediate success, decisions may be made that will satisfy the demands of program critics but neglect projects that might ultimately provide a reliable solution to the issues faced in developing nations. To abandon a short-run perspective in development programming often requires acts of faith since many years may be needed before program outcomes can be known.

Beyond our impatience, our ill-advised demands for early successes, and even our occasional lack of appreciation for the complexity of the issues entwined in world hunger and poverty, public apathy remains the most dangerous deterrent to future success. Clearly, the American public supports efforts to alleviate suffering and privation resulting from an emergency shortfall of food such as occurred in Ethiopia and the Sudan. The level of willingness to help runs high in America, and the response from both individuals and the government justifies applause.

Few Americans, however, seem to understand that starvation in Ethiopia or the Sudan or Bangladesh is not the crux of the problem, although they are amenable to sensational coverage by television cameras and commentators. It is the insidious and relentless advance of malnutrition and deprivation, resulting from the incapacity of masses of people to either produce food or earn money to buy it for their families, that most threatens world stability. Nor do many Americans understand how long and arduous is the task that must be attempted and how substantial must be the financial support given to it.

The historical absence of a strong public alliance with official foreign development assistance reflects a general dislike of the long-term perspective. As a nation, we compassionately react to stark hunger and starvation but would prefer that others exert the patience needed to solve the less dramatic underlying problems.

There have been no widespread, popular national movements protesting badly conceived development policies in poor nations. U.S. citizens have taken to the streets to protest apartheid in South Africa, yet no citizen group has similarly pressed the issue of inadequate development policies (in Ethiopia or elsewhere) that sentence large numbers of people to starvation and death. Is one issue really substantially different from the other? Is not the right to feed and clothe one's family as basic as any civil or human right conceived by man? Does it not deserve the same level of national awareness and public debate by the American people as they have given to more sensationally publicized social and moral issues? With hundreds of millions of people still shackled by poverty and hunger, there should be no thought of turning aside from the challenge. No physical or natural resource insufficiencies dictate that the world's people cannot all be adequately fed. The world hunger problems are man-made and so must be their solutions. Future success in finding solutions to this enemy of mankind will be as much a matter of public commitment as of technical achievements.

# THREE

# U.S. Economic Assistance And International Trade

## E. Boyd Wennergren

The average standard of living in the United States ranks among the highest in the world, and this country's long-run productive capacity is also a leader in the community of nations.

This material wealth could not be maintained if the United States chose to isolate itself and did not engage in a wide range of international trade. These activities can spawn controversy, but the historical record demonstrates that the welfare of nations has been consistently improved by their participation in the trading process. By its very nature, trade can benefit all partners. This is fortunate since no nation can be completely self-sufficient.

The complex issues of world trade lie at the base of the present balance-of-payments difficulty faced by the United States. To help clarify the factors that determine how and what trade occurs among nations, some general principles of trade are considered in this chapter. The focus, however, is on the importance of LDCs to the international trade patterns of the United States, the extent to which nations who receive U.S. assistance function in this nation's foreign trade, and the nature of their impact.

## ECONOMIC DEVELOPMENT AND TRADE

When an LDC becomes an active commercial trading partner with developed nations, it is signaling progress in its process of economic development. In general, the economic evolutionary process begins with significantly rising agricultural productivity, which usually requires additions to and replacements for traditional agricultural inputs. Rarely can agricultural output be expanded and farm profitability improved without an infusion of new methods and technology. In turn, these methods and technologies are based in agricultural research that is popularized through extension efforts. Once set in motion, the process generates a chain of reactions throughout the LDC's economy. Regrettably, the adjustments are not all automatic and self-sustaining, and proper public policies, investment mechanisms, and other economic factors must be in place and attended to.

Ideally, the series of changes proceeds in the following way. First, as agricultural production rises and becomes more efficient, the necessary labor force can be reduced, and the agricultural sector can release to nonagricultural employment those who are no longer needed while it continues to meet the food needs of the nation.

Second, as agricultural output increases, net farm incomes also rise. The results include higher levels of rural purchasing power and demands for additional agricultural and nonagricultural goods. In addition, the new surplus of income over consumption can be mobilized as savings to be invested in either industrial or further agricultural modernization.

Third, as food output improves, food prices fall relative to other prices. Consumers in the nonagricultural sector (as well as those in agriculture itself) are then able to use the savings to buy more food in greater variety (thus improving nutrition) and/or to purchase nonfood items. Because people with low incomes tend to spend a large part of their income on food, the decline in relative food prices induced by greater agricultural production can significantly improve the welfare of the impoverished. Rising agricultural output may also assist general economic development by creating either higher tax revenues as the tax base grows or loan capital to nonagricultural businesses.

The possibility of trade with other nations extends the linkages associated with rising agricultural output. Initially, as agricultural production continues to improve, so does its efficiency. Unit production costs decline, and the LDC's agriculture becomes more competitive on a world basis. As a consequence, exports increase. Concomitantly, industrial production can become more efficient and competitive as labor and investment resources are transferred from agriculture. The result is an improved export base and an expanded capacity to pay for imports. Rising exports and imports may also lead to increased public revenues via taxation. Imports and exports are important sources of taxes in most LDCs.

In the normal course of events, more goods, equipment, and raw materials are needed and most have to be imported. Thus, the development of an LDC begins to affect world markets and requires access to trading partners.

As an LDC prospers and its people begin to become more affluent, it demands more quality and variety in he products and services it buys. Where domestic production is inadequate, the requirements for consumer foods from abroad can rise dramatically. To some extent, local producers can be a factor in meeting this demand. But in most LDCs, local production will have to be supplemented by imports. It is primarily the developed nations that are positioned to fill the rising demand by LDCs for consumer goods, food products, and industrial items.

The trade relationships that result from this process benefit all concerned. For LDCs, strategic imports such as fertilizers, petroleum, irrigation equipment, and raw materials that support existing (but usually limited) industrial plants are basic to their development progress. In addition, the consumer goods imported to satisfy the nation's emerging middle- and upper-income families can be paid for only if LDC exports provide international exchange. Even in the poorer nations where food production remains a major concern, exportable goods are essential in creating the viable trade system that must help support economic progress.

For developed nations, trade is equally important. Pressures to import are substantial, due mainly to strong domestic demands for foreign goods and services. Critical metals and minerals are often unavailable in developed nations or may be less expensive if procured from another nation. Most developed nations depend on other nations (many of which are LDCs) to provide various classes of raw materials that are strategic to their needs. Like LDCs, developed nations must export goods in amounts comparable to their quantities of imports or suffer the economic damages to their economy that accompany negative trade balances.

The developmental process that results in rising demands for agricultural and nonagricultural imports in LDCs is based on the increased agricultural output in LDCs and on their improved ability to export. Therefore, developed nations do well to nurture the trade and market potentials of developing nations. Even during their initial stages of development, LDCs must engage in trade. As economic development proceeds, however, their needs expand significantly. The potential trade benefits are obvious enough to offer an important rationale for economic support from richer nations. One indication of the importance of LDC economic growth to U.S. exports and the overall economy has been provided by the UN. According to a UNDP estimate, 500,000 new jobs would have been created in the United States if the economic growth rates for LDCs in the 1970s had persisted into the 1980s. USAID reports that between 1980 and 1985, reduced U.S. exports to Mexico alone cost the United States an estimated 300,000 jobs. In other words, the slowing progress of LDCs can have a detrimental effect on U.S. exports and jobs.

## PRINCIPLE OF COMPARATIVE ADVANTAGE

The process of international trade sharpens the efficiency of the productive capabilities of all participating nations since they must compete in the production of similar products. The pressures of this competition usually lead to discoveries of the "best" and "most profitable" ways to produce. At the same time, a nation can evaluate which products it should import and which it could most profitably produce for home consumption or export.

It is a common notion that a nation should export goods it can produce at an absolutely lower real cost at home and import goods for which other nations have a similar advantage. This view is based on the concept of an "absolute" advantage in production. In actual practice, however, a nation may import (rather than produce) certain items for which it has an absolute advantage. By doing so, the nation encourages domestic producers to concentrate on goods for which it has the highest possible or a comparative advantage.

To illustrate, suppose a businessperson is expert in both managing a business and doing accounting work. In other words, he has an absolute advantage over his accountant for both sets of tasks. Why does he then hire someone to perform these duties? Because even though he can do both tasks better than someone else, it is most efficient and productive for him to concentrate his limited time on the task that yields the greatest value to his business and to "buy" the services of an accountant to do the work that would have provided lower returns on his time.

The same logic applies to nations. For example, if the United States was more efficient than Japan in producing both wheat and television sets, it might still make economic sense for the United States to concentrate on producing wheat. If wheat provided the highest returns relative to television sets, the United States could profitably exchange part of its wheat for television sets.

This is called the "law of comparative advantage." Today, world trade is governed by comparative and not by absolute advantage. Adherence to the concept of comparative advantage has very important implications for nations involved in international trade. It means that these nations are not necessarily restricted to exporting either all of or only the goods they can produce most efficiently.

A nation's comparative advantage is determined by four general factors, all of which affect the cost per unit of output for domestic products: its natural resource advantage; its location advantage relative to markets; its production efficiency as measured by the ratio of inputs to outputs; and its institutional advantages as expressed in trade-related items such as import or export tariffs, subsidies, and currency exchange rates. Although the nation's natural resources and location are difficult to manipulate for economic gain, most of the ways production is accomplished are susceptible to human ingenuity.

In recent years, changes in the international economy have heightened the relative importance of institutional factors associated with trade policy. Nations are much more interdependent now than they were after World War II, when a limited volume of trade was carried on by only a few autonomous nations. Since 1970, this nation's economy has become vastly more dependent on world trade. In fact, U.S. dependence on world trade doubled from 1970 to 1979. In the 1980s, the U.S. economy's dependence on world trade approximated that of Japan and Western Europe.

The trade system is substantially different in the 1980s from what it was in 1970. One important change of direct consequence to U.S. trade occurred in 1973 when U.S. fixed exchange rates were replaced by floating U.S. dollar exchange rates. Another major change was the emergence of a large, well-integrated international capital market. This market, which strongly influenced the trade system of the 1980s, hardly existed in the 1950s. It is estimated that $40 trillion flowed through this market in 1984, only a small part of which financed international trade in goods. This enormous capital market is composed primarily of funds that flow among nations for investment in monetary instruments and multinational businesses. Because this international flow of funds is so much larger than the trade-oriented flow of funds, the capital market rather than the trade sector essentially determines the exchange rate of many currencies. This may help explain why the United States can have a large trade deficit and a strong dollar exchange rate at the same time.

This situation means that, for example, if the United States has higher interest rates, a stable economy, and more promising investment alternatives than other nations, large amounts of capital may move into the country. This makes the U.S. dollar strong relative to other currencies. A high U.S. dollar exchange rate causes U.S. exports to be more expensive and imports to be less costly than they would be with a lower exchange rate. This leads to a declining and perhaps eventually negative trade balance for the United States. With a floating exchange rate and without an international capital market, the situation would, theoretically, correct itself. A negative balance of payments would cause a decline in the dollar exchange rate, making U.S. exports cheaper and imports more expensive and thereby reversing the pressures that have led to a negative trade balance. However, in the 1980s, the flow of funds into the United States through the international capital market has kept the dollar exchange rate high even though the U.S. trade balance has been and continues to be substantially negative.

These international market realities do not, however, alter the basic importance or application of the principle of comparative advantage. Nations still produce the goods they are relatively good at producing. By so doing, all nations benefit, be they developed or developing, and all nations can identify some type of product or mix of products that is in their best interest to trade. The difference now as opposed to pre-1973 is that a nation's comparative advantage is constrained, or in some sense more directly influenced, by trade policies, domestic subsidies, and currency exchange rates. Policy changes either in the United States or in other countries now can have much greater implications for the

U.S. economy and its trade options. A process that was once slow-moving and limited has become fastmoving and highly competitive. To remain competitive, nations must understand the complex operation of international markets and be able to adjust production and resource use to conditions that change in response to foreign markets.

## U.S. TRADE EXPERIENCE

The record of the past 35 years confirms the mutual benefits that both developed nations and LDCs derive from trade relationships. It also demonstrates that through economic development, LDCs can become active and beneficial trade partners whose existence complements the activities of other nations. Certainly, the United States operates within a world community that supplies critical imports and simultaneously serves as a market for our exports, and LDCs are an important subset of that community.

### Classes of Imports

There are two broad classes of imports, each with a different implication for groups within the United States. The first involves goods that "complement" the national resource and skill base of the United States. A significant number of natural resources essential to U.S. industry and commerce either are not produced domestically in sufficient quantity or are simply not available in the United States. Developing nations are often the principal suppliers of these key commodities.

The second class of imports involves goods that compete with products readily produced in the United States. These imports are much more controversial since a decision to bring them into the country may result in a displacement of U.S. production.

**Complementary Imports.** The United States is highly dependent on other nations for several complementary imports (table 3.1). For example, in 1986, 100 percent of columbium, graphite, manganese ore, and strontium; 97 percent of bauxite; and 77 percent of tin consumed in the United States were imported. Most of these quantities came from developing nations. These and other comparable imported materials are critical to U.S. industrial production, and their uninterrupted availability is a persistent concern.

## Table 3.1    U.S. Imports of Selected Metals and Minerals, 1986

| Metals and Minerals | U.S. Reliance on Imports 1986 (percent) | Developing Countries' Share of U.S. Market in 1985 (percent) | Principal Suppliers, (1982–85) (Share of Total U.S. Imports) |
|---|---|---|---|
| Strontium | 100 | 100 | Mexico (97%), Spain (3%) |
| Graphite | 100 | 88 | Mexico (50%), China (24%), Brazil (8%) Madagascar (6%) |
| Columbium | 100 | 83 | Brazil (73%), Canada (13%), Thailand (5%) |
| Manganese ore | 100 | 80 | Gabon (36%), Brazil (22%), South Africa (15%) |
| Platinum | 98 | 37 | South Africa (43%), United Kingdom (17%), USSR (12%) |
| Bauxite & Alumina | 97 | | |
| Bauxite | | 89 | Guinea (45%), Jamaica (32%), Brazil (6%) |
| Alumina | | 15 | Australia (76%), Jamaica (10%), Suriname (7%) |
| Diamond | 92 | 62 | South Africa (41%), United Kingdom (26%), Ireland (18%), Belgium-Luxembourg (10%) |
| Cobalt | 92 | 55 | Zaire (40%), Zambia (16%), Canada (13%), Norway (6%) |
| Tantalum | 91 | 0 | Thailand (34%), Brazil (10%), Australia (8%), Malaysia (6%) |
| Flourspar | 88 | 70 | Mexico (47%), South Africa (30%), China (9%), Italy (7%) |
| Chromium | 82 | n.a. | South Africa (59%), Zimbabwe (11%), Turkey (7%), Yugoslavia (5%) |
| Nickel | 78 | 10 | Canada (40%), Australia (14%), Norway (11%), Botswana (10%) |
| Potash | 78 | 0 | Canada (90%), Israel (6%), E. Germany (1%), USSR (1%) |
| Tin | 77 | 96 | Thailand (22%), Brazil (20%), Indonesia (15%, Bolivia (12%) |
| Zinc | 74 | | |
| Ore concentrates | | 40 | Canada (38%), Mexico (23%), Honduras (14%) |
| Metals | | 16 | Canada (55%), Mexico (8%), Peru (7%), Australia (5%) |
| Silver | 69 | 39 | Canada (28%), Mexico (25%), United Kingdom (17%), Peru (14%) |
| Cadmium | 69 | 8 | Canada (39%), Australia (24%), Mexico (8%), W. Germany (7%) |
| Barite | 66 | 88 | China (46%), Morocco (16%), India (10%), Chile (7%) |
| Tungsten | 62 | 62 | Canada (17%), China (17%), Bolivia (12%), Portugal (7%) |
| Mercury | 51 | 41 | Spain (27%), Algeria (18%), Japan (12%), Turkey (11%) |
| Iron Ore | 37 | 28 | Canada (62%), Liberia (13%), Brazil (12%), Venezuela (11%) |
| Gypsum | 36 | 16 | Canada (69%), Mexico (20%), Spain (10%) |
| Silicon | 35 | 42 | Brazil (23%), Canada (19%), Norway (16%), Venezuela (13%) |
| Copper | 27 | 60 | Chile (40%), Canada (29%), Peru (8%), Mexico (6%) |
| Gold | 21 | 13 | Canada (56%), Uruguay (12%), Switzerland (5%) |

**Table 3.1   U.S. Imports of Selected Metals and Minerals, 1986**

| Metals and Minerals | U.S. Reliance on Imports 1986 (percent) | Developing Countries Share of U.S. Market in 1985 (percent) | Principal Suppliers, (1982–85) (Share of Total U.S. Imports) |
|---|---|---|---|
| Lead | 20 | | |
|   Ore concentrate | | 100 | Peru (67%), Honduras (22%), Mexico (4%), Canada (3%) |
|   Metals | | 29 | Canada (54%), Mexico (23%), Australia (6%), Peru (6%), Honduras (2%) |
| Fixed Nitrogen | 17 | 29 | Canada (32%), USSR (28%), Trinidad & Tobago (20%), Mexico (15%) |
| Beryllium | 16 | 96 | Brazil (51%), China (27%), South Africa (6%), Switzerland (6%) |

*Sources:* Adapted from U.S. Department of the Interior, Bureau of Mines, *Mineral Commodity Summaries 1987 and Minerals Yearbook (1985),* as cited in John W. Sewell, Stuart K. Tucker, et.al., *Growth, Exports, and Jobs in a Changing World Economy: Agenda 1988,* Overseas Development Council (New Brunswick, N.J.: Transaction Books, 1988), 218.

Agricultural crops (mostly tropical fruits and vegetables) constitute a second major source of complementary imports. The production of these crops often coincides with special climatic conditions that give the nations involved a comparative advantage. Coffee, cocoa, bananas, coconuts, and some classes of spices are examples of agricultural crops not produced in the United States but imported as complementary items for domestic consumption.

Typically, LDCs that trade with the United States have a limited export base that depends heavily on these primary metals, minerals, and agricultural commodities (table 3.2). One or two items commonly account for more than 50 percent of exports from LDCs. For example, Lesotho export earnings are 90 percent from wool, Burundi earns 94 percent from coffee, and Namibia earns 92 percent from three primary metals. Generally, the value of these single-product exports is not adequate to carry the full burden of a nation's foreign trade, and negative trade balances are common. (In 1986, the composite deficit for all LDCs was $21.3 billion; see chap. 2.)

Overall world trade relies heavily on primary commodity exports from developing countries. For the most part, these are staple food items or critical minerals or metals. As examples, more than 90 percent of the world's trade in coffee, rubber, and cocoa is supplied by LDCs (appendix table 3.1). Bananas, tea, and palm oil are also supplied largely by developing nations.

## Table 3.2  Export Dependency on Primary Commodities for Selected Developing Nations, 1975-77 (in percentage of total export earnings)

**Over 90 percent**

| | |
|---|---|
| Lesotho* | Wool 90, Wheat 10 |
| Zimbabwe* | Tobacco 59, Sugar 18, Cotton 13 |
| Burundi* | Coffee 94 |
| Botswana* | Beef 54, Copper 43 |
| Zambia* | Copper 92 |
| Uganda* | Coffee 84 |
| Namibia* | Copper 65, Lead 14, Zinc 13 |
| Kiribati* | Phosphate 95 |
| Zaire* | Copper 64, Coffee 18 |
| Liberia* | Iron ore 71, Rubber 12 |
| Mauritania* | Iron ore 87 |
| Gambia, The* | Groundnuts 56, Groundnut oil 34 |

**80 to 90 percent**

| | |
|---|---|
| Malawi | Tobacco 47, Tea 20, Sugar 11 |
| Swaziland* | Sugar 62, Iron ore 14 |
| Togo* | Phosphate 56, Cocoa 17, Coffee 11 |
| Rwanda* | Coffee 68 |
| Guinea-Bissau* | Groundnuts 78 |
| Reunion* | Sugar 82 |
| Ghana* | Cocoa 68, Timber 11 |
| Guinea* | Bauxite 76 |
| Peru | Copper 19, Fishmeal 13, Zinc 13, Sugar 12 |

**70 to 80 percent**

| | |
|---|---|
| Guadeloupe | Bananas 42, Sugar 37 |
| Guyana | Sugar 38, Bauxite 30, Rice 10 |
| Burma | Rice 46, Timber 20 |
| Equatorial Guinea | Coffee 43, Cotton 24 |
| Mauritius* | Sugar 73 |
| Ivory Coast | Coffee 33, Cocoa 19, Timber 17 |
| Honduras | Bananas 25, Coffee 22, Timber 11 |
| Sudan* | Cotton 51, Groundnuts 18 |
| Belize* | Sugar 65 |
| Sri Lanka* | Tea 51, Rubber 17 |
| Central African Republic | Coffee 34, Timber 21, Cotton 14 |
| Dominican Republic | Sugar 43, Coffee 13 |
| Ethiopia* | Coffee 56, Hides/skins 10 |

**60 to 70 percent**

| | |
|---|---|
| Colombia* | Coffee 57 |
| El Salvador* | Coffee 52, Cotton 10 |
| Fiji* | Sugar 64 |
| Nepal* | Rice 56 |
| Cameroon | Coffee 29, Cocoa 22, Timber 10 |
| Chile* | Copper 56 |

| Table 3.2 | Export Dependency on Primary Commodities for Selected Nations, 1975–77 *(Cont.)* |
|---|---|

**60 to 70 percent** *(Cont.)*

| | |
|---|---|
| Papua New Guinea | Copper 32, Coffee 14 |
| Solomon Islands | Timber 30, Copra 29 |
| Nicaragua | Cotton 24, Coffee 23 |
| Tanzania | Coffee 33, Cotton 14 |
| Costa Rica | Coffee 29, Bananas 21 |
| North Yemen | Cotton 41, Coffee 22 |
| Guatemala | Coffee 35, Sugar 12, Cotton 10 |
| Mali | Cotton 45, Groundnuts 10 |
| Philippines | Sugar 19, Coconut oil 12 |

**50 to 60 percent**

| | |
|---|---|
| Martinique* | Bananas 57 |
| Madagascar | Coffee 46 |
| New Hebrides | Copra 43 |
| Haiti | Coffee 36, Bauxite 14 |
| Senegal | Groundnut oil 35, Phosphate 15 |
| Kenya | Coffee 35, Tea 13 |
| Thailand | Rice 16, Sugar 11 |
| Benin (Dahomey) | Cotton 29 |
| Morocco | Phosphate 45 |
| Chad | Cotton 46 |

*Source:* World Bank, *Commodity Trade and Price Trends (1979)*, as cited in report of the Presidential Commission on World Hunger, *Overcoming World Hunger: The Challenge Ahead* (Washington, D.C., 1980), 57.
*Heavily dependent on a single commodity.

Such specialization reflects the law of comparative advantage as influenced mostly by natural resource conditions that favor production of one or two products. Either the minerals and metals are in place as decreed by nature, or the crops are especially fitted to local climates and production has become stabilized over a long period of adaptation. In most LDCs, only continued developmental progress can put a broader production or export base into place.

Their dependence on primary commodity exports carries extreme risks for LDCs. prices of primary commodities tend to be highly variable, and LDCs often suffer from declining prices. Also, primary products are vulnerable to technological changes that may give major cost advantages to substitute commodities. A good example involves the synthetic materials that have displaced wool, cotton, and other natural fibers in textile manufacturing. Finally, agricultural crops originating in the tropics (as do most from

LDCs) are especially susceptible to damage from disease and insects. The sudden decline of cocoa production in Ecuador and the destruction of banana production throughout much of Central America from Panama disease in the 1950s are just two examples of the widespread havoc that can suddenly eliminate or materially reduce an export base.

Lack of diversity in agricultural production also creates another major danger in most LDCs. Beyond limiting export flexibility, producing only a few different crops reduces domestic consumption options. Thus, nutrition in LDCs suffers, and national diets are commonly deficient in essential vitamins and minerals.

If these nations are to diversify their total agricultural production and export mix, they must find market outlets. LDCs face a difficult task as they attempt to enter the highly competitive world of international commerce. Most of the markets available to them are located in developed nations. Development of the LDCs is conditioned by the degree to which they can penetrate these markets.

The success of U.S. assistance to LDCs may be significantly determined by the degree to which portions of the LDCs' increased production can be marketed (whether in the United States or in other donor nations). This is the essence of the North-South dialogue (see chap. 5), in which developing nations located in the southern hemisphere are calling for a restructuring of the world's economic order. One of their requests is for better access to markets in developed nations, which are mostly located in the northern hemisphere. The issues are complex but must be dealt with promptly if the problems of world hunger and economic development are to be adequately addressed.

To help stabilize prices of agricultural commodities traded by LDCs and to provide for more orderly marketing, the United States participates in a noncompetitive quota system for selected products. The most important crops included by the United States under this procurement process are coffee, sugar, rubber, cocoa, and some spices. In 1987, all noncompetitive imports, mostly from LDCs, accounted for 32 percent of U.S. farm imports. Since 1980, the percentage of noncompetitive imports has ranged from 40 percent to 32 percent.

**Competitive Imports.** The imports that most commonly compete with U.S. products are manufactured goods from other developed nations or the more advanced LDCs. However, several classes of agricultural exports from LDCs are competitive with U.S. agriculture. Important among these are beef, pork, dairy, poultry, fruits and vegetables, and oilseed products. In recent years, cereal grain exports from some LDCs (such as rice and corn from Thailand and wheat from India) also have become competitive in world markets.

Because such imports by their very nature compete with U.S. products, they can generate controversy. Their intrusion often leads to pressures for protectionist policies whereby tariffs and other regulations limit entry of foreign goods into U.S. markets. The truth, however, is that imports generally, and competitive ones in particular, produce benefits for both the United States and its LDC trading partners.

One benefit from imports arises from their interrelationship with exports. When the United States imports commodities, the process provides foreign exchange dollars to other nations; these dollars are commonly used to finance purchases of U.S. exports. It is obvious that had the United States not permitted competitive imports—from either LDCs or other nations—to enter its domestic markets, related jobs and production levels would not have been threatened in recent years. But such a policy would also have initiated a chain of reactions that would have yielded limited export sales and foreign exchange earnings in LDCs. Consequently, jobs in export-related production in the United States would have suffered. Additionally, limiting imports would have reduced the dollars held by other nations and thus would have restricted their ability to buy U.S. products. Such trade-offs are not always one for one, but they do occur.

A second benefit from importing is based on the principle of comparative advantage. It makes no sense for the United States to produce everything it can when some products are available at a lesser cost through trade arrangements. Admittedly, from time to time this policy will affect existing industries and require adjustments in resource use and production, especially where competitive imports are involved. Some see these impacts as being purely negative because they cause stress for certain U.S. workers and their companies. But they can also be positive because they sharpen the discipline of producers and encourage them to improve efficiency and redirect their resources toward more productive ends. Achieving the new structure takes time, and it may involve severe adjustments in people's lives. But this is the nature of competitive trade. Some of the best recent examples are the hard times faced by copper producers in Utah, steel factories in Pennsylvania, and textile mills in Georgia.

Finally, competitive imports can give domestic consumers a price advantage. Imported goods increase the quantity and variety of available goods and tend to reduce consumer prices. U.S. consumers have realized significant savings by having access to relatively inexpensive imports. This option is especially important to low-income Americans. Savings associated with purchases of lower-cost imports are not lost to the U.S. economy; they are generally redirected toward personal savings or toward the purchase of other domestically produced goods.

Furthermore, the very importation of goods and services opens job opportunities for Americans. When jobs are lost in one section of the economy due to competitive imports, additional workers tend to be required in another section that markets and handles the sale of these imports. These trade-offs may or may not be one for one in new jobs and other adjustments, but the employment impacts are not necessarily all negative and do tend to balance out over time. Still, if Americans are willing to pay higher prices for a U.S.-produced commodity, jobs that would have been affected by foreign imports can be maintained by protectionist policies.

In the long run, however, it seems apparent that the United States must keep its economy efficient and competitive if prosperity is to continue. Failure to meet trade issues head-on and adjust to them continually permits problems to become masked in import restrictions Knowing that the possibility of losing markets to more efficient foreign producers is part of reality can be a powerful catalyst for eliminating inefficiency in high-cost production units and for rewarding productive employees.

Today's international trade relationships ar characterized by a number of protectionist policies an government subsidies. Unencumbered conditions an truly free trade are nonexistent. Fair competition rather than free trade is the realistic goal. To achieve fair trade worldwide, without retribution and trade wars, the rules of the game with respect to protectionism must be reasonably consistent among nations. No nation, including LDCs, can routinely protect its producers with tariff regulations or subsidies and expect other nations to insist that their producers compete unprotected.

The cost of allowing competitive imports to enter the United States is a widely discussed topic. People losing jobs and industries being challenged or closed are newsworthy events. One of the principal hidden costs of U.S. protectionism that limits exports is the loss of jobs in export sectors such as agriculture: other nations have fewer dollar credits with which to buy U.S. products, and they often establish import barriers of their own in response to such protectionist policies.

To help ease the kind of domestic transition on industry and people caused by competitive imports, the U.S. government enacted the Trade Act of 1974. Under the Trade Act, people who lose their jobs or businesses that lose their investments to unfair import competition can qualify for federal assistance. Individuals can receive unemployment insurance payments for up to one year, relocation allowances to cover moving expenses to a new job, and training and job counseling under existing federal programs. Firms affected by import trade can qualify for tax credits and for low-interest loans or guarantees to modernize or retool plants and equipment, plus free technical advice.

This response by the federal government recognizes the "real" cost of encouraging competitive trade. By assisting people and businesses to adjust to competition-induced changes, the United States has acknowledged that negative as well as positive impacts are associated with foreign trade. As it offsets some of the negative burden in this manner, the nation permits the rest of society to benefit from the positive aspects of international trade.

## Composition of U.S. Imports

In 1975, total U.S. imports were valued at $103.4 billion. They grew to $273.4 billion in 1981. In 1986, they reached $370.0 billion (figure 3.1 and appendix table 3.2). The share of U.S. imports coming from LDCs declined over that period from 42.4 percent to 33.8 percent, but the value of these imports rose from $43.8 billion in 1975 to $125.1 billion in 1986. The highest percentages of imports from LDCs in 1986 were for fuel (mostly petroleum); food, feed, and beverages; and consumer goods. Despite the high percentage of food items coming from LDCs (55.5 percent), their dollar value was one of the lowest among all classes of U.S. imports. The shares of total imports filled by food, feed, and beverages, as well as by industrial supplies, have remained fairly constant since

### Figure 3.1a  Total U.S. Imports[1] 1975 and 1986

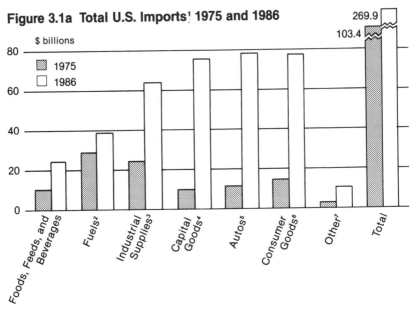

Notes and sources: See appendix table 3.2

### Figure 3.1b  Developing Countries' Share of U.S. Imports[1] 1975 and 1986

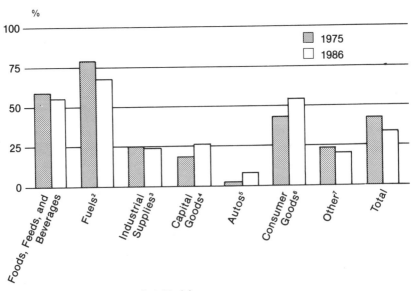

Notes and sources: See appendix table 3.2

1975. The most dramatic changes, in terms of both market share and annual growth, have been in autos, capital goods, and consumer goods.

In 1987, 32 percent of all U.S. agricultural imports were classified as noncompetitive; the rest were competitive. Since 1980, noncompetitive imports have ranged from 32 percent to 40 percent of total agricultural imports. In 1987, 55.8 percent of all agricultural imports (both competitive and complementary) came from LDCs (figure 3.2). This is a slight reduction from the 63 percent in 1982. The developing nations most involved in exporting agricultural products to the United States are Indonesia, Colombia, the Philippines, Malaysia, the Ivory Coast, Ecuador, Guatemala, and Honduras.

It should be kept in mind that many of the nations classified as LDCs in these data are, in fact, emerging nations that are creating their own industrial production and export bases. Among the 20 largest U.S. trading partners in 1987, the 9 classified as LDCs supplied 25.4 percent of all U.S. imports (table 3.3). The 3 most important LDC exporters to the United States were Mexico, Taiwan, and South Korea, all of which are upper middle-income

**Figure 3.2  Sources of U.S. Agricultural Imports, 1987**

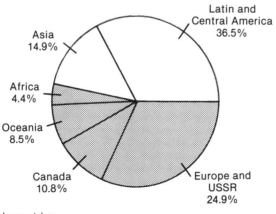

▓ Developed countries
☐ Developing countries

Source: Bureau of the Census, *Highlights of U.S. Export & Import Trade* (Washington, D.C.: U.S. GPO, 1987), tables C-12 and -13.

LDCs. Of the 9 LDCs, only China is classified as a lower-income nation. It is noteworthy that most of these 9 LDCs have benefited from U.S. assistance, with some such as South Korea, Brazil, and Taiwan having become "graduates" of the U.S. economic assistance program. The increased importance of these formerly assisted nations as U.S. trading partners was brought about by their economic progress. This situation illustrates the interrelationship between a country's economic development and international trade, as discussed earlier in this chapter.

**U.S. Export Trade**

Exports are important to the prosperity of the U.S. economy. Despite a large domestic market that consumes much of its production, the United States needs sales abroad to earn foreign exchange to pay for the high level of imports demanded by its citizens.

Between 1975 and 1981, U.S. exports increased from $107.7 billion to $233.7. They dropped slightly to $212.9 billion in 1986 (and then rebounded to $252.9 billion in 1987) (appendix tables 3.3 and 3.4). Capital goods and industrial supplies were the two most valuable classes of exports. Capital goods grew at an annual rate of 10.5 percent during the period. Consumer goods, while representing a lower dollar value, grew at 10.6 percent annually. The fastest growing export class was the composite group of "other," which includes military-type goods.

**Exports to Developing Nations.** The export success of the United States is closely tied to its relationships with developing nations. Of the $107.7 billion worth of goods the United States exported in 1975, 38.2 percent went to LDCs (appendix table 3.3). U.S. exports to developing nations fell to 34.2 percent in 1986, but total U.S. exports had almost doubled by that year, which meant that the value of exports to LDCs rose from $41.1 billion to $72.8 billion on 1986. (In 1987, the percentage fell to 32.1 but the value of exports to LDCs rose to $81.2 billion.) With the exception of autos and "other" exports, developing nations took between 30 percent and 40 percent of all other classes of U.S. exports.

The annual growth in value of exports to LDCs for 1975–86 was 7.0 percent, somewhat less than the 8.9 percent rise in all U.S. exports for the period. Exports of fuels and consumer goods had the highest annual growth rates among exports to LDCs. However,

### Table 3.3   Twenty Largest U.S. Trading Partners, 1987 ($ billions)

|  | Total Transactions | Exports[a] | Imports[a] |
|---|---|---|---|
| Canada | 131.3 | 59.8 | 71.5 |
| Japan | 116.3 | 28.2 | 88.1 |
| West Germany | 39.7 | 11.7 | 28.0 |
| **Mexico**[b] | 35.1 | 14.6 | 20.5 |
| **Taiwan** | 33.8 | 7.4 | 26.4 |
| United Kingdom | 32.1 | 14.1 | 18.0 |
| **South Korea** | 26.1 | 8.1 | 18.0 |
| France | 19.1 | 7.9 | 11.2 |
| Italy | 17.2 | 5.5 | 11.7 |
| **Hong Kong** | 14.5 | 4.0 | 10.5 |
| Netherlands | 12.4 | 8.2 | 4.2 |
| **Brazil** | 12.4 | 4.0 | 8.4 |
| Belgium and Luxembourg | 10.6 | 6.2 | 4.4 |
| **Singapore** | 10.5 | 4.1 | 6.4 |
| **China** | 10.4 | 3.5 | 6.9 |
| **Venezuela** | 9.5 | 3.6 | 5.9 |
| Australia | 8.8 | 5.5 | 3.3 |
| **Saudi Arabia** | 8.3 | 3.4 | 4.9 |
| Switzerland | 7.6 | 3.2 | 4.4 |
| Sweden | 6.9 | 1.9 | 5.0 |
| Total, 20 Countries | $562.6 | $204.9 | $357.7 |
| Total, 9 Developing Countries | 160.6 | 52.7 | 107.9 |
| Total U.S. Trade | $677.0 | $252.9 | $424.1 |
| 9 Developing Countries as Percentage of Total U.S. Trade | 23.7 | 20.8 | 25.4 |

*Source:* Bureau of the Census, *Highlights of U.S. Export and Import Trade* (Washington, D.C.: U.S. GPO, 1987), tables B-22 and -23, and C-26 and -27.

*Notes:* [a]All export figures are f.a.s. (free alongside ship) transaction values; import figures are c.i.f. (customs, insurance, and freight) transaction values.
    [b]Developing nations are boldface.

the dollar value of these increases was low compared with that of other export classes.

Many of the nations that are most important to U.S. import trade are also among the nation's significant export markets. This supports the prior claim of mutual advantage from trade relationships. In 1987, Mexico purchased goods worth about $14.6 billion from the United States. This equaled 18.0 percent of all U.S. sales to

LDCs, putting Mexico at the head of the list of LDC markets (figure 3.3 and appendix table 3.4). South Korea (10.0 percent) was the second most important, followed by Taiwan (9.1 percent). Overall, in 1987 the 10 largest LDC traders accounted for 67.6 percent of U.S. exports to all developing nations, or $54.9 billion, and 21.7 percent of all U.S. exports. These figures are slightly above those of 1984, which suggests a significant level of stability in U.S. trade relations with these nations.

From 1975 to 1986, China was the fastest-growing LDC market for U.S. exports (appendix table 3.4). Exports rose from $0.3 billion to $3.5 billion. Singapore, Hong Kong, and Taiwan also had significant growth in the purchase of U.S. exports. As with imports, the largest LDC markets for U.S. exports—with the exception of China—are the upper-income developing nations (table 3.3).

U.S. export trade with the poorer LDCs does not approach that involving the more economically advanced ones, but the aggregate amounts are still impressive, and for some nations this trade is very important. Exports to 35 "very poor" LDCs in 1987 approximated $7.5 billion, with about 46.5 percent going to China (appendix table 3.5). India, Pakistan, and Haiti were the next most important export markets among this group. Overall, exports to all these very poor nations represented 3.0 percent of all U.S. exports. (U.S. imports from these same nations were also 3.0 percent of its total from all nations.) Of these nations, 9 had export trade and 8 had import trade with the United States in excess of $100 million.

Among the 34 "poor" LDCs, U.S. exports totaled $16.8 billion worth of goods, or 6.7 percent of all 1987 exports. Egypt, Thailand, and Turkey were the 3 largest export markets among this group, and 22 of these nations had export trade with the United States in excess of $100 million in 1987. (U.S. imports from these poor LDCs totaled $25.3 billion, or 6.0 percent of all U.S. imports.)

It is interesting to note that some of the very poor nations, such as Bangladesh and Zaire, have fairly important volumes of trade with the United States, even at their present early stages of development. Moreover, trade activities tend to increase, even with the limited economic improvement that takes a nation from very poor to poor in the classification. For example, 30 of the 34 nations in the poor group (88 percent) had trade transactions (imports plus exports) with the United States of more than $100 million. By

**Figure 3.3a  Ten Largest Developing Country
Markets for U.S. Exports, 1975 and 1987**

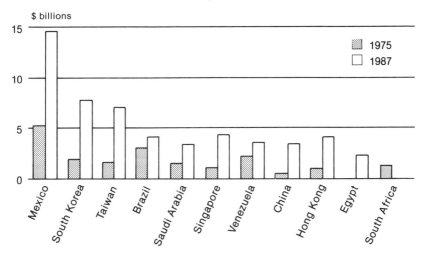

Notes and sources: See appendix table 3.4.

**Figure 3.3b  Share of U.S. Exports to All
Developing Countries, 1975 and 1987**

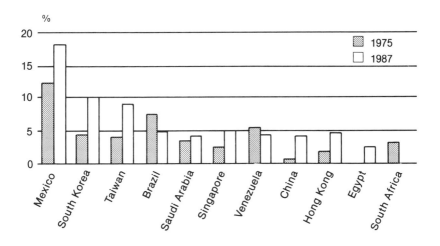

Notes and sources: See appendix table 3.4.

contrast, only 13 of the 35 very poor nations (37 percent) engaged in trade of this magnitude.

**Agriculture's Role.** Agriculture plays an important role in U.S. exports. In 1972, the value of agricultural exports approximated $10 billion and rose consistently to a peak of about $43 billion by 1981 (figure 3.4). The value fell to about $29.1 billion in 1987. During much of the same period, U.S. imports of agricultural products rose at a slower rate, allowing agriculture to amass a large trade surplus. The agricultural sector has shown a positive trade balance each year since 1960, and the balance has averaged around $20 billion annually since 1979 (figure 3.5). However, the recent trend has been downward. These trade surpluses have been used to offset the purchase of nonagricultural goods and services, which as a group have created negative overall trade balances for the United States each year since 1970. The huge trade deficits since the late 1970s reflect serious imbalances in the U.S. trade situation and are so large that there is virtually no hope that an improved agricultural trade balance could even come close to offsetting them. In 1987, the trade deficit for the United States reached about $170 billion. However, the deficit has shown some reduction in 1988 as the value of the U.S. dollar has become cheaper and U.S. exports have become less expensive in world markets. Official data are not yet published.

The United States depends on world agricultural markets for goods and services and is a significant seller in these markets. Market export potentials are especially important for a select group of primary agricultural products produced in the United States (figure 3.6). Since 1954, the production percentages of several major U.S. crops that are exported abroad have risen but show annual variations. In 1988, more than 80 percent of the wheat produced in the United States was exported. Further, between about 35 percent and 45 percent of all soybean, rice, cotton, and corn production was shipped abroad.

Agricultural exports are not equally shared by all states. California, Iowa, and Illinois typically lead the list of states exporting agricultural products. Most of the important exporting states are in the Midwest, reflecting the limited group of agricultural crops that most affect the level of U.S. agricultural exports.

U.S. export levels of these few crops represent a large part of the total volume passing through world markets (appendix table 3.6).

## Figure 3.4 U.S. Export and Import of Agricultural Products

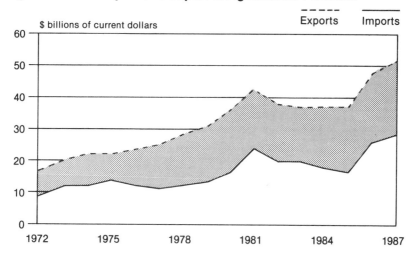

Source: USDA, *Foreign Agricultural Trade of the United States* (Washington, D.C.), January-February 1985 and various other issues, as cited in World Food Institute, *World Food Trade and U.S. Agriculture, 1960-1984,* 5th annual ed. (Ames: Iowa State University, October 1985), 41; Bureau of the Census, *Highlights of U.S. Export and Import Trade*

## Figure 3.5 Net U.S. Trade Balance, 1960-87

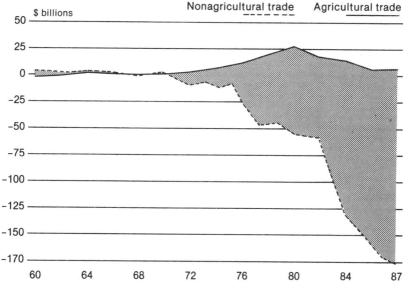

Source: See figure 3.4.

### Figure 3.6 Proportion of Production Exported for Selected Agricultural Products, 1954 and 1988

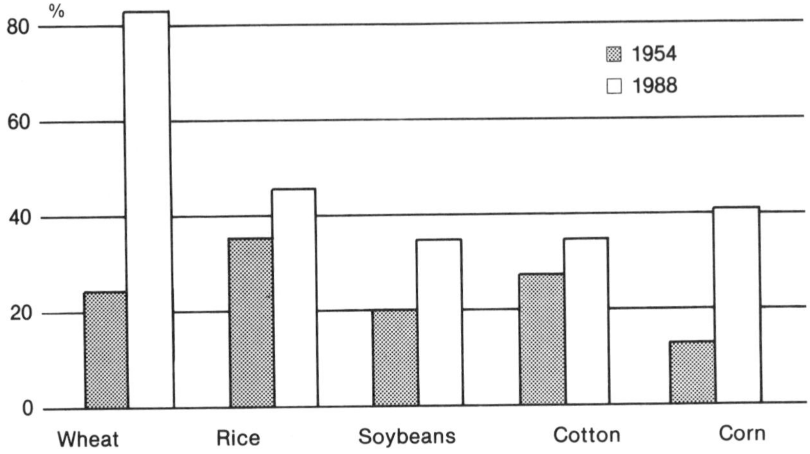

Source: USDA, 1967, 1981a, as cited in Larry Lev, Michael T. Weber, and H.C. Bittenbender, *Michigan Agriculture and Its Linkages to Developing Nations* (East Lansing: Institute of International Agriculture, Michigan State University, March 1984), 35; ERS/USDA, Agriculture and Trade Indicators Branch, March 1989, personal correspondence.

In 1981–82, the United States held 59 percent of the world's wheat market, 74 percent of the coarse grains market, and 71 percent of the soybeans market. The market shares fell to 31, 57, and 47 percent, respectively, in 1986–87. These export sales have important effects on the U.S. employment picture. An estimated 1 million jobs in the United States depend on agricultural exports. Half of them are on-farm jobs; the other half are off-farm jobs related to agriculture. It is also estimated that for each dollar generated by farm exports, two additional dollars are created in economic activity elsewhere in the U.S. economy.

**Importance of Developing Nations.** U.S. agricultural exports to developing nations represent a significant and growing proportion of total U.S. agricultural exports. Since 1975, agricultural exports destined for LDCs have almost doubled in dollar value, and the percentage of the total has also increased (figure 3.7 and appendix table 3.7). In 1984, the dollar value of this nation's agricultural exports to LDCs was about $15 billion, which amounted to about 39.7 percent of the $38 billion worth of all U.S. agricultural exports. During this same period, the percentage of U.S. farm exports going to developed nations declined from 57.5 percent to 49.2 percent.

## Figure 3.7  Where U.S. Farm Exports Go

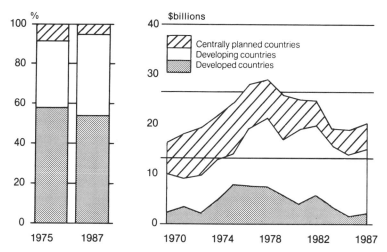

Sources: USDA, 1982, as cited in Larry Lev, Michael T. Weber, and H.C. Bittenbender, *Michigan Agriculture and Its Linkages to Developing Nations* (East Lansing: Institute of International Agriculture, Michigan State University, March 1984): USDA, *Foreign Agricultural Trade of the United States* (Washington, D.C.: O.E. GPO, 1985) and *1987 Supplement* (Washington, D.C.: O.E. GPO, 1987), 27.

In 1987, total agricultural exports declined to $28.6 billion, but the percentage to developing nations increased slightly to 40.6 percent. Early reports for 1988 (not yet officially available) indicate the possibility of a continuing rise in agricultural exports.

This rising trend in agricultural exports to developing nations indicates the ever-increasing importance of LDCs to U.S. trade, and there are two basic reasons why this growth rate might exceed that to developed nations and become even more important with time. The first is sheer population numbers. As was pointed out in chapter 1, more than 70 percent of the world's population is now located in LDCs, and the trend is upward. Growing numbers of people need food and food products in ever greater amounts. Second, most people in developing nations have low incomes, and the income of poor families is spent mostly for food and less for other consumables. During the 1980s, for example, 60 percent or more of the people's income in India, Tanzania, and Niger, went for food purchases (figure 3.8). As individual incomes in such nations begin to rise, these relationships generally persist. There is a strong tendency to satisfy food needs more adequately before increasing spending on nonfood items.

**Figure 3.8 Income Spent on Food in Selected Countries**

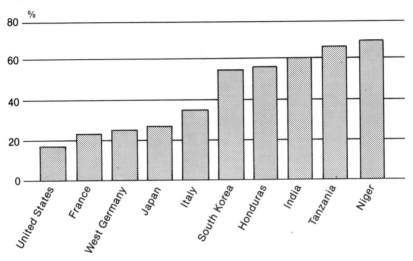

Source: Arthur B. Mackie, "The U.S. Farmer and World Market Development (Washington, D.C.:
ERS/USDA, October 1983, Mimeographed), 16, as adapted by and cited in Larry Lev,
Michael T. Weber, and H.C. Bittenbender, *Michigan Agriculture and Its Linkages to
Developing Nations* (East Lansing: Institute of International Agriculture, Michigan
State University, March 1984).

Rising food demands that cannot be met by domestic production must be satisfied by purchases on world markets. Evidence suggests that as developing nations become less poor, their demand for food imports also increases, at least until (and if) local production can better respond to the demand. But even with enhanced local production, only selected crops will be affected. No nation satisfies its total food needs, and once the principle of comparative advantage has helped define the products to be produced in-country, other nations will fill the demand gap. Of course, LDCs' nonfood demands also represent an important export market potential for the United States since the capacity of LDCs to fill such demands is usually limited. Given the anticipated levels of population and income growth in LDCs, their importance as trading partners for the United States can only improve.

To illustrate, consider the history of U.S. exports to nations that have progressed developmentally since World War II (table 3.4). For example, U.S. agricultural exports to Brazil between 1969–71 and 1987 increased by 708 percent, to Taiwan by 912 percent, and to South Korea by 1,733 percent. These and the "developing nations" listed in table 3.4 have benefited from U.S. economic

### Table 3.4    U.S. Agricultural Exports to Selected Countries, 1969–71 and 1987

| | Years | | |
| Country | 1969–71 ($ millions) | 1987 ($ millions) | increase (percent) |
|---|---|---|---|
| **Developed Countries** | | | |
| Japan | 1,076 | 5,700 | 430 |
| Netherlands | 514 | 1,975 | 284 |
| West Germany | 505 | 1,284 | 154 |
| United Kingdom | 418 | 654 | 56 |
| France | 169 | 523 | 91 |
| **Developing Countries** | | | |
| Colombia | 20 | 131 | 555 |
| Brazil | 36 | 291 | 708 |
| Nigeria | 15 | 38 | 153 |
| South Korea | 100 | 1,833 | 1,733 |
| Taiwan | 127 | 1,285 | 912 |

*Source:* Larry Lev, Michael T. Weber, and H.C. Bittenbender, *Michigan Agriculture and Its Linkages to Developing Countries* (East Lansing: Institute of International Agriculture, Michigan State University, March 1984), 44; USDA, *Foreign Agricultural Trade of the United States, 1987 Supplement* (Washington, D.C.: U.S. GPO, 1987).

assistance at some time during the past four decades. On the other hand, the highest rate for U.S. agricultural exports sent to developed nations was 430 percent with Japan, while agricultural exports to the United Kingdom, a traditional trading partner, increased by only 56 percent.

U.S. agricultural export markets in traditional areas such as Europe do not appear to have significant growth potentials because of the limited growth in domestic demand found in these countries as well as their increasing domestic agricultural production, which meets most of their own needs. The best likelihood for improving U.S. agricultural exports lies with developing nations. If policy accommodations can be developed, Japan, the Soviet Union, and the Eastern European countries also can be important growth markets.

The rise in U.S. agricultural exports to LDCs during a period when the agricultural output of these nations has also been increasing suggests that U.S. agricultural exports generally have not been adversely affected by their production improvements. Yet total U.S. agricultural exports have shown important declines in recent years, even to most of these nations. Justifiably, one might ask why.

As previously indicated, one of the most important causes of the decline in U.S. agricultural exports has been the strength and high value of the dollar relative to other nations' currencies. This relationship has made U.S. exports more expensive than those of competing nations, thus shifting market demand away from the United States. But, as suggested above, there are indications that a decline in the value of the dollar has resulted in increased U.S. agricultural exports in 1988. Second, U.S. domestic agricultural policies have resulted in some world commodity prices rising to levels that are higher than they would be otherwise. This has allowed some nations to profitably grow and competitively export commodities that they could not grow and export at lower world prices. Third, the European Economic Community (EEC) has increasingly produced some commodities in excess of their internal demands, and the surplus has been exported in competition with U.S. exports. Their market shares have been enhanced by the strength of the U.S. dollar. Finally, total world agricultural trade has declined somewhat in the 1980s, and part of the reduction in U.S. agricultural exports reflects this trend. It is apparent, therefore, that the reduction in U.S. agricultural exports has been more a consequence of these factors than of U.S. assistance helping LDCs improve their agricultural productivity.

## U.S. Trade Balance

Problems of trade balance are a constant concern to the United States. Since 1970, the U.S. trade balance has been negative for all but about three years, and the trend has been worsening (figure 3.5). The trade relationships among various nations and groups of nations illustrate the role played by non-OPEC developing nations (figure 3.9). In 1981, U.S. trade with non-OPEC LDCs accounted for 30.2 percent of U.S. exports and 26.4 percent of this nation's imports. The U.S. trade surplus with these nations was about $1 billion. With only three other groups of nations did U.S. trade yield a positive balance for 1981, the principal one being the EEC.

The major sources of the U.S. trade deficit for 1981 were the OPEC nations ($28 billion) and Japan ($16 billion). The overall U.S. trade deficit was $28 billion. However, in 1987, the worsening

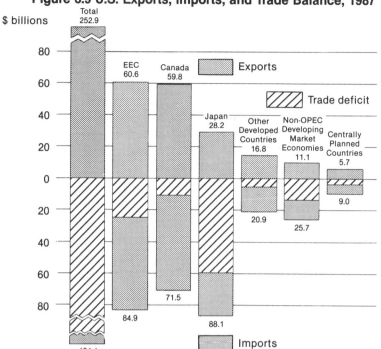

**Figure 3.9 U.S. Exports, Imports, and Trade Balance, 1987**

Source: Bureau of the Census, *Highlights of U.S. Export and Import Trade* (December 1987), tables B-22 and C-26.

Notes: Total world export and import figures include U.S. trade with unidentified countries not otherwise shown on this table. Export and import figures are f.a.s. (free alongside ship) transaction values.

trade situation was reflected in trade relationships with all nations. The United States experienced a negative trade balance with all groups (figure 3.9), as the trade deficit reached about $170 billion. Japan still represents the largest trade deficit for the United States.

Changes in the U.S. trade balance are influenced as much by the value of the dollar relative to other nations' currencies as by most other factors. It is improper, therefore, to generalize about trade relationships based on only one year. When the value of the dollar is low relative to other currencies, U.S. exports become relatively less expensive and the volume of goods leaving the United States expands. During the late 1970s this happened, and U.S. exports, especially those from the agricultural sector, enjoyed a sharp upswing (figure 3.4). In more recent years (1983-84), however, the value of the dollar rose relative to other currencies.

U.S. exports became more costly and foreign imports became less expensive, so the net trade balance worsened dramatically. In 1987, the deficit approximated $170 billion, almost six times that for 1983. Unpublished reports indicate that the deficit for 1988 has declined somewhat in response to the weakening value of the U.S. dollar.

Virtually every sector in the U.S. economy (including agriculture) is now subject to pressures from vacillations in world markets; in turn, U.S. public policy influences international relationships. Even the debt management problems of LDCs mentioned in chapter 2, for example, can be important to U.S. trade balances. The debt obligations facing developing nations such as Mexico and Brazil mean that resources previously available for buying U.S. imports must be redirected to debt repayment. Mexico's imports from the United States were reduced from $17.8 billion in 1981 to $14.6 billion in 1987 due partly to that nation's fiscal austerity programs.

## SUMMARY COMMENTS

There are three primary reasons why it is important for the United States to assist developing nations. The first reason is humanitarian. Nations able to do so have a moral obligation to help those whose people are malnourished, subject to high death rates and excessive infant mortality, and facing limited life expectancy. Most Americans embrace this obligation. The second reason is that such assistance can promote world peace and international political stability (see chap. 5). The third reason is the potential for the United States to realize economic benefits if LDCs have healthy economies. The evidence presented in this chapter supports such a premise. Developing countries are important suppliers of various commodities to the United States. For many important metals and minerals, the United States must rely primarily on LDCs, who also provide many of the complementary agricultural imports demanded by U.S. citizens. In addition, the LDCs as a whole represent one of the primary growth markets for U.S. exports, especially for agricultural products. Evidence suggests that for low-income nations to be viable importers of U.S. agricultural commodities, they must improve their domestic agriculture. To do so gives rise to broad income increases and export sales where foreign exchange can be earned to pay for imports. The benefits are measurable, and they represent visible outcomes that should counter certain pragmatic concerns expressed by some Americans about U.S. foreign assistance.

Admittedly, by promoting economic development abroad, the United States may assist other nations to become more competitive in the world community of nations, which would force U.S. producers to use their ingenuity to meet the competition. This applies to competitive imports. In the case of complementary imports, however, development progress in LDCs may make these goods more economically available to the United States and/or raise their quality. The U.S. industries most likely to be affected by the foreseeable adjustments in the competitive import picture will be those that depend on skills that can be more cheaply duplicated in LDCs. In this age of intimate international interdependence, market shares will shift among nations as competitive factors change.

Before the causal factors responsible for these shifts can be managed, they must be understood. Today, fiscal, monetary, and trade policies—especially those of the United States but also those of other trading nations—may have more to do with losses of foreign markets for U.S. products (especially in agriculture) than with anything LDC producers are able to do to alter the structure of comparative advantage. It is hard to imagine that U.S. agricultural producers could not meet most competitive challenges for LDC producers if fair competition prevailed and if trade policies allowed comparative advantages to determine outcomes rather than distort the relative value of either group's outputs. As an example, the reduction in U.S. agricultural exports is less a reflection of any decline in agricultural efficiency among U.S. farmers than it is of the ramifications of public fiscal and trade policies that have made U.S. agricultural exports more costly in world markets than those exports of competing nations. Before condemning U.S. development assistance to LDCs for fear of its destructive impact on U.S. producers, care should be exercised to understand the complexities, realities, and forces that drive present-day world markets, as well as the factors that most directly cause U.S. producers to lose markets.

Regardless of arguments about the advisability of maintaining U.S. development assistance, the long-run outlook for the world is gloomy indeed unless the productive potentials of LDCs are developed. The most obvious short-term impact on Americans (and others) if LDCs were cut adrift would be higher food prices as the global food supply began to fall ever further behind population and other demand pressures. Further, ignoring the plight of the Third World would certainly have a detrimental effect on international stability. Many fear a future North-South global conflict as much as one between the superpowers, despite the persistent concern about a nuclear holocaust. In the long run, without donor assistance, the poorest LDCs will increasingly experience the outrageous human costs of starving populations. In other regions, malnutrition will continue its insidious march. The developed world, including the United States, will not be able to escape the effects of such tragedies on their own economies. Such devastation and lingering deprivation can only be avoided if the LDCs are able to develop their productive potentials through international cooperation.

Despite the significant self-interest potentials, to justify U.S. economic assistance entirely on the basis either of values arising from trade relationships with developing countries or, for that matter, of any direct benefits (be they economic or political) that serve the particular interests of this nation is to ignore the enormity of the predictable consequences. The world must create the means to feed its people, wherever they live. Accepting the moral imperative does not preclude self-interest factors. In fact, the two should be amalgamated as the basis for U.S. economic assistance. Broader popular support of U.S. efforts may be forthcoming if Americans could be helped to see how U.S. assistance promotes equality and justice for all people while they pursue their fundamental right to be free of hunger. Stability within the international world order will remain elusive until all of the world's people have opportunities to control their own lives and to achieve their innate potentials.

Most Americans can empathize with this vision of a future world, but the unsensational, plodding progress characteristic of long-range development may lose their interest and support. Many U.S. citizens may be only dimly aware of the dimensions of world hunger and what it means to their personal futures and to those of their children. Many react with horror and resolution to television coverage of starvation in Ethiopia but tend to lapse into apathy when these crises disappear from the television screen. Thus, few voters actively encourage their governmental representatives to place elimination of world hunger high on the list of national priorities. This lack of pressure may explain why much of what is classified as foreign assistance is not being directed to nations with the most critical food needs. Only an enlightened public can help establish such a goal as a national priority, and only a committed people can keep its government on target.

# FOUR

# Benefits of International Collaboration in Agricultural Research

## Donald L. Plucknett and Nigel J. H. Smith

One lesson many countries have learned in recent years is the importance of scientific research to sustainable and productive agriculture. The United States learned this basic lesson long ago, but today we have come to recognize that much of the research needed to produce new agricultural technology can only be effectively carried on through international contacts and collaboration. And, in fact, over the past two decades, agricultural research has developed into a global enterprise and may well be now the most international of all scientific endeavors.

### A GLOBAL ENTERPRISE

How did the establishment of an international agricultural research system come about? No government has planned it and no international organization has willed it, yet many pieces are already in place and operating, despite the lack of a common budget or—in most cases—formal agreements. Who is involved in such work, and how is the work being carried out?

Ultimately, of course, all scientific research is conducted by individual scientists. So it was among individuals that international cooperation started. Scientists in different countries with common interests began to exchange ideas and materials and to plan joint research. However, since such activities relied heavily on individual initiative and received uncertain financial support, they tended to be opportunistic and sporadic.

It was not until after World War II that a cooperative global effort really got under way, and it is only in the past 20 years or so that all the major developments have taken place. The Rockefeller and Ford foundations can take much of the credit for originating today's system since their joint initiative in starting international agricultural research centers gave intellectual leadership, impetus, and worldwide dimension to work that had previously been mostly individual and fragmented.

Once the effort began on a larger scale, others joined in areas where they had particular interest, and their successes led to still greater collaboration. The Consultative Group on International Agricultural Research (CGIAR) was established by a group of foreign aid donors. New international centers—and initiatives— took shape; some new centers were started by the CGIAR, others began as independent bodies. More countries joined in, taking on research that responded to their local needs. LDC institutions forged working relationships with developed country institutions, such as universities and even private laboratories, as well as with international agricultural research centers. Foreign assistance organizations, private and public foundations, and individual governments all contributed financial support. And so an "international fellowship of science" emerged that has brought about not only technical results but also social and political advances as well.

In the United States, USAID has been a focal point for such efforts, providing special funding to the USDA and to U.S. universities so that work could be started and continued. During the past decade, U.S. university involvement has been fostered by BIFAD, the presidential board that works with USAID and that promotes and supports international research through its Collaborative Research Support Programs (CRSPs). These programs, the first of which was established in 1978, seek to match the interests of U.S. university research programs with similar interests at developing country institutions for the benefit of all parties. At present, seven CRSPs bring together 40 U.S. universities and 66 agricultural institutions in 30 LDCs to work collaboratively to conduct research on beans and cowpeas, peanuts, sorghum and millet, small ruminants, management of tropical soils, pond dynamics, and fisheries stock assessment.

Other countries have also established institutions to promote international research. For example, Canada has established its International Development Research Centre; Australia, the Australian Center for International Agricultural Research; and the Federal Republic of Germany, the Deutsche Gesellschaft für Technische Zusammernarbeit. Special institutions have also been set up in France, Japan, the Netherlands, Sweden, and the United Kingdom.

Whatever the name of the mechanism used, the basic idea is the same—that agricultural research can and does benefit from international cooperation. The cooperation may be simple, with two or three scientists corresponding and visiting periodically to keep in touch on a common problem. Or one institution may serve the special needs of another by crossbreeding special plants to incorporate resistance to diseases or pests not yet present in the latter's country or by growing out a generation of breeding lines during a season when the crop could not be grown in that country. Or dozens of institutions and hundreds of scientists in several countries may be working cooperatively in carefully linked research. Through many kinds of collaboration the international research effort is active and expanding.

## SHARING THE GERMPLASM

One vitally important area of cooperation is the international exchange of germplasm. Germplasm can be defined as seeds or living organisms (plants or animals), or parts of living organisms, bearing hereditary characteristics that can be passed along to succeeding generations. Long before today's global research system came into being, of course, germplasm was moving around the world. Sugarcane, for example, was originally a Southeast Asian crop, yet today it provides a major base to the economies of Brazil, the Caribbean islands, Peru, and South Africa. Sunflower came originally from North America; now it has become a major crop in the Soviet Union and China. And rice, a crop whose major cultivated form is indigenous to Asia, has become important throughout the world.

But today the sharing—and the constant improvement of germplasm—has become highly sophisticated. Plant germplasm exchange has developed into a bustling, worldwide activity involving public and private research organizations in both developed and developing countries, as well as international organizations. An international network of plant genetic resource centers has been established, mostly through the efforts of the International Board for Plant Genetic Resources, to ensure that germplasm necessary for future plant breeding is located, characterized, safely stored in gene banks, and made available to all interested countries. The plant germplasm system in the United States is a key participant in this work, especially through such facilities as the U.S. Seed Storage Laboratory at Fort Collins, Colo., and four regional plant introduction stations in Pullman, Wash.; Ames, Iowa; Geneva, N.Y.; and Experiment, Ga.

The worldwide germplasm effort includes internationally funded collecting trips to the centers of origin of important crops and international programs of plant breeding. Through a network of international nurseries, the performance of individual entries is carefully noted and communicated to scientists worldwide. Traits such as disease and insect resistance, tolerance to drought or other environmental stresses, and other factors are identified and used in future breeding efforts.

Mankind has benefited greatly from such work. Yields of major food crops have risen and continue to rise when such techniques have been used cooperatively, and responses to new problems have been quicker since international testing and rapid communication of results have been employed.

In recent years, the question of the ownership of germplasm has become a matter of international contention. Traditionally, germplasm has been considered to be a resource that is, and should be, available to all countries. Indeed, almost all gene banks operate on the principle of free exchange in response to bona fide requests.

But today those who are questioning the current germplasm system point out that germplasm is largely held in gene banks in the developed countries, even though most of the basic germplasm of our important crops was obtained from Third World countries. Their solution is to place the international germplasm system under intergovernmental control.

Those defending the present system point out that although scientific plant breeding and systematic collection and use of germplasm began and have been highly refined in some developed countries, today developing countries are rapidly improving their own capacities to store and use germplasm of major interest to them, in most cases with the help of developed countries. Further, they point to the return by gene banks in developed countries of germplasm that has disappeared in those countries where the plants originated. The solution of the germplasm issue lies not in intergovernmental oversight and political control, they argue, but in international cooperation and the free exchange of germplasm between scientists and technical people in all countries.

## HISTORY OF U.S. INVOLVEMENT
## IN GERMPLASM EXCHANGE

If you were to go shopping at a supermarket and buy only foods indigenous to the United States, your basket would be virtually empty. Only a handful of food crops—notably sunflower, cranberry, and pecan—originated in North America, and none of them is of major importance in commerce or subsistence. As is true in other countries, agriculture in the United States has always depended heavily on the importation of foreign plant germplasm to introduce new plants and to boost the yield and hardiness of existing crops.

Political and scientific leaders in the United States early recognized the importance of obtaining plant germplasm from other countries. While Thomas Jefferson was minister to France, for example, he sent seeds of cereal crops, vegetables, and grasses, and cuttings of olive and fruit trees to correspondents and organizations back home. In 1819, the U.S. secretary of the treasury issued a circular calling attention to the importance of new crop plants and requesting that consuls and naval officers send home useful examples. In 1839, the U.S. Patent Office started providing direct financial support for the acquisition of plant germplasm.

After the USDA established the Office of Foreign Seed and Plant Introduction in 1898, legendary plant hunters scoured distant lands gathering plants of potential economic value to the United States; one man alone was responsible for 2,500 plant introductions to this country. Over the years more than 200 plant-collecting missions have been organized to the centers of crop diversity. To quarantine and evaluate the ever-growing stream of incoming plant material, the Office of Foreign Seed and Plant Introduction built facilities on the Washington Mall and established plant introduction stations throughout the country. By 1910, five such stations were operating, including one in Chico, Calif., that concentrated on stone fruits and another in Miami that specialized in tropical plants.

Today the United States has perhaps the most highly developed plant germplasm storage and improvement system in the world. And the flow has not been all one way. For example, the cooperative efforts of the USDA have enabled French scientists to collect wild grape germplasm in the Mississippi Valley to improve French grapes, have enabled the Soviet Union to collect wild sunflowers in the Midwest to improve their sunflower crops, and have returned to Ethiopia seeds of teff (a cereal important to the local diet) that were collected by an international team in 1967 and safely held in cold storage in the United States.

## BENEFITS OF INTERNATIONAL COLLABORATION IN GERMPLASM WORK

In the long term, of course, all countries benefit from having basic germplasm such as primitive cultivars (varieties that have originated and persisted under cultivation) and wild relatives safely preserved for future use. But there are also immediate benefits from having world collections of germplasm of important crops, collections that can be tapped in the continuing search for desirable genes that could confer useful and often robust traits to crop plants. For example, the germplasm from the global wheat collection held by the International Maize and Wheat Improvement Center headquartered near Mexico City—Centro Internacional de Mejoramiento de Maiz y Trigo (CIMMYT)—has been useful as a source of improvements both in semidwarf varieties and in resistance to rust. Using germplasm from several countries, CIMMYT develops semidwarf and other varieties of wheat for the Third World. The ancestry of the semidwarf wheat it produced in 1966 that helped spark the "green revolution" in Asia can be traced back to Norin 10, a Japanese variety brought back to the United

States after World War II, and to breeding efforts at Washington State University.

One might ask how the United States benefits specifically from international germplasm work. For the answer, one might look to the production of semidwarf wheats, which are winning converts around the world both because more growth goes into the grain rather than into the stems and because they do not topple over under increased fertilization. Research scientists at U.S. universities and at CIMMYT's headquarters in Mexico have been working on semidwarf crosses since the 1950s to promote the use of short-stemmed wheat. The first successful use of a semi-dwarf variety was in 1962 with the Gaines variety, a cross using Norin 10, on one-fourth of the wheat area in California. The first semidwarf CIMMYT crosses were introduced in 1968, and the use of Mexican crosses spread rapidly. By 1979, 147 semi-dwarf wheat varieties had been adopted in the United States. Of these, 18 were introduced directly from Mexico, 34 were selected from Mexican crosses, and of the 95 selections from crosses made in the United States, 14 had Mexican varieties in their pedigrees. By 1984, an additional 72 semidwarf wheat varieties had been planted in this country, 25 of which contained germplasm from the CIMMYT collection or from the Mexican national program. In all, short-statured wheat varieties containing germplasm from the CIMMYT collection were planted on an estimated 15.6 million acres of U.S. farmland during that year, and the proportion is growing. Some 60 percent of U.S. wheats now contain dwarfing genes originating in Asia.

Germplasm from the collection held by CIMMYT has been widely adopted in the midwestern and western United States. In 1984, for example, all of the spring wheat planted in the Pacific Northwest and West contained CIMMYT germplasm, as did half of the hard red winter wheat planted in Kansas, a third of the same variety sown in Oklahoma, and nearly a third of the acreage planted to soft red winter wheat in Indiana (table 4.1). Overall, a fifth of the area sown to this latter variety of wheat in the United States now embodies such genetic material; for hard red winter wheat, the proportion is close to a third.

Semidwarf rices are also gaining popularity in the United States, and many trace their pedigrees to the tropical rice collection held by the International Rice Research Institute (IRRI) at Los Banos in the Philippines. Close to a quarter of the U.S. rice area is

### Table 4.1    Estimated Percentage and Area of U.S. Wheat Lands Occupied by Varieties with Germplasm from the World Collection, 1984

| State/Region | % Wheat Area | Acres Planted |
|---|---|---|
| **Hard Red Winter Wheat** | | |
| Kansas | 50 | 6,817,500 |
| Oklahoma | 32 | 2,487,100 |
| Colorado | 22 | 828,400 |
| Nebraska | 16 | 515,200 |
| Texas | 10 | 740,000 |
| Total | 32 | 11,388,200 |
| **Soft Red Winter Wheat** | | |
| Indiana | 30 | 351,000 |
| Illinois | 26 | 468,000 |
| Ohio | 15 | 186,000 |
| Missouri | 11 | 263,200 |
| Total | 19 | 1,268,200 |
| **Hard Red Spring Wheat** | | |
| California | 100 | 770,000 |
| Idaho | 100 | 400,000 |
| Washington | 100 | 210,000 |
| Oregon | 100 | 80,000 |
| Arizona | 100 | 63,000 |
| Utah | 100 | 39,000 |
| Nevada | 100 | 16,000 |
| Montana | 16 | 347,600 |
| South Dakota | 15 | 255,000 |
| Minnesota | 14 | 308,000 |
| North Dakota | 8 | 430,550 |
| Total | 22 | 2,919,150 |

*Source:* CIMMYT, internal document, 1985.

currently planted to semidwarfs. In 1984, two-thirds of this semi-dwarf rice area contained varieties or lines from the IRRI collection. One variety released in California in 1977, M-9, contains an IRRI variety, IR8, in its parentage. By 1979, M-9 occupied 60 percent of California's semidwarf rice area (about 5 percent of total U.S. rice lands). Its importance is now waning, however, a typical fate even for successful varieties; they become obsolete either because they succumb to rapidly changing diseases or pests or because superior varieties become available. In 1981, for example, M-9 occupied only 32 percent of California's semidwarf rice area— about half of the total acreage occupied just two years earlier—and by 1984 its proportion had further slipped to 11 percent. However, another rice with IR8 in its parentage, M-201, is replacing M-9. Released in 1982, M-201 covered 46 percent of California's short-statured rice area by 1984. Like its predecessor, M-201 is highly productive, with an average yield of 8,460 pounds per acre.

Considering that both the germplasm collection at IRRI and its breeding program are geared to tropical (indica) rices, its impact on California agriculture is remarkable. Rice farmers in California, the most important rice-producing region in the United States, plant temperate sinica (japonica) rices, and breeders there use tropical germplasm mainly as a source of dwarfing genes. (Other dwarf rices planted in California trace their short stature to mutants produced through irradiation.) Similarly, all semidwarf rices grown in the southern United States, the other important rice-growing region of the country, also contain tropical germplasm from the IRRI collection.

Bean germplasm from other countries has also helped U.S. farmers. Plant breeders in Michigan, for example—the nation's leading producer of the common bean (also known as the bush of field bean)—have employed bean germplasm from Colombia, Mexico, Puerto Rico, Chile, and Venezuela during the last two decades. Genes for an erect plant type highly suited to Michigan's farming environment were obtained from a Costa Rican variety, San Fernando, which is derived from a radiation-induced mutant. Similarly, bean breeders at Michigan State University have found germplasm from the collection maintained at the Centro Inter-nacional de Agricultura Tropical (CIAT) in Colombia especially useful for such traits as resistance to mosaic virus disease, but national programs in Latin America have also been helpful. Bunsi-ICA, a navy bean developed by Colombia's national program, has proved to be a good source of tolerance to white mold and has been approved for release in Michigan.

Michigan's common bean crop was worth $120 million in 1982, accounting for close to a third of U.S. bean production. Its continued vigor depends on unhampered access to a broad germplasm base, particularly from Latin America where the crop was domesticated.

Potatoes are an important crop in many parts of the United States, and virtually every American eats potatoes in some form during the course of a week. The Peruvian-based International Potato Center—Centro Internacional de la Papa (CIP)—maintains a large collection of potato germplasm, which consists of 6,500 accessions of distinct samples (5,000 clones and 1,500 accessions of wild relatives kept as botanical seed). A major duplicate collection of these wild potato relatives from Latin America is housed at Sturgeon Bay, Wis., and is useful to potato breeders in the United States. At Cornell University, for example, germplasm resistant to golden nematode (a class of parasitic worms) has been used to develop potato varieties that have been grown in New York for a decade. And with financial support from international research funds provided by CIP, doctoral students at the University of Wisconsin in Madison have perfected potato breeding techniques that have also benefited red clover and alfalfa breeders in the United States.

Corn was domesticated in Mexico, and its greatest genetic diversity is found in the American tropics. However, for U.S. breeders developing temperate corn, such material presents formidable problems such as poor yields, adverse response to day-length conditions in cooler climates, and the need for repeated backcrossing to advanced breeding methods to shed undesirable genes. But despite these difficulties, corn germplasm from LDCs has made its way into commercial hybrids in the United States. Funks G-4734 and G-4949A and Pioneer 3160 and 3328 contain corn germplasm from the Caribbean; DeKalb hybrids XL73 and XL309 contain germplasm from Mexico; and big agribusinesses such as Cargill, DeKalb, Migro, and Hoegemeyer market hybrids with small amounts of Argentine material.

Numerous crop varieties that contain germplasm produced in international agricultural research centers or in collaborative research efforts involving U.S. and Third World national programs are in the pipeline for U.S. farmers. In the case of peanut, for example, germplasm from the collection at the International Crops Research Institute for the Semi-Arid Tropics (ICRISAT) is being tested by breeders at Texas A&M University, the University of Florida, and North Carolina State University. A scientist at Texas A&M is using the collection's lines tolerant to drought and resistant both to foliar diseases and to *Aspergillus flavus*, a seed fungus that produces a carcinogen. A scientist at the University of Florida's research station at Marianna is testing ICRISAT's collection lines that are resistant to leaf spot; he also plans to use material that does not "nodulate" (i.e., form nodules or swellings on the plant roots containing symbiotic bacteria that enable the plant to make use of nitrogen in the air) in experiments on the physiology of nitrogen nutrition. And a plant breeder at North Carolina State University is using in his crossing program ICRISAT materials that tolerate drought, resist leaf spot, mature early, and are superior fixers of nitrogen. He estimates that the university will have a peanut variety containing such germplasm ready for release within five years.

Soybean, introduced to the United States from China at the turn of the nineteenth century, has recently been improved by germplasm from Korea. At present, raw soybeans contain within them a substance that inhibits their digestibility for livestock. Thus, they must be cooked to inactivate this substance, a costly procedure that also reduces their nutritional value. However, U.S. breeders have been using Korean materials to develop soybean lines that lack the inhibiting compound, and this breeding development is expected to heighten demand for soybean in the livestock industry.

The cowpea CRSP has made several contributions to California agriculture, and more are on the way. The program facilitated the discovery of heat-tolerant germplasm, which is now being used to develop improved varieties of black-eyed pea (as the cowpea is known in the United States) that thrive in hot temperatures. The searing summers in many parts of California will soon no longer prove an obstacle to black-eyed pea growers in the state.

Wild species will be used increasingly in plant breeding, particularly with further refinements in biotechnology. For example, wild relatives of peanut are helping upgrade yield stability of the crop. The world's largest collection of peanut varieties and wild relatives—over 11,000 accessions—is housed in India at ICRISAT, and scientists there have crossed peanut with 13 wild relatives, thereby considerably widening the peanut germplasm base. Similarly, CIP's crossing program using potato relatives is likely to provide benefits to farmers throughout the world. Potato scientists have crossed the cultivated potato with 22 wild species containing such useful traits as resistance to diseases and pests and tolerance to adverse soils and weather. And a Cornell University scientist is using germplasm from the CIP collection to develop potato varieties resistant to late blight and potato virus Y. Cultivars are expected to be ready for farmers in New York State within five to ten years.

## OTHER SCIENTIFIC AND TECHNOLOGICAL ADVANCES

Although most scientific benefits to U.S. farmers and consumers from international collaboration in agricultural research stem from the exchange and use of plant germplasm, livestock research and other aspects of crop research in the United States have also benefited.

This is particularly true in the area of animal disease research. One such disease, the foot-and-mouth virus, has been the focus of extensive international research attention—including collaborative efforts between U.S. researchers and foreign colleagues—to the great benefit of the United States. With Argentine colleagues, for example, USDA scientists have produced a technology for processing meat so it can be shipped worldwide free of virus. The Pan-American Foot-and-Mouth Disease Center in Argentina has produced new formulations of vaccines that give longer-lasting immunity to animals, while research conducted with Dutch colleagues has enabled USDA scientists to study the longevity of animal immunity to the disease. Tests developed at USDA's Plum Island Animal Disease Center at Greenport, N.Y., can distinguish between the immune response to natural infections of foot-and-mouth disease and to vaccination for it by singling out a specific enzyme, replicase, that is present in naturally infected animals but not in vaccinated ones. This method, which has been field tested, can also be used to test semen imported for breeding purposes, and it was the main serological method used in studies that led to Chile being declared a country free of foot-and-mouth disease.

Another dreaded disease requiring international research is African swine fever (ASF). While not yet in the United States, this disease has been found in the Caribbean in recent years. A virus disease like foot-and-mouth, ASF, if found in a new location, can be controlled only by destroying infected animals. In the 1950s a USDA scientist from Plum Island working in Kenya developed a laboratory test for ASF. This was a very important discovery since

ASF cannot be distinguished from hog cholera, another serious disease, except through field studies. Later, through a research agreement support by P.L. 480 funds, the procedure was field tested in Spain in collaboration with Spanish animal scientists.

The Plum Island laboratory has also collaborated with Italian researchers on four swine viruses commonly found in Italy but not in the United States. The work involved studying the survival of the viruses during the processing of hams into prosciutto, a process that requires some 400 days. Since it was determined conclusively that the viruses do not survive this period, the processed meat can be shipped and consumed safely.

International research on insects and diseases that are not yet found in the United States but that could accidentally arrive one day helps to provide advance knowledge of the problems such insects or diseases could cause. In addition it supplies information on the direction and speed of their spread and on conditions that encourage—or might discourage—rapid infestation of croplands. For example, results from the peanut CRSP are likely to benefit U.S. farmers in the future. The fact that peanut mottle disease, also known as rosette disease, is caused by a pair of viruses was uncovered in research conducted in Nigeria in collaboration with several U.S. universities. Although the disease in not yet present in the United States, it may spread here. Fortunately, researchers at the University of Georgia have developed methods to detect the presence of the viruses in seeds; this helps prevent the spread of the disease when plant material is exchanged from one region to another.

Efforts are currently being made to establish a world data bank on plant diseases at Fort Detrick, Md., to keep track of all that is known about crop diseases, their present locations, their special characteristics, and their potential for increased virulence. Other world data bases have already been established or are being planned, and they will all require broad international cooperation and support.

International collaboration has also been of tremendous value in the biological control of insects, weeds, and other pests. Biological control involves finding natural enemies of pests, testing them carefully to determine that they will not damage desirable plants or animals, and then growing and releasing them into a new environment to act as biological agents against a target species.

Successful biological control requires a constant search for pests or predators of problem plants or insects. This is the work of the USDA's Beneficial Insects Laboratory at Beltsville, Md., which also supports four laboratories overseas to look for, study, and ship beneficial organisms. The laboratories include one in Rome, established in 1959 for the biocontrol of weeds; one in Buenos Aires, established in 1962 for the biocontrol of both weeds (especially water weeds) and insects; the European Parasite Laboratory in Paris, established in 1919 to study natural enemies of insect pests in Europe that are also important to the United States; and the laboratory in Seoul (originally founded in Japan in the 1930s), which devotes its major effort to the study of natural enemies of insect pests from Asia. USDA is also considering a working relationship with the biological quarantine laboratory in China and a similar arrangement with the USSR.

For some weeds, especially aquatic ones, the only effective control measure may be biological. For example, alligator weed, an aquatic weed from South America that infests Florida waterways, has been controlled by a flea beetle introduced from Argentina. Similarly, water hyacinth, another South American aquatic weed, has been controlled by a weevil brought from South America that interacts with a kind of fungus to control the beautiful but pesky plant.

Some states, such as Florida, Hawaii, and California, have been involved in biological control for many years. For example, Hawaii has been introducing biocontrol agents since 1895 to control pests in pasture lands as well as croplands. In California, two wasps brought in from Asia have provided biocontrol of black scale and mealybug on citrus, with a savings of some $4 million annually to the California citrus industry. And in the mid-Atlantic states, control of the alfalfa weevil by wasps identified by the USDA European Parasite Laboratory in Paris and introduced into the United States has resulted in an annual savings estimated at $8 million.

A technique known as integrated pest management is also being used increasingly in U.S. agriculture, particularly in Hawaiian sugarcane plantations and California citrus groves. With this program, harmful insects are kept in check by such measures as releasing predators, rotating crops, and dispersing species-specific hormones into the air to disrupt breeding; thus, the need for pesticides is reduced or even eliminated. Agricultural systems in

LDCs, most of which have never employed pesticides, provide useful models for scientists devising agronomic practices for integrated pest management in the United States.

## SUMMARY COMMENTS

The few examples given above of benefits from international collaboration in agricultural research tell only a small portion of the story. Many more could be cited, not only in the area of crops, but also in livestock and in social science methodology, such as the "farming systems" approach to research, extension, and economic planning in rural development.

The United States has been dependent historically on the international exchange of germplasm. Without access to wild species and cultivars from abroad, U.S. agriculture would not have reached its current high level of productivity; possibly our entire economy would not have developed as it has, since the country's early growth resulted from advances on the farm.

In more recent years, as cooperative activities have increased, we have come to recognize our dependency in other areas as well—or, at least, the great advantages to be gained from collaboration in agricultural research, of all kinds, by all parties to the collaboration. As noted, even in the case of research focusing specifically on needs of countries in the Third World, the ancillary benefits to American agriculture have been significant. And these scientific and technological benefits are in addition, of course, to the economic and political advantages discussed elsewhere in this book. If the past is prologue to the future, it is clear our interest lies in open lines of communication, in sharing our expertise, and in financial investment to promote international research on an ever wider scale.

# FIVE

## Hunger, Poverty, And Political Instability

### William L. Furlong

T he rapid proliferation of independent nations during the twentieth century is unprecedented. At the end of 1945, the UN recognized 52 nations. In 1989, there were 160 members. There are more power centers, more decision-makers, and more interacting public policies affecting the lives of the world's people than ever before.

Both domestic and international political conflicts abound. These are a result not just of ideological differences but also of cultural diversity, racism, and competition for power, land, natural resources, and economic advantage. The competition between the United States and the Soviet Union is perhaps the best known and most critical, but it is certainly not unique. These worldwide conflicts pervade all attempts to reduce poverty, alleviate hunger, slow population growth, and improve agricultural production. The configuration of U.S. foreign assistance therefore reflects these conditions.

### AID AND SECURITY

The evidence presented in the preceding chapters supports one fairly clear conclusion: relieving world hunger and solving food supply problems claim a very small portion of U.S. foreign assistance funds. Political and security aspects of U.S. foreign policy quite often take precedence over such purely humanitarian efforts (see appendix table 2.6).

Most foreign assistance funds are not being used to directly combat hunger in the poorest nations of the world. Even food aid and economic development monies are often subject to the broader needs of U.S. political, economic, and security interests. This occurs because the priorities of U.S. foreign policy reflect a wide spectrum of concerns beyond just hunger and poverty.

U.S. administrations after that of President Truman have stressed some or all of the following goals in this more comprehensive view of American foreign policy: 1) to maintain peace and avoid nuclear war, 2) to limit Soviet expansion throughout the world, 3) to encourage an international economic system that ensures the United States access to markets and resources while promoting economic development, and 4) to seek a world in which other nations have values that are similar to those of the United States and have political systems that are stable and compatible with our own (as shown by President Carter's emphasis on human rights and by President Reagan's and now President Bush's defense of democracy).

President Truman began significant post–World War II foreign assistance with the Marshall Plan to rebuild Europe. In his 1949 inaugural address, he suggested expanding that program as part of his Point Four program to make the benefits of the developed and industrialized world available for improvement and growth in the developing nations. However, eradication of world hunger was not explicitly set forth in his four-point program or in any of the other post-Truman U.S. foreign policy pronouncements. Instead, efforts to eliminate world hunger have been seen mainly as a means of helping to accomplish the more overreaching foreign policy objectives.

As discussed in chapter 2, views of U.S. defense security have conditioned much of U.S. economic assistance since 1950. Revolution and major political instability anywhere in the world are perceived to have a direct impact on U.S. security interests, especially if the revolution or instability might lead to the establishment of a Marxist government. Some analysts believe, however, that poverty and hunger can compound problems that lead to political violence and revolution. In that context, it is reasoned that reducing hunger through food support will also reduce political instability and violence, thereby allowing the United States to fulfill its major foreign policy objectives, especially that of limiting

Communist expansion. Thus, although the popular perception of technical and food assistance is that the largest amounts go to the poorest, the most underdeveloped, and the hungriest nations, in reality, this assumption is incorrect. Economic and food aid recipients are identified more by the security and other foreign policy interests of the United States than by their levels of need and poverty.

This chapter discusses food and economic assistance and their relationships with LDC development, food sufficiency, and political instability. The analysis is concerned mostly with recent events and some of the causes of political violence and revolution. Unfortunaltely, although U.S. foreign assistance to the less developed world has helped nations and peoples, it has not been able to create long-term solutions to world hunger, poverty, and political problems.

## ASSISTANCE AND DEVELOPMENT

Many U.S. policymakers believe that economic assistance can help Third World nations on their path to development. Assistance programs to date have engendered progress in a number of areas. Schools, hospitals, medical centers, water and sewage systems, and housing complexes have been erected; new factories and industries have been built; roads, airfields, port facilities, dams, and irrigation systems have been constructed; advanced technologies have been introduced; illnesses have been eradicated; and food production has increased. However, as indicated in chapter 1, much of this progress has unfortunately had an urban bias as even agricultural advances have benefited city populations more than rural ones.

Moreover, despite agricultural progress in many LDCs over the past 30 years, food production has generally not kept pace with population growth, as was also detailed earlier. This is due not only to the urban bias of development assistance but also to many other factors, including ownership of land concentrated in the hands of a few, mechanization and technology concentrated on export crops rather than on domestic food production, and government policies benefiting export producers while penalizing domestic food producers. Other relevant factors are the low level of education of most rural inhabitants; the low visibility and influence of most ministries of agriculture; and the restraints imposed by poor soil, erosion, bad weather, and lack of irrigation networks. Development assistance has been unable to resolve these problems.

Nevertheless, continued economic assistance to LDCs from developed nations is necessary if world food production is to improve. Many U.S. policymakers also believe that, with development, nations will become more stable and more democratic as the ills of poverty, food shortages, and unemployment are reduced. Put another way, this rationale depends on the following scenarios: Economic assistance will enable the LDC to develop, which will thus lead to improvements in the standard of living; this in turn will foster greater political stability and with it greater democracy, resulting finally in a political system more supportive of and friendly to the United States. On the other hand, hunger and poverty in an LDC, if allowed to go unchecked, will create political instability, a prime condition for the intervention of Communist influences, which would then result in a nation that is more of a threat to U.S. interests and to world peace. Both rationales are used extensively to justify food aid as well as economic assistance to LDCs.

Ironically, as many experts in political and social development also point out, economic development often causes major dislocations in society even while it improves some conditions. It can threaten established processes and relationships and create new power centers, changes that can also lead to violence. Governmental elites can be threatened as new groups become more economically viable and make additional demands on the political system. Landowners can become concerned when proposals are made for land and agrarian reforms. Middle classes worry as labor becomes more organized and militant. Economic development and improvements in education and social systems often threaten the established elites and the political systems that they influence and from which they benefit. Clearly, development is disruptive. Yet change is necessary if human suffering is to be reduced.

Obviously it is hoped that economic assistance will aid development, reduce hunger and poverty, and improve social and political stability. It is also expected that through this process nations will be less prone to political violence, revolution, and eventual Communist influence. Thus, the goals of foreign assistance are not only to help people but also to encourage the economic development of LDCs and enhance the likelihood of their evolving toward democratic-type governments. These coincide with the main goals of American foreign policy mentioned above.

Without assistance from the United States and other donor nations, the world probably would be suffering from even more poverty, hunger, illiteracy, illness, and misery, and would be more anti-American than it is today. Yet despite the levels of aid already given, these tragic conditions persist. Continued political violence and instability within and among the LDCs therefore seem likely.

## NORTH-SOUTH CONFLICT

Since the 1970s, there has been much talk of future North-South conflict. The rationale is that the northern half of the world is developed and that its people are well fed and healthy at the expense of the exploited southern half, where the population is hungry, ill housed, unhealthy, and poor.

Most LDCs do lie below the 30th degree north latitude (figure 5.1). The only major LDC north of this line is China. The explanation for this distribution of rich and poor nations involves too many economic, political, geographic, cultural, and historical events to be detailed here. It is enough for our purposes to know that an inequitable distribution exists and is the source of considerable debate about claims that northern nations exploit those in the South.

Many political leaders in the LDCs perceive that the developed North is exploiting them through trade, aid, and other relationships. They claim the northern industrialized nations keep the South underdeveloped and dependent for their own northern economic advantage. In much of the world, this is known as the "dependency" explanation of underdevelopment (see "The Question of Dependency" below). This concept further complicates North-South relations and exacerbates conditions of conflict.

The North-South conflict is further aggravated by the debt crisis of the 1980s. External pressures continue to build against LDCs to force them to pay debts that may consume as much as 50 percent of their foreign currency. The resultant domestic austerity measures have a direct, negative impact on the poor. The situation then reinforces the belief that the rich are getting richer and the poor are getting poorer due to a conspiracy among developed

**Figure 5.1**

**World**

# Map

countries, which in turn furthers the conflict and the belief in the dependency theory.

The indebted LDCs are attempting to improve their economic conditions by renegotiating their debts, requesting new forms of aid, and examining nontraditional trade agreements. They are seeking new, large loans on a more concessional and less conditional basis. They also want debt forgiveness or at least more favorable terms for their extensive external debts. In addition, they want improved access to foreign markets for their exports; better terms of trade, including higher and more stable prices for their exportable raw materials; and major transfers of technology. To achieve these objectives, they are asking for a fundamental restructuring of existing international trade and the world monetary system. The envisioned changes would give these countries a much more significant operational role in the international economic system, including management of such key institutions as the International Monetary Fund (IMF). This is often referred to as the North-South dialogue and the quest for a "new international economic order."

In addition to debt and lack of development, food production, as noted above, is not keeping pace with population growth in many developing areas of Africa, South and Southeast Asia, and Latin America. While the world experienced an increase in grain production of 367 million metric tons between 1970 and 1984, the least developed nations' share was less than 36 million tons, or less than 10 percent of the increase. This occurred while their populations were growing at a more rapid rate.

The gap between the developed and the less developed nations continues to expand in technology, industry, and the standard of living. It is illustrated here by a deterioration in the per capita caloric intake in the poorest nations (figure 5.2 and table 5.1). Although some developing nations have improved, the least developed have declined as the poorest get poorer and hungrier.

It is not surprising that hunger and poverty are related. Table 5.2 lists 16 nations with an average annual per capita income of less than $400 in 1987; in 1985 these nations consumed an average daily per capita intake of less than 2,000 calories. This is less than the 2,400 calories that are considered to be the required daily intake to maintain the organism.

Not only do the poorest people have a difficult time feeding themselves, but the countries with the largest percentage of their

## Figure 5.2 Average Daily Caloric Intake per Person, as a Percentage of Requirement

Not only is there a gap between developed and developing countries in caloric intake, but there is also considerable variance among developing countries. By the end of the 1970s, the least developed countries were worse off than they were at the beginning, and they continued to decline through 1985.

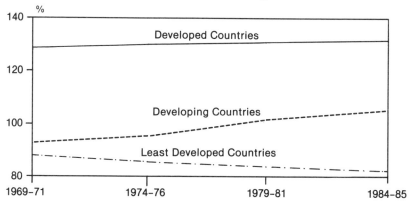

Source: FAO, *Current World Food Situation,* April 1984, as cited in John W. Sewell, Richard E. Feinberg, and Valeriana Kallab eds., *U.S. Foreign Policy and the Third World: Agenda 1985-86,* (Washington, D.C.: ODC, 1985), 233; World Bank, *The World Bank Atlas 1988* (Washington, D.C.: 1988).

## Table 5.1 Average Daily Caloric Intake: The African Diet Worsens

The mid-1980s witnessed deep declines in African food consumption. In 1984, average caloric intake per person was well below the standard requirement for an active working life and less than two-thirds of the caloric intake in industrial countries.

| | Percentage of Daily Caloric Requirement | | | | | Annual Rates of Change | |
| --- | --- | --- | --- | --- | --- | --- | --- |
| | 1970 | 1975 | 1980 | 1982 | 1984 | 1970–80 | 1980–84 |
| **Developing Countries** | 92.7 | 94.6 | 101.8 | 103.9 | 104.9 | 0.9 | 0.8 |
| Africa | 93.1 | 92.9 | 95.6 | 94.5 | 87.3 | 0.4 | −2.4 |
| Far East | 91.5 | 90.7 | 97.7 | 99.1 | n.a. | 0.7 | n.a. |
| Latin America | 105.3 | 106.8 | 110.8 | 110.2 | 114.5 | 0.5 | 0.9 |
| Middle East | 98.4 | 107.8 | 116.3 | 118.9 | 122.3 | 1.7 | 1.3 |
| **Developed Countries** | 128.1 | 130.0 | 132.1 | 132.4 | n.a. | 0.3 | n.a. |

*Sources:* Adapted from the UN World Food Council, "Current World Food Situation" (March 1982 and April 1986); FAO, "Current World Food Situation" (May 1987).

*Note:* Annual index numbers are based on three-year averages centering on the year indicated. Figures refer to the calories required for an active working life in the regions concerned.

Table 5.2    Relationship Between Poverty and Hunger:
The Poorest Nations and Their Daily Caloric Intake

| Country | Per Capita GNP in U.S. Dollars 1987 | Per Capita Daily Calorie Supply 1985 |
|---|---|---|
| Ethiopia | 120 | 1,650 |
| Mozambique | 150 | 1,550 |
| Chad | 150 | 1,700 |
| Bhutan | 150 | 2,500 |
| Bangladesh | 160 | 1,900 |
| Nepal | 160 | 2,000 |
| Zaire | 160 | 2,100 |
| Laos | 160 | 2,300 |
| Malawi | 160 | 2,400 |
| Burkina Faso | 170 | 2,000 |
| Mali | 200 | 1,800 |
| Madagascar | 200 | 2,400 |
| Sierra Leone | 300 | 1,800 |
| Haiti | 360 | 1,800 |
| Ghana | 390 | 1,800 |
| Guinea | — | 1,750 |

*Source:* World Bank, *The World Bank Atlas 1988* (Washington, D.C.: 1988).

people working the land are also among the hungriest. The 45 nations in which over 30 percent of their gross domestic product (GDP) was produced by agriculture in 1987 are at the same time among those nations with the lowest daily per capita calorie consumption in 1985. While most nations (approximately 65 percent) have a per capita consumption of over 2,600 calories, these 45 nations consume an average of less than 2,300. Ten nations that generate an average of 55.2 percent of their GDP in agriculture average only 2,100 calories intake per capita per day (table 5.3). Without some major alterations in the present world economic system, growth in poverty and increased hunger will continue and could result in increased violence and political instability.

## CAUSES OF POLITICAL INSTABILITY

### Economic and Social Theories

One accepted economic theory of political instability is elaborated by James Davies. He claims that it is not just poor

**Table 5.3 Daily Caloric Intake of Countries with Highest Percentage of GDP in Agriculture**

| Country | Share of Agriculture in GDP (percent) 1987 | Per Capita Daily Calorie Supply 1985 |
|---|---|---|
| Uganda | 76 | 2,300 |
| Somalia | 60 | 2,050 |
| Tanzania | 58 | 2,250 |
| Burundi | 58 | 2,100 |
| Nepal | 55 | 2,000 |
| Bhutan | 52 | 2,500 |
| Ghana | 50 | 1,800 |
| Mali | 50 | 1,800 |
| Laos | 48 | 2,300 |
| Bangladesh | 45 | 1,900 |

*Source:* World Bank, *The World Bank Atlas 1988* (Washington, D.C.: 1988).

conditions that cause revolutions but also conditions that worsen after a period of improvement while expectations continue to rise. A similar situation occurs when expectations rise quickly with few or no changes in actual conditions (figure 5.3).

Another popular economic and social theory centers on relative deprivation as contributing to violence. This concept stands in contrast to universal deprivation, in which everyone is suffering equally, thus making the common plight easier to accept and enabling a sense of camaraderie to result. Under relative deprivation, however, some suffer while others enjoy the benefits of society. When the severely disadvantaged can compare themselves with a less poor group, their level of frustration may increase. And when an individual's problems can be blamed on someone else's doing well or can even be said to have been *caused* by this someone else, violent behavior may result. A rich landlord, for example, may become the target of his poverty-ridden peasants' frustrations and eventually of their violence.

Another theory focuses on land ownership. In many LDCs the principal economic activity is working in agriculture. Most rural inhabitants directly work on the land but not on land they themselves own. Instead, the best land is owned by the landed aristocracy, who allow the peasants to work it either for very low wages– in which case they give most of the production to the

## Figure 5.3 Need Satisfaction and Revolution (Davies Curve)

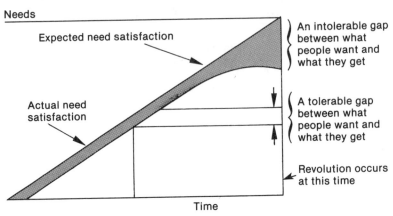

A: A Declining Economic or Political Condition

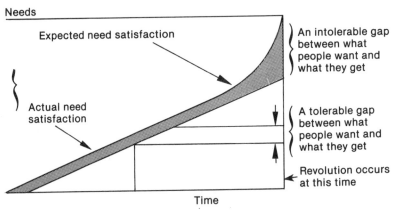

B: A Condition of Rapidly Rising Expectations

Source: As adapted from James C. Davies, "Toward a Theory of Revolution," *American Sociological Review* 27 (February 1962): 5-19.

landowner—or for the privilege of working a miniplot for their own subsistence. In these situations, the peasants who are deprived and hungry become frustrated and eventually resort to violence to alter their condition. If major changes do not occur, the rebellion becomes more violent and a major revolution can occur. According to this theory, this is what causes most radical revolutions.

Similarly, if a government is repressive and exploits its people or supports the exploiters, it too can become the target of violence. If a dictator can be blamed—a Fulgencio Batista, an Anastasio

Somoza, a Shah Reza Pahlavi—that political leader becomes the symbol marked for violence.

### Food Shortages

Many experts and government officials believe that continued economic crises that include inadequate food supplies and/or rising food prices can affect political stability. Hungry people do not necessarily rebel, but if conditions become extreme, they often do. In addition, people who have a fairly good quality of life may turn violent if that lifestyle is threatened by the prospect of hunger and deprivation, as indicated by Davies' theory. Food riots in Egypt in 1977, in the Dominican Republic in 1984, and in many other parts of the world such as Poland, Bolivia, Brazil, and the Sudan clearly illustrate that hunger or a precipitous rise in food prices can be related to political violence.

The volatility of such populations can endanger the security not only of their nations but of regions as well. The *Kissinger Commission Report on Central America* in 1984 dedicated significant attention to this problem and concluded that the United States must act in Central America to reduce the risk of revolution. Overt threats to regional security anywhere in the world can be perceived by U.S. policymakers as threats to U.S. security. A Vietnam or a Nicaragua can elicit a defensive response from liberal as well as conservation politicians.

But inadequate food production and distribution, which create major food shortages, do not alone cause revolutions, any more than adequate food supplies ensure political tranquility. True, food shortages or a severe and sudden rise in prices certainly can spark acts of violence and attacks on the government: the often-remembered statement of Marie Antoinette in response to food shortages—"Let them eat cake"—helped bring on the French Revolution; and the Mexican, Russian, and Chinese revolutions included food shortages among their many causes. Further, since World War II, food riots have rocked various governments throughout the world, and in the last 20 years, they have been prevalent in many LDCs. But other conditions must also exist—for instance, a lack of land ownership by the peasants.

It is a truism to say that the United States must become more aware of and constructively responsive to the various conditions throughout the world that can lead to violence. Food aid and economic assistance sometimes can alleviate many of these conditions, but only temporarily. Such aid, along with assistance to improve food production, serves best when used as a step toward lasting reforms, structural changes, and new institutions. For instance, domestic food supplies in affected LDCs must be increased simultaneously with food imports, and this can only be done by improving incentives to in-country farmers.

The many factors that influence food production include levels of technology, weather, natural resources, infrastructure, land ownership and use, production incentives, the skills of human resources (see chap. 1), and public policy. This last is particularly important to the present discussion.

For example, in most developing nations, the ministry of agriculture is the ugly stepsister in the governmental family when compared with agencies such as those concerned with the military, urban planning, and industrial development. Often the military absorbs more investment resources than any other institution or program. Associated negative impacts on domestic agricultural production and rural life have caused people to migrate to the cities in search of the rewards of "modern" life.

As populations continue to increase rapidly and migration from rural to urban areas continues unabated, governments try to implement food policies that often conflict with each other. Farmers are subsidized and given inexpensive fertilizers and insecticides to promote production at the same time that the demand for more and cheaper food by urban populations leads to price controls and price ceilings. The urban influences predominate as they are more articulate and are closer to the seats of government. This results in generally reduced prices paid to farmers and peasants, which removes any incentive for them to produce more. Many such affected people either join the flight to the cities or switch their production to export crops.

### Export/Import Interactions

Large agricultural operations in the developing world tend to specialize in export crops. They are more profitable than crops intended for domestic consumption, more credit is available for investment, and they bring the country necessary foreign exchange. In addition, there is more infrastructure (roads, railroads, port facilities, and storage capacity) available to exporters. Other advantages include favorable exchange rates, financial incentives, and higher profits for exported items than for domestic foodstuffs. The current debt crisis in most LDCs further encourages agriculturalists to produce for the export market. Moreover, price controls on domestically consumed food products, weak domestic markets, and poverty-stricken consumers all militate against production for domestic markets. Thus, sugar, coffee, tobacco, palm oil, animal feed, soybeans, and even cocaine are grown in areas where grains, fruits, vegetables, and other domestic foods could be produced.

As a result, many developing countries whose principal exports are agricultural products must nevertheless import significant amounts of their basic food needs, such as wheat, corn, rice, and soybeans. In other words, nations that produce 20 to 50 percent of their GDP in agriculture are importing large amounts of food and are thereby spending their scarce foreign exchange on these consumables rather than on imports that could assist in long-term development (table 5.4).

The situation is compounded in Latin American and African LDCs by overwhelming international debts. Pressure to meet their interest payments compels such countries to increase export commodity production and to decrease foreign imports, including foodstuffs. Both actions reduce the availability of food and increase prices. At the same time, the IMF is requiring that such indebted governments reduce all expenditures. Thus, government support for food subsidies and agricultural outlays, as well as support to farmers in the form of inexpensive fertilizers and insecticides, may disappear. These policies all effect domestic food production negatively and tend to push prices upward.

## Some Additional Causes

The concept that well-fed people are more likely to be happy and satisfied, and are therefore less likely to participate in political violence and to threaten national security, has a logical, common-sense ring to it. Unfortunately, it does not necessarily hold true. The world's poor and starving, often without the basic necessities of shelter, clothing, and securities, seldom have enough energy to initiate revolutionary, terroristic, or otherwise politically violent

**Table 5.4    Percentage of Agricultural Share of GDP Among High Food Importers**

|              | Percent of GDP in Agriculture (1987) | Percent Food of Total Imports (1985) |
|--------------|:---:|:---:|
| Somalia      | 60 | 29.6 |
| Burundi      | 59 | 16.7 |
| Nepal        | 56 | 10.3 |
| Burma        | 52 | 10.6 |
| Ghana        | 50 | 16.9 |
| Bangladesh   | 45 | 21.6 |
| Burkina Faso | 44 | 38.5 |
| Niger        | 43 | 25.5 |
| Sudan        | 38 | 45.5 |
| Liberia      | 38 | 38.2 |
| Ivory Coast  | 33 | 22.0 |
| North Yemen  | 33 | 18.4 |
| Togo         | 32 | 38.9 |
| Senegal      | 22 | 47.4 |
| Egypt        | 22 | 36.4 |
| Nicaragua    | 21 | 14.2 |

*Source:* UN Conference on Trade and Development, *Commodity Yearbook* (New York: UN, 1987), and UN, *National Account Statistics: Analysis of Main Aggregates, 1985* (New York: 1987).

behavior. The poor, wherever they live, usually are more concerned about survival and family needs than about philosophies, ideas, and revolution. Their despair and frustration are more often evidenced by inaction than by violence. The starving thousands of Ethiopians are characteristic in their apathy and acquiescence. During 1984–85, they sat around refugee camps waiting to greet death like an old friend. At the same time, their less poverty-stricken compatriots in Northeast Ethiopia were in rebellion against the government. The leaderless poor seldom organize to commit violent acts, but when there is little to lose, leaders can find avid followers among the poverty stricken and downtrodden.

The instigators and leaders of any type of political violence are, in most cases, better educated than the general public. They are also better off economically and usually come from urban areas. Thus, the middle class and professionals can become the leaders of the nation's poor and hungry peasants, who have no land and little food.

At the same time, however, many revolutions also attract followers from groups that are not on the bottom of the socioeconomic ladder. Fidel Castro drew much of his support from among the middle class and professionals in Cuba, as did Thomas Borge and the Sandinistas in Nicaragua in 1979. Many of the leaders who support Iran's Ayatollah Khomeini are graduates of Western Europe and U.S. universities.

Similarly, the middle-class demonstrations and turbulence created the political atmosphere needed for both the bloodless coup in Brazil in 1964 and the bloody and violent coup in Chile in 1973. However, while ideology, military self-interest, and widespread economic problems caused the downfall of Haile Selassie in Ethiopia in 1974, the African food crisis of 1984–85 has not had a similar result.

Still, violence-prone leaders usually can find numerous followers from the poorer classes. Food problems and poverty can reach such crisis levels as to motivate the masses to participate in political upheaval and unrest. Mao Tse-tung, for example, used the Chinese peasants as his political base. Leaders in Vietnam, Algeria, Mexico, and Nicaragua have also used peasant followers extensively. The dissatisfied, the frustrated, the outcast, and those who have little to lose characteristically follow charismatic, better-educated leaders.

Although social conditions and hunger can lead to group action, the preconditions for and causes of political violence are varied, complex, and interrelated. Rarely does a single condition create an atmosphere of instability. Economic, social, political, and international elements are generally all implicated to varying degrees.

Economic conditions that can lead to violence include 1) a widening gap between the few who are very rich and the majority who are very poor, 2) severe exploitation of one group by another, 3) a declining economy, 4) a rapid rise in expectations without a commensurate rise in capacities to attain them, 5) conflicts between rich landlords and poor peasants, 6) bad labor conditions, and 7) high unemployment, among other associated economic problems.

Social conditions that can be important factors include 1) minimal or no education, 2) lack of health care, 3) inadequate housing, 4) ethnic differences, 5) cultural incompatibilities, and 6) little prospect of future improvements.

Some of the most critical political factors leading to violence are 1) a fragmented or polarized political community, 2) a corrupt political system, 3) a weak and ineffective government, 4) a government that lacks legitimacy and popular support, and 5) a government that is identified as a cause of the social and economic problems.

International factors that can have an impact include 1) a neighboring country that is experiencing political upheaval, 2) a group from outside bent on subversion, 3) an ideology that blames all social ills on the old system and also claims to have a solution to these problems, and 4) a major war.

**Today's Political Realities**

Of the above, it is the political factors that are often ignored, most notably those dealing with political fragmentation and polarization and with governmental legitimacy. The issue of political fragmentation is particularly important and in need of attention since the present U.S. leadership seeks to encourage democratic governments in LDCs. Americans see democracy as the preferred type of government because it provides for freedom of action and participation in government processes for each individual. As viewed from the experience of the United States and other Western democracies, the point is well taken. People in democracies are more free than those living under any other form of government, and they have more power to influence their government. Within limits, their elected leaders respond to public pressures.

Democracy works in nations like the United States because the political community is not excessively fragmented or polarized. A majority consensus can be reached; the government can govern, and most citizens consider it legitimate and support it.

Consider, however, the realities of political fragmentation in many LDCs. In Bolivia, for example, the United States pressed for open elections in 1978 and the result was catastrophic. More than 20 candidates representing special groups vied for the presidency, and the candidate who was finally elected had only about 35 percent of the popular vote and no majority of popular or political support. This resulted in a government that could not govern. Issues could not be resolved, and stalemate and stagnation occurred. This in turn left problems unsolved and eventually led to a military coup d'état in 1980.

This same condition has prevailed in other South American countries that moved toward democracy in the 1980s, including Peru, Argentina, and Ecuador. Further, the political freedom guaranteed all groups under democracy allows individual groups to pursue their special interests and refuse to compromise. Governments are thus precluded from making decisions and resolving problems. Today, such politically fragmented nations are in trouble economically and are being confronted by food shortages and many similar public policy problems.

In many cases, excessive fragmentation is accompanied by extreme polarization. The moderate or middle-of-the-road segment of the political spectrum becomes very small in comparison with the radical Right and Left. Polarized politics makes compromise and accommodation extremely difficult and vastly increases the potential for violence and/or repression. This condition existed in Bolivia in the late 1970s, in Guatemala in the 1980s, and is currently seen in many other LDCs.

A polarized system also has major problems with stagnation, stalemate, and resulting violence. A current example is El Salvador. There were few moderates or middle-of-the-road politicians in El Salvador by 1989. The left-wing radical guerrillas continued their decade-long civil war while the right wing, which some claim included elements of the "death squads," won the March 1989 elections. These two elements cannot compromise and work together so in all likelihood they will continue to fight, to kill each other, and to destroy the nation. The problems of economic development, land reform, increased agricultural production, and education, among others, will remain unresolved as this polarized system continues its violent confrontations.

Several complex reasons account for this present state of affairs in Ghana, Nigeria, Bolivia, El Salvador, Peru, Brazil, and other nations that have actually started to move toward democracy. They include high levels of illiteracy, unfamiliarity of people and leaders with the concept of democracy, and absence of the political tradition of cooperation that is so essential to the success of a democratic form of government. Given time and experience, democracies may flourish in LDCs. Evidence suggests, however, that the concept is not a panacea for these nations and that considerable effort and maturing must precede its introduction.

## THE QUESTION OF DEPENDENCY

LDCs are struggling to feed their growing populations and to cope with external influences that direct them to alter their food policies and to pay their international debts. These dual pressures reinforce their belief that the developed world is, in part, responsible for their critical plight.

One of today's most popular economic theories in Latin America (and repeated in other forms elsewhere) is the *dependencia* (dependency) theory. As noted earlier, it claims that the developed world purposely keeps other nations underdeveloped to exploit them. Under this theory, aid is seen as imperialism in disguise as the developed industrialized nations, led by the United States, conspire against the Third World to keep it poor and illiterate. This is done to benefit the richer nations so they can buy raw materials and agricultural products more cheaply and, at the same time, sell their manufactured goods at higher profits. This theory is accepted throughout much of the Third World today.

Dependency theorists argue that economic assistance and even food aid are part of this conspiracy and that the giver benefits much more than the receiver. Some say, for example, that P.L. 480 food aid is provided not to help starving people, but to give American farmers income, to dispose of surpluses, and to ensure that the international price of food remains above a predetermined level. The believers cite a number of countries—such as Iran, Chile, Mexico, Japan, India, and South Korea—that received food aid and continued to import food at high levels after the crisis. The implication is that the United States obtains a broader market for food than it had before.

For example, Iran imported only $15 million of American wheat in 1965. Shipments of P.L. 480 aid ended in 1973, yet by 1975 Iran was importing $325 million worth of wheat, mostly from the United States. At the same time, Iran's own production of wheat declined drastically. Similar situations have been reported in other nations.

It is also charged that wheat is substituted for more traditional grains in many nations to promote markets for U.S. cereals. After years of P.L. 480 grain imports, many Latin American nations, which traditionally consumed corn and potatoes, have turned more and more to imported U.S. wheat. This reliance (dependency) on American grains can make a nation more vulnerable to external pressures politically as well as economically. For example, before 1970 Chile imported between 400,000 and 600,000 tons of wheat each year, with U.S. assistance. When Socialist Salvador Allende was elected president in 1970, the United States cut off government credit for food purchases, and Chilean wheat imports dropped to only 8,800 tons during 1971-72. This reduction in U.S. imports had a critical impact on the Allende government and helped induce its eventual downfall.

The dependency arguments are supported by trade, economic assistance, and monetary exchange statistics. These data can offer a perceived rationale for poorer nations to argue that they are being dominated by richer nations and to press for a new international economic order that ensures a greater equality for LDCs.

Given current revolutionary philosophies and the problems of food supply, developed nations could become increasingly popular as targets of terrorists, revolutionaries, and other perpetrators of violence. Governments of LDCs may use the argument of relative deprivation to avoid responsibility for their own mistakes. By equating developed nations with oppressors, LDCs have someone to blame for their ills. Right or wrong, these claims are a force to be reckoned with and understood in managing U.S. foreign assistance programs. In the long run, the North-South conflict could be as important to U.S. security as the highly publicized East-West debate.

Nearly all LDC governments suffer from instability, inefficiency, corruption, and other internal malfunctions. The causes of poverty thus tend to thrive, and the poor may seek change through violence since they have little to lose. It is always tempting to think that maybe a new group will be better. For those further up the social and political ladder, the spoils of office look attractive. Those clinging to office in the face of developmental failures need a scapegoat for their failures to engage the passions of the people and divert their attention. The Americans, the French, or the Communists are at fault. Or the Jews, the Christians, or the Muslims are causing the problem. Outside help is often sought to solve an immediate crisis, but at the same time, blame is laid on those who provide the outside assistance.

The provision of aid and assistance does not guarantee that a recipient nation will be more stable, less violent, and more friendly to the United States. Withholding assistance and restraining development, however, virtually guarantee conditions that are ripe for a terrorist or revolutionary to exploit, while the established government becomes more repressive to maintain political stability. According to economist John Kenneth Galbraith, "The poor countries are the focus of internal disturbance, insecurity, interracial friction and international conflict because these are intimately a part of the politics of privation."

## SUMMARY COMMENTS

U.S. economic assistance is not totally humanitarian in nature, nor is it aimed purely at economic and social development. Aid is a political tool used for many purposes, especially to guard our own security. It is hoped by policymakers that the major goals of U.S. foreign policy will be enhanced through economic and food assistance.

Economic assistance and food aid help nations through crises and may even improve social and human conditions, but only on a short-term basis. Such aid does not ensure that a nation will avoid political violence, nor does it ensure stability and a pro-American stance. To refuse to give aid in a crisis, on the other hand, may lend unanticipated support to the fomenters and leaders of revolution. Thus, aid is given to help people and to increase governmental stability, thereby reducing the threat of Communist takeovers.

Relationships between food scarcity and political stability cannot be conclusively demonstrated by the historical record, as the causes are too complex and include a mix of political, social, economic, and international factors and conditions. In some cases, political instability has occurred in the presence of apparent food sufficiency, yet in others food scarcity has been directly linked with riots, violence, and even revolution. Logic seems to suggest that the probabilities of achieving world peace and stable political systems will be heightened if people in want are properly fed and their basic physical needs are met. Unfortunately, recorded history gives us few examples with which to prove the logic either right or wrong.

Terrorism, political violence, and revolutionary activities appear to be on the rise as we enter the 1990s. Food shortages, hunger, and famine are also more evident and more publicized, while natural forces of bad weather, earthquakes, and volcano eruptions add to the plight of growing world populations. Poverty and hunger have not been eliminated among the developed nations, let alone among the lesser-developed ones. Although reasons for optimism exist—world food production capabilities are sufficient to alleviate most world hunger, technology holds hope for future green revolutions, and alterations in traditional farming methods and crops could do much—the political realities of today's world prevent a more equitable distribution of food and a significant reduction in human suffering.

The world's instances of poverty, hunger, excessive population growth, social inequities, political instability, and repression clamor for attention. A more dedicated U.S. and international endeavor is needed to confront these conditions. And while even the most imaginative and consistent effort to resolve these issues may not produce a utopia, it will certainly ease the suffering of millions of innocents and perhaps divert their potential for protest and violence.

While these challenges will be very difficult to meet, they provide the United States with a tremendous chance to improve the world and make it more politically compatible, while at the same time they provide America's farmers and businesses with a major economic opportunity. As the LDCs develop and improve their quality of life, their peoples will demand more food and other products. This could mean expanding markets and growth for the United States. It is possible that American farmers could experience their most significant expansion since the 1970s as they make more food available to the developing nations of the world in the 1990s and beyond.

# SIX

# Determining the Impact of U.S./ Third World Interdependence On a Local Economy

## Joan H. Joshi

The ties that bind the United States to the rest of the world have so proliferated since World War II that economic and political policies formulated abroad now have a profound impact on this country. As evidence, we can point to the explosive growth over the last several decades in international trade; the development of an international capital market; the vast increase in international travel for business, pleasure, and educational purposes; and the infusion of new waves of immigrants. Our involvement in political struggles abroad that have critical international implications is another case in point. These ties are as strong with countries in the Third World as they are with the industrialized West. Indeed, we can foresee a future in which developing countries will have even greater significance for our economic and political well-being, not least because 75 percent of the world's people live there. By the year 2050, when the children of today's college students reach their middle years, that figure will likely be 86 percent.

It is vital that Americans begin to comprehend this interdependence as a context for many of the decisions they will make as citizens, and educators and politicians alike are stepping forward to proclaim the importance of this understanding. To make these complex issues more relevant—and thus more meaningful—some educators have found it useful to help students view them from a local perspective—that is, to document the how our multifaceted ties to the Third World directly affect a local economy and to demonstrate the local impact of development assistance programs.

This educational concept arose from an experiment conducted by former foreign correspondent and World Bank official John Maxwell Hamilton. Several years ago, Dr. Hamilton proposed to his journalist colleagues that news organizations with limited resources could still cover the poor nations that comprise the developing world; journalists had only to look to their own communities. In fall 1984, he set out to test his premise in collaboration with the editor of the *Hattiesburg* (Miss.) *American,* producing a series of front-page articles on a surprising diversity of links between that community and countries in the Third World. The articles attracted wide local attention. The experiment's success led to the publication of a book of model news stories from dailies large and small across the country. Entitled *Main Street America and the Third World* (see bibliography), the book is widely used in schools of journalism as well as in undergraduate courses in other disciplines.

Research into local ties is an exercise that can be integrated into a number of classroom settings. Faculty in a variety of disciplines, some focusing only on those ties related to the discipline in question, have guided their students in an investigation of local links and assigned them the task of presenting their findings in the form of journalistic articles. In some cases, the best of the articles have been submitted for publication in the community's local newspaper or broadcast over local radio or television. This type of exercise accomplishes three objectives: it contributes to the students' global education (as well as to their skills in research and writing); it provides an opportunity for institutions to serve their local communities and be recognized for doing so; and it helps educate the local populace on the issues of interdependence and development.

The guidelines for the exercise below are designed to highlight those areas in which the impact is most visible and most easily quantifiable. They are in the form of questions and are divided into two parts:

    a) evidence of interdependence, and
    b) local impact of development assistance.

The same questions can be asked from the perspective of a local community, a region of a state, or an entire state. They can also be answered with statistics, case studies, or a blend of the two. The choice should depend on the interest of the student, the objectives of the class, and/or the audience for which the material is intended. In any event, data collection will probably require considerable legwork, including visits to local financial institutions, agribusiness organizations, and industries, as well as to institutions of higher education, especially the state's land-grant universities. Statistics will be most readily available from state departments of trade and commerce or of agriculture, from the U.S. Departments of Agriculture and Commerce, and from USAID.

Initial contact should be made through the following offices:

- Information Division
  Office of International Cooperation and Development
  U.S. Department of Agriculture
  Washington, DC 20250
  (Tel. 202/653-7589)

- Office of Public Affairs
  U.S. Department of Commerce
  Washington, DC 20230
  (Tel. 202/377-3263)

- Office of Public Inquiries
  Bureau for External Affairs
  U.S. Agency for International Development
  Washington, DC 20523
  (Tel. 202/647-1850)

## EVIDENCE OF INTERDEPENDENCE

1. Exports *
   a. Which locally produced goods (agricultural and industrial) are exported?

---

*In making export calculations, it is useful to note the methodology described in a brochure put out by Virginia Polytechnic Institute and State University, Blacksburg, Va., entitled *What the Agricultural Export Boom Means to Virginians:*

> Determining which U.S. agricultural exports were actually grown on Virginia farms is about like trying to determine which part of the pond the water in the drain pipe is coming from. In a market economy, commodities, like pond water, seek a new level once some is removed.
>
> In view of this market fluidity, estimates of Virginia's share of U.S. exports have been made by relating Virginia's sales of commodities to U.S. sales of the respective commodities. Such a procedure for estimating export shares assumes that U.S. exports have a proportionate impact on each state producing the commodity. Although the product of a given state may not actually be exported, the product of that state has the opportunity to meet the demand for such a product that otherwise would be met by the exported item.

   b.  How much do they earn?
   c.  What percentage of local industry or agriculture do they
       represent?
       *Examples:* Percentage of acreage producing for export,
       percentage of crop X or manufactured product Y
       exported.
   d.  How many jobs are directly involved?
   e.  What are the indirect benefits to the local community/
       state?
       *Examples:* Dollars circulating in the local economy as a
       secondary result of export earnings, number of jobs these
       create.
2.  Imports
   a.  What raw materials are imported for use in local industry
       or agriculture?
   b.  Why are they imported?
       *Examples:* Materials not produced, grown, or mined in the
       United States; an import price substantially below the
       domestic price.
   c.  How does the local consumer benefit from imports?
       *Examples:* Prices moderated due to competition from
       foreign goods, goods available (coffee, diamonds) that
       cannot be produced locally.
   d.  What negative impact do imports have on the local
       economy?
       *Examples:* Number of jobs lost through foreign competi-
       tion, dollar losses to local industry and agriculture.
3.  Financial ties
   a.  How much and in what industries have local industries
       invested abroad? Example: Overseas subsidiaries.
   b.  What are the earnings on these investments?
   c.  Has this had a positive or negative effect on the local
       economy?
       *Examples:* Jobs created or lost, increase or decrease of
       dollars in circulation.
   d.  How much have local financial institutions loaned to
       foreign governments and institutions?
   e.  What are the earnings (or losses) on these loans?
   f.  How much foreign capital has been invested in the local
       economy and in which industries?

g. How has this investment affected the local job market and the dollars in circulation?
4. Educational ties
   a. How many foreign students are enrolled in local institutions of higher education?
   b. What positive and negative impacts do they have on the local economy?
      *Example:* Their expenditure for tuition, room, and board versus local government subsidies for their tuition.
   c. What ties do local educational institutions and their faculties have with institutions abroad?
      *Examples:* Formal institution-to-institution affiliations, collaborative research projects, consultancies.
5. Cultural ties
   a. Is there local participation in the Sister Cities or Partners of the Americas programs?
   b. What international programs in the arts does the local population patronize?
      *Examples:*Foreign movies, imported television shows, performances of visiting artists, museum exhibits from abroad.
   c. What restaurants serving Third World cuisine operate locally?
   d. What local religious institutions have close ties with Third World cultures?
6. Ethnic mix of the population
   a. From what parts of the world did the local population immigrate to the United States?
   b. Is there a recent immigrant population?
   c. Why and how did they come to the United States?
   d. What are immigrants contributing to the local community/state, or what problems are created by their presence?

## LOCAL IMPACT OF DEVELOPMENT ASSISTANCE PROGRAMS

1. Project dollars spent in the local community/state for goods and services
   a. How much is paid to local people, especially university staff, to participate in USAID projects?

    b. What locally produced goods or services are purchased for use in USAID projects (or those of other funding agencies, such as the World Bank)?
*Examples:* Trucks, fertilizers, irrigation equipment, shipping services.

    c. How many P.L. 480 dollars are spent on the purchase of local agricultural products?

    d. How many of the foreign students at local institutions participate in USAID training programs?

2. Byproducts of development assistance activities

    a. What germplasm, originating abroad and identified in development assistance projects, has been introduced into local agriculture?

    b. Are there any methodologies developed through development assistance projects that have been useful to local agriculture?
*Examples:* Farming systems methodology, increased understanding of technology transfer to agricultural producers, new cropping systems.

3. Impact on trade

    a. How have local industry and agriculture been affected by development abroad in the last decade, two decades, three decades?

    b. Has development in certain countries led to competition with local products?

    c. Has increased purchasing power in certain countries led to their import of local products?

    d. Has lack of development in certain countries or their decreased purchasing power had any effect on the local economy?
*Examples:* Decreases in exports, disappearance of foreign goods from the market, immigration of competitive (or needed) foreign labor?

# References and Bibliography

The initial five chapters in this book constitute an amalgamation of the ideas and data of a number of people and institutions concerned about the world hunger problem and U.S. foreign assistance. Few primary data were developed. Although a few summary tables were prepared by the authors, most tables, charts, and selected points of discussion that could be attributed to others were taken from their published works, which are listed below. Similarly, where information concerning specific research procedures and findings was obtained through the authors' personal communication with particular researchers and scientists (as is frequently the case in chap. 4), these sources and their affiliations are listed below as well. In the interest of keeping the text and presentation as unencumbered and elemental as possible, however, it was decided to refrain from extensive footnoting within the manuscript. Insofar as this takes license with accepted standards of documentation and attribution, apologies are extended to the authors, sources, and organizations. Their contributions are clearly acknowledged and appreciated since the availability of their work made this effort possible, especially given the limited time and other resource constraints presented by the project.

The manual is not intended to represent a consensus of thought and evidence, nor is it meant to encompass the totality of issues and information on world hunger and poverty and U.S. foreign assistance. These topics are too broad and too widely debated for their sum total to be contained in one limited writing. Primarily, this is a teaching manual that summarizes many current ideas and facts about these topics in the hopes of catalyzing widespread discussion among the populace of the United States.

The following list of references was used extensively in preparing this manual and is recommended as supplemental reading, as are the sources listed under "Additional Reading," which follows.

Ahluwalia, Montek S. "Inequality, Poverty, and Development." *Journal of Development Economics* 3 (1976).

Board for International Food and Agricultural Development (BIFAD). *Budget Recommendations: 1985.* Washington, D.C.: U.S. Agency for International Development (USAID), February 1984.

Bureau of the Census. *Highlights of U.S. Export and Import Trade.* Report FT990/December 1984 and 1987. Washington, D.C.: U.S. GPO.

_____. *Statistical Abstract of the United States, 1980* and *1984.*

Callis, Jerry. U.S. Department of Agriculture (USDA) Plum Island Animal Disease Center, Greenport, N.Y. Personal communication.

Chilcote, Ronald H., and Joel C. Edelstein, eds. *Latin America: The Struggle with Dependency and Beyond.* New York: John Wiley and Sons, 1974.

Cockcroft, James D., Andre Gunder Frank, and Dale Johnson. *Dependence and Underdevelopment: Latin America's Political Economy.* Garden City, N.Y.: Doubleday and Company, Inc., 1972.

Commission on Security and Economic Assistance. *A Report to the Secretary of State* (Carlucci Report). November 1983.

Coulson, Jack R. USDA Beneficial Insects Laboratory, Beltsville, Md. Personal communication.

Cunningham, I. S. *Frank N. Meyer: Plant Hunger in Asia.* Ames: Iowa State University Press, 1984.

Curtis, Byrd. International Maize and Wheat Improvement Center (CIMMYT), El Batan, Mexico. Personal communication.

Dalrymple, D.G. "The Demand for Agricultural Research: A Colombian Illustration: Comment." *American Journal of Agricultural Economics* 62, no. 3 (1980): 594–596.

———. *Development and Spread of Semi-dwarf Varieties of Wheat and Rice in the United States: An International Perspective.* USDA/USAID, Office of International Cooperation and Development, Washington, D.C., 1980.

Davies, James C. "Toward a Theory of Revolution." *American Sociological Review* 27 (February 1962): 5–19.

*Development Assistance Committee Aid Review* 78 (September 1978).

*Development Cooperation Review,* 1982 and 1983. Paris: Organization for Economic Cooperation and Development (OECD).

Eldridge, Albert F. *Images of Conflict.* New York: St. Martins Press, 1979.

Extension Research Service. U.S. Department of Agriculture (ERS/USDA). Agriculture and Trade Indicators Branch, January 1989.

Feierabend, Ivo K., et al., eds. *Anger, Violence, and Politics.* Englewood Cliffs, N.J.: Prentice-Hall, Inc., 1971.

Food and Agriculture Organization (FAO). "Current World Food Situation" (May 1987).

FAO. *Production Yearbook, 1976* and *1986.* Rome.

*A Framework for Development Education in the United States.* Paper prepared by the Joint Working Group on Development Education of the American Council of Voluntary Agencies for Foreign Service and Private Agencies in International Development (now merged and known as INTERACTION), April 1984.

Frank, Andre Gunder. *Lumpenbourgeoisie: Lumpendevelopment: Dependence, Class, and Politics in Latin America.* New York: Monthly Review Press, 1972.

Goodman, M. M. "Exotic Maize Germplasm: Status, Prospects, and Remedies." *Iowa State Journal of Research* 59, no. 4 (1985): 497–527.

Gurr, Ted Robert. *Why Men Rebel.* Princeton, N.J.: Princeton University Press, 1970.

Habeck, Dale. University of Florida, Gainesville, Fla. Personal communication.

Hamilton, John Maxwell. *Main Street America and the Third World.* 3rd ed. Cabin John, Md.: Seven Locks Press, 1988.

———. "Seed Migration to U.S. Heartland Marches On: Movement That Started in Fertile Crescent Is Still Improving Crop Strains." *Christian Science Monitor,* 22 December 1985, 29–30.

Hollist, W. Ladd, and E. LaMond Tullis, eds. *Food, Politics and Society in Latin America.* Lincoln: University of Nebraska Press, 1985.

*Information Please Almanac 1985.* New York: Houghton Mifflin Company, 1985.

International Maize and Wheat Improvement Center (CIMMYT). Internal document, 1985.

Jones, Q. "A National Plant Germplasm System." In *Conservation of Crop Germplasm: An Internal Perspective.* Edited by W. L. Brown, et al., 27–33. Madison, Wis.: Crop Science Society of America, 1984.

———. "The National Plant Germplasm System." *Hortscience* 16 (1981): 737–739.

Kellogg, Earl D. "Agricultural Developing Countries and Changes in U.S. Agricultural Exports." Washington, D.C.: Consortium of International Cooperation in Higher Education (CICHE), March 1987.

Lev, Larry, Michael T. Weber, and H.C. Bittenbender. *Michigan Agriculture and Its Linkages to Developing Nations.* East Lansing: Institute of International Agriculture, Michigan State University, March 1984.

Lewis, John P., and Valeriana Kallab, eds. *U.S. Foreign Policy and the Third World: Agenda 1983.* Washington, D.C.: Overseas Development Council, 1983.

Linz, Juan. *The Breakdown of Democratic Regimes: Crisis, Breakdown and Reequilibration.* Baltimore, Md.: The Johns Hopkins University Press, 1978.

Loup, Jacques. *Can the Third World Survive?* Baltimore, Md.: The Johns Hopkins University Press, 1983.

Megargh, Edwin I., and Jack Eokanson. *The Dynamics of Aggression.* New York: Harper and Row, 1970.

Morgan, Dan. *The Merchants of Grain.* New York: Viking Press, 1979.

Paarlberg, Robert L. "Developing Country Farm Production and U.S. Farm Exports: The Decisive Role of Policy." Washington, D.C.: CICHE, March 1987.

Park, William M. "World Food Supply: Problems and Prospects." Staff Paper 84-01. University of Tennessee Agricultural Experiment Station, September 1984.

Plucknett, D.L., et al. "Crop Germplasm Conservation and Developing Countries." *Science* 220 (1983): 163–169.

Population Reference Bureau, Inc. "World Population Data Sheet," 1985 and 1988.

Presidential Commission on World Hunger. *Overcoming World Hunger: The Challenge Ahead.* Washington, D.C., 1980.

Rothberg, John C. "U.S. Foreign Assistance, A.I.D. and BIFAD— An Introduction." BIFAD Staff Paper, 1984. Mimeographed.

Schuh, G. Edward. "Changes in the International Economy: Implications for the United States." Washington, D.C.: CICHE, March 1987.

———. "International Extension Programs for U.S. Citizens." Presented at the Conference on the International Role of Extension, Michigan State University, 31 March–2 April 1985.

Sewell, John W., Richard E. Feinberg, and Valeriana Kallab, eds. *U.S. Foreign Policy and the Third World: Agenda 1985–86.* Washington, D.C.: Overseas Development Council, 1985.

Sewell, John W., Stuart K. Tucker, et al. *Growth, Exports, and Jobs in a Changing World Economy: Agenda 1988,* Overseas Development Council (New Brunswick, N.J.: Transaction Books, 1988).

Todaro, Michael P. *Economic Development in the Third World.* 4th ed. New York: Longman, 1989.

Tullis, E. LaMond, and W. Ladd Hollist. *Food, the State, and International Political Economy: Developing Country Dilemmas.* Lincoln, Neb.: University of Nebraska Press, 1985.

United Nations (UN). *National Account Statistics: Analysis of Main Aggregates 1985.* New York: 1987.

———. *The World Population Situation in 1983.* New York, 1984.

UN Conference on Trade and Development. *Commodity Yearbook.* New York: UN, 1987.

UN World Food Council. "Current World Food Situation" (March 1982 and April 1986).

USAID. *AID Highlights.* Washington, D.C., Summer 1984.

———. *1983 AID Presentation to Office of Management and Budget.* Washington, D.C., October 1982.

———. Office of Personnel, 1989.

———. *U.S. Overseas Loans and Grants.* Washington, D.C., 1945–86 and 1987.

U.S. Congress. House of Representatives. *Report of the Task Force on Foreign Assistance to the Committee on Foreign Affairs.* Washington, D.C.: U.S. GPO, February 1989.

USDA. *Foreign Agricultural Trade of the United States.* Washington, D.C., 1985 and 1987 supplement.

———. *1988 Agricultural Chartbook,* Handbook no. 673.

U.S. Department of Commerce. *Survey of Current Business.* Washington, D.C., July 1987.

Wennergren, E. Boyd, and Morris D. Whitaker. "U.S. Universities and the World Food Problem." *Science* (October 1976).

"What the Agricultural Export Boom Means to Virginians." Virginia Polytechnic Institute and State University, Blacksburg, Va. Undated brochure.

White, T. Kelley. "The Global Food System and the Future U.S. Farm and Food Supply." ERS/USDA, 1984.

Whitt, Steven C. *Brief Book: Biotechnology and Genetic Diversity.* San Francisco: California Agricultural Lands Project, 1985.

*The World Almanac and Book of Facts 1985.* New York: Newspaper Enterprise Association, Inc., 1984.

World Bank. *The World Bank Atlas 1988.* Washington, D.C., 1988.

————. *World Development Report 1982, 1983, 1984, 1985,* and *1988.* New York: Oxford University Press.

World Food Institute. *World Food Trade and U.S. Agriculture, 1960–1984.* 5th annual ed. Ames: Iowa State University, 1985.

## ADDITIONAL READING*

### 1. Nonfiction

Brown, Lester. *The State of the World.* New York: W. W. Norton and Co.

Annual publication of the Worldwatch Institute, which analyzes major trends and developments in world resources and the way they relate to each other.

De Silva, Leelananda. *Development Aid: A Guide to Facts and Issues.* Geneva: Third World Forum in Cooperation with the United Nations Nongovernmental Liaison Service, n.d. (Contact the Nongovernmental Liaison Service, United Nations, New York, N.Y. 10017.)

A comprehensive compilation of data on development assistance. Includes history of official development assistance and comparative analysis of types and levels of assistance being given by countries and international organizations. Organized for quick access to information. Includes suggestions for reform.

Fenton, Thomas, and Mary Heffron. *The Third World Resource Directory: A Guide to Organizations and Publications.* Maryknoll, N.Y.: Orbis Books.

An encyclopedia of material and organizations with geographical as well as issue indices: e.g., food, hunger, agribusiness, human rights, women. Updated biannually.

Gran, Guy. *Development by People: Citizen Construction of a Just World.* New York: Praeger Publishers, 1983.

---

*Prepared by Communications for Development for its multimedia development education package, "What's a Developing Country?" and reprinted by permission.

Analyzes why the poor in Third World countries remain poor and discusses how this process can be reversed through participatory development, so the poor can become aware of the choices open to them and of how they themselves can take the initiative in improving their lives. Bibliography of over 2000 titles.

Higgens, Benjamin. *Economic Development of a Small Planet*. New York: W.W. Norton and Company, 1979.

Proposes a global approach to international development, considering the interactions among events and trends in both developed and developing countries and how the economics of the former must change if development is to occur in the latter. Policy recommendations incorporate strategies emphasizing growth, quality of life, and basic human needs.

Huston, Perdita. *Third World Women Speak Out*. New York: Praeger Publishers, 1979.

Interviews with Third World women at the grassroots level. Their eloquent discussion of their everyday lives underlines the need to recognize and enhance women's productive roles if development is to occur.

Jesus, Carolina Maria de. *Child of the Dark*. New York: E.P. Dutton and Company, 1962. (Also available in paperback from Signet Books.)

The diary of a simple, uneducated black woman who wrote on scraps of paper picked up from the gutter about her daily fight for survival for herself and her three illegitimate children in a Brazilian slum. Hailed by criticsas "possibly one of the best books to come from a Brazilian in this century."

Kidron, Michael, and Ronald Segal. *The New State of the World Atlas*. New York: Simon and Schuster, 1984.

A colorful and graphic representation of basic international data and statistics. Through the use of graphics, the authors interpret political, economic, social, and cultural indicators, identifying topics of public concern and explaining linkages among international events.

Kristensen, Thorkil. *Development in Rich and Poor: A General Theory with Statistical Analysis*. New York: Praeger Publishers, 1975.

Suggests that because all countries are developing, there is currently no one theory of development that is applicable to all countries. Proposes another general theory of development covering the economic, social, cultural, political, and environmental aspects of development.

Lappe, Francis Moore, and Joseph Collins. *Food First: Beyond the Myth of Scarcity.* Boston: Houghton Mifflin Company, 1977.

Discusses why world hunger is not due to a lack of food, but rather to how food is controlled by both traditional landed elites and corporate agribusiness. Offers strategies for improving this situation.

Nyerere, Julius K. *Freedom and Development.* New York: Oxford University Press, 1973.

A selection from speeches and writings, 1968–73, by the president of Tanzania, who has been described as "one of the rare philosopher-kings." Nyerere relates the problems and possibilities facing an African nation in the processes of maturation and development.

Sewell, John W., Richard E. Feinberg, and Valeriana Kallab, eds. *U.S. Foreign Policy and the Third World: Agenda, 1985–86.* New York: Praeger Publishers, 1985.

Annual publication of the Overseas Development Council with a series of articles on both global interdependence and international development. Among issues discussed: U.S. macroeconomic policy and the developing countries, trade with developing countries, and reordering priorities in U.S, foreign aid. Over 120 pages of statistical tables relevant to development.

Shoemaker, Dennis E. *The Global Connection: Local Action for World Justice: A Development Education Handbook.* New York: Friendship Press, 1977.

Looks at development from a Christian perspective. Discusses the root causes of the gap between rich and poor nations and how Christians can become direct participants in bridging this gap. Identifies fundamental weaknesses in local development efforts of Christian groups and highlights responsible models for improving these efforts.

Singer, W. Hans, and Javed A. Ansari. *Rich and Poor Countries.* Baltimore, Md.: The Johns Hopkins University Press, 1977.

A look at some of the fundamental aspects of the relationship between rich and poor countries, focusing on both the general situation of the international economy as well as the effect of international trade and multinational corporations on Third

World development. Includes chapters on the quantitative and qualitative aspects of development aid.

Sivard, Ruth Leger. *World Military and Social Expenditures.* Leesburg, Va.: WMSE Publications.

An annual accounting of the use of world resources for social and military purposes, and an objective basis for assessing relative priorities.

Sommer, John G. *Beyond Charity: U.S. Voluntary Aid for a Changing Third World.* Washington, D.C.: Overseas Development Council, 1977.

Assesses the role of U.S. private voluntary organizations in contributing to both emergency relief and human resource development. Stresses the need to focus on the problems of the very poor and to adopt more participatory and self-reliant approaches to development. Gives concrete recommendations for how private voluntary organizations can be more effective overseas and in the United States.

Tendler, Judith. *Inside Foreign Aid.* Baltimore, Md.: The Johns Hopkins University Press, 1975.

An insider's view of the problems surrounding foreign aid. Discusses usual criticisms and recommendations about development assistance. Adds finding that development assistance is often the product of how organizational output is defined—i.e., how governmental organizations adapt to the constraining effects of policies imposed by the legislative and executive branches.

Weaver, James H., and Kenneth P. Johnson. *Economic Development: Competing Paradigms, Competing Parables.* Development Studies Program Occasional Paper, no. 3. Washington, D.C.: USAID, n.d.

Clear and concise summary of the various theories of economic development. Includes, among others, Adams, Ricardo, Mill, Keynes, Marx, Lenin, Mao, Frank, Grant, and Muller. Bibliography contains a full citation of the relevant works of the authors cited.

World Bank. *Toward Sustained Development for Sub-Saharan Africa: A Joint Program for Action.* Washington, D.C.: World Bank, 1984.

The third in a series of recent reports by the Development Committee of the World Bank analyzing Africa's prospects and problems in the coming decade and the role of international development assistance in addressing those problems.

World Bank. *World Development Report 1978.* New York: Oxford University Press.

Annual publication containing the latest socioeconomic statistics for every country in the world. Includes an annual review of global economic developments plus a substantive essay on a current development issue. The 1984 edition focuses on population change and its link with development.

## II. Fiction

Achebe, Chinua. *No Longer at Ease.* New York: Fawcett Premier, 1960.

Explores the dilemma of a man who leaves his rural African community to face the pressures of an urban center. Reconciling these pressures, however, may imply corruption and loss of high ideals.

Lederer, William J., and Eugene Burdick. *The Ugly American.* New York: Norton and Company, Inc., 1958.

Written in the late 1950s as a critique of U.S. economic and military aid in Southeast Asia, this novel dramatically portrays what happens to human beings affected by the political intent and cultural impact of foreign aid. Recommendations in this book later formed the basis of the U.S. Peace Corps.

Marquez, Gabriel Garcia. *The Autumn of the Patriarch.* New York: Harper and Row Publishers, 1975.

The nightmarish story of a Latin American dictator, initially loved by his people but slowly, as his rule tightens, despised and eventually assassinated. A profound look at dictatorship, corruption, and distrust.

Naipaul, V.S. *A Bend in the River.* New York: Vintage Paperbacks, 1980.

A major work by a Third World author acknowledged as one of the greatest living writers in the English language. This novel deals with themes of national independence, development assistance, modernization, and race relations in a hypothetical central African country.

Soyinka, Wole. "The Lion and the Jewel." In *Wole Soyinka: Five Plays.* London: Oxford University Press, 1964.

This play by an award-winning Nigerian playwright, poet, and novelist revolves around the choice of a village beauty. The two contestants: the schoolteacher, a symbol of progress and civilization, and the king, who proves to have a better notion of general progress.

White, Margaret B., and Robert N. Quigley, eds. *How the Other Third Lives: Third World Stories, Poems, and Songs.* Maryknoll, N.Y.: Orbis Books, 1977.

A compendium of works by Third World authors who write vividly of their lives and concerns.

## III. Periodicals

*Development.* Society for International Development, Palazzo Civilta del Lavoro, 00144 Rome, Italy.

The quarterly journal of the Society for International Development, an independent, nongovernmental organization, the purposes of which are to provide a forum for collecting reflections and to encourage a mutually educating dialogue on development at all levels. (Many universities and larger cities in the United States have local chapters.)

*The Economist.* P.O. Box 904, Farmington, N.Y. 11737.

A weekly British periodical now also published in the United States. Although its chief focus is on American and European affairs, it has excellent weekly coverage of Third World political and economic developments. (Available in most libraries.)

*Finance and Development.* International Monetary Fund, Washington, D.C. 20431.

A free quarterly publication of the International Monetary Fund and the World Bank. It contains brief, technical but readable articles on current issues and problems of international development and development assistance.

*Journal of Developing Areas.* Macomb, Ill.: Western Illinois University Press, 1966.

A well-rounded quarterly that discusses various issues in development. Includes several book reviews in each publication.

*Journal of Development Studies.* London: Frank Cass and Company, Ltd., 1964.

Quarterly journal devoted to economic, political, and social development.

*The New Internationalist.* 70 Bond Street, Ground Floor, Toronto, Ontario M5B 929, Canada.

A monthly periodical published in Great Britain and distributed in North America through Canada. An excellent source of information on development concerns with outstanding graphics useful for educators.

*South: The Third World Magazine.* South Publications Limited, Suite 319, Helmsley Building, 230 Park Avenue, New York, N.Y. 10169.

Monthly news magazine similar in format to *Time and Newsweek* but featuring Third World news. Available in many university and public libraries and by subscription.

*Third World Quarterly.* London: Third World Foundation, New Zealand House, 1979.

Diverse array of articles dealing with the intellectual, economic, and social development of Third World peoples and with the evolution of a fundamentally equitable relationship among all countries.

*World Development.* New York: Pergamon Press, 1975.

A monthly journal encouraging new insights into many development issues, including malnutrition, disease, illiteracy, foreign investment, scarcity of resources, world inflation, and appropriate science and technology.

*World Development Forum Newsletter.* P.O. Box 21 126, Washington, D.C. 20009.

A free report of facts, trends, and opinion in international development published twice monthly as a public service by The Hunger Project.

*World Press Review.* Stanley Foundation, P.O. Box 915, Farmingdale, N.Y. 10169.

A monthly publication of news and views from the foreign press.

# Appendix Tables

## Appendix Table 1.1    Basic Development Indicators

| GNP Rank | Country | Population (millions) Mid-1988 | Area (thousands of square kilometers) | GNP/ Capita (dollar) 1986 | Adult Literacy (percent) 1980 | Life Expectancy at Birth (years) 1980 | Percentage of Labor Force in Agriculture 1980 |
|---|---|---|---|---|---|---|---|
| **Low-Income Economies** | | | | | | | |
| 1 | Ethiopia | 48.3 | 1,222 | 120 | 15 | 46 | 80 |
| 2 | Bhutan | 1.5 | 47 | 150 | — | 45 | 93 |
| 3 | Burkina Faso | 8.5 | 274 | 150 | 5 | 47 | 82 |
| 4 | Nepal | 18.3 | 141 | 150 | 19 | 47 | 93 |
| 5 | Bangladesh | 109.5 | 144 | 160 | 26 | 50 | 74 |
| 6 | Malawi | 7.7 | 119 | 160 | 25 | 45 | 86 |
| 7 | Zaire | 33.3 | 2,345 | 160 | 55 | 52 | 75 |
| 8 | Mali | 8.7 | 1,240 | 180 | 10 | 47 | 73 |
| 9 | Burma | 41.1 | 677 | 200 | 66 | 59 | 67 |
| 10 | Mozambique | 15.1 | 802 | 210 | 33 | 48 | 66 |
| 11 | Madagascar | 10.9 | 587 | 230 | 50 | 53 | 87 |
| 12 | Uganda | 16.4 | 236 | 230 | 52 | 48 | 83 |
| 13 | Burundi | 5.2 | 28 | 240 | 25 | 48 | 84 |
| 14 | Tanzania | 24.3 | 945 | 250 | 79 | 53 | 83 |
| 15 | Togo | 3.3 | 57 | 250 | 18 | 53 | 67 |
| 16 | Niger | 7.2 | 1,267 | 260 | 10 | 44 | 91 |
| 17 | Benin(Dahomey) | 4.5 | 113 | 270 | 28 | 50 | 46 |
| 18 | Somalia | 8.0 | 638 | 280 | 60 | 47 | 82 |
| 19 | Central African Republic | 2.8 | 623 | 290 | 33 | 50 | 88 |
| 20 | India | 816.8 | 3,288 | 290 | 36 | 57 | 69 |
| 21 | Rwanda | 7.1 | 26 | 290 | 50 | 48 | 91 |
| 22 | China | 1,087.0 | 9,561 | 300 | 69 | 69 | 69 |
| 23 | Kenya | 23.3 | 583 | 300 | 47 | 57 | 78 |
| 24 | Zambia | 7.5 | 753 | 300 | 44 | 53 | 67 |
| 25 | Sierra Leone | 4.0 | 72 | 310 | 15 | 41 | 65 |
| 26 | Sudan | 24.0 | 2,506 | 320 | 32 | 49 | 72 |
| 27 | Haiti | 6.3 | 28 | 330 | 23 | 54 | 74 |
| 28 | Pakistan | 107.5 | 804 | 350 | 24 | 52 | 57 |
| 29 | Lesotho | 1.6 | 30 | 370 | 52 | 55 | 87 |
| 30 | Ghana | 14.4 | 239 | 390 | — | 54 | 53 |
| 31 | Sri Lanka | 16.6 | 66 | 400 | 85 | 70 | 54 |
| 32 | Mauritania | 2.1 | 1,031 | 420 | 17 | 47 | 69 |
| 33 | Senegal | 7.0 | 196 | 420 | 10 | 47 | 77 |
| 34 | Afghanistan | 14.5 | 648 | — | 20 | 37 | 79 |
| 35 | Chad | 4.8 | 1,284 | — | 15 | 45 | 85 |
| 36 | Guinea | 6.9 | 246 | — | 20 | 42 | — |
| 37 | Kampuchea (Cambodia) | 6.7 | 181 | — | — | — | — |

## Appendix Table 1.1    Basic Development Indicators (Cont.)

| GNP Rank | Country | Population (millions) Mid-1988 | Area (thousands of square kilometers) | GNP/ Capita (dollar) 1986 | Adult Literacy (percent) 1980 | Life Expectancy at Birth (years) 1980 | Percentage of Labor Force in Agriculture 1980 |
|---|---|---|---|---|---|---|---|
| **Middle-Income/Lower Middle-Income Economies** | | | | | | | |
| 38 | Laos | 3.8 | 237 | — | 44 | 50 | 75 |
| 39 | Vietnam | 65.2 | 330 | — | 87 | 65 | 71 |
| 40 | Liberia | 2.5 | 111 | 460 | 25 | 54 | 70 |
| 41 | South Yemen | 6.7 | 333 | 470 | 40 | 50 | 45 |
| 42 | Indonesia | 177.4 | 1,919 | 490 | 62 | 57 | 55 |
| 43 | North Yemen | 2.4 | 195 | 550 | 21 | 46 | 75 |
| 44 | Philippines | 63.2 | 300 | 560 | 75 | 63 | 46 |
| 45 | Morocco | 25.0 | 447 | 590 | 28 | 60 | 52 |
| 46 | Bolivia | 6.9 | 1,099 | 600 | 63 | 53 | 50 |
| 47 | Zimbabwe | 9.7 | 391 | 620 | 69 | 58 | 60 |
| 48 | Nigeria | 111.9 | 924 | 640 | 34 | 51 | 54 |
| 49 | Dominican Republic | 6.9 | 49 | 710 | 67 | 66 | 49 |
| 50 | Papua New Guinea | 3.7 | 462 | 720 | 32 | 52 | 87 |
| 51 | Ivory Coast | 11.2 | 323 | 730 | 35 | 52 | 79 |
| 52 | Honduras | 4.8 | 112 | 740 | 60 | 64 | 63 |
| 53 | Egypt | 53.3 | 1,001 | 760 | 44 | 61 | 50 |
| 54 | Nicaragua | 3.6 | 130 | 790 | 90 | 61 | 43 |
| 55 | Thailand | 54.7 | 514 | 810 | 86 | 64 | 76 |
| 56 | El Salvador | 5.4 | 21 | 820 | 62 | 61 | 50 |
| 57 | Botswana | 1.3 | 600 | 840 | 35 | 59 | 70 |
| 58 | Jamaica | 2.5 | 11 | 840 | 90 | 73 | 21 |
| 59 | Cameroon | 10.5 | 475 | 910 | — | 56 | 56 |
| 60 | Guatemala | 8.7 | 109 | 930 | — | 61 | 55 |
| 61 | Congo | 2.2 | 342 | 990 | — | 58 | 34 |
| 62 | Paraguay | 4.4 | 407 | 1,000 | 84 | 67 | 44 |
| 63 | Peru | 21.3 | 1,285 | 1,090 | 80 | 60 | 39 |
| 64 | Turkey | 52.9 | 781 | 1,110 | 60 | 65 | 54 |
| 65 | Tunisia | 7.7 | 164 | 1,140 | 62 | 63 | 35 |
| 66 | Ecuador | 10.2 | 284 | 1,160 | 81 | 66 | 52 |
| 67 | Mauritius | 1.1 | 2 | 1,200 | 85 | 66 | 29 |
| 68 | Colombia | 30.6 | 1,139 | 1,230 | 81 | 65 | 26 |
| 69 | Chile | 12.6 | 757 | 1,320 | — | 71 | 19 |
| 70 | Costa Rica | 2.9 | 51 | 1,480 | 90 | 74 | 29 |
| 71 | Jordan | 3.8 | 98 | 1,540 | 70 | 65 | 20 |
| 72 | Syria | 11.3 | 185 | 1,570 | 58 | 64 | 33 |
| 73 | Lebanon | 3.3 | 10 | — | 86 | — | 11 |
| **Middle-Income/Upper Middle-Income Economies** | | | | | | | |
| 74 | Brazil | 144.4 | 8,512 | 1,810 | 76 | 65 | 30 |
| 75 | Malaysia | 17.0 | 330 | 1,830 | 60 | 69 | 50 |
| 76 | South Africa | 35.1 | 1,221 | 1,850 | — | 61 | 30 |
| 77 | Mexico | 83.5 | 1,973 | 1,860 | 83 | 68 | 36 |
| 78 | Uruguay | 3.0 | 176 | 1,900 | 94 | 71 | 11 |
| 79 | Hungary | 10.6 | 93 | 2,020 | 99 | 71 | 21 |
| 80 | Poland | 38.0 | 313 | 2,070 | 98 | 72 | 31 |
| 81 | Portugal | 10.3 | 92 | 2,250 | 78 | 73 | 28 |
| 82 | Yugoslavia | 23.6 | 256 | 2,300 | 85 | 71 | 29 |

## Appendix Table 1.1   Basic Development Indicators (Cont.)

| GNP Rank | Country | Population (millions) Mid-1988 | Area (thousands of square kilometers) | GNP/ Capita (dollar) 1986 | Adult Literacy (percent) 1980 | Life Expectancy at Birth (years) 1980 | Percentage of Labor Force in Agriculture 1980 |
|---|---|---|---|---|---|---|---|
| 83 | Panama | 2.3 | 77 | 2,330 | 85 | 72 | 27 |
| 84 | Argentina | 32.0 | 2,767 | 2,350 | 93 | 70 | 13 |
| 85 | South Korea | 42.6 | 98 | 2,370 | 93 | 69 | 34 |
| 86 | Algeria | 24.2 | 2,382 | 2,590 | 35 | 62 | 25 |
| 87 | Venezuela | 18.8 | 912 | 2,920 | 82 | 70 | 18 |
| 88 | Gabon | 1.3 | 268 | 3,080 | 65 | 52 | 65 |
| 89 | Greece | 10.1 | 132 | 3,680 | — | 76 | 37 |
| 90 | Oman | 1.4 | 300 | 4,980 | 20 | 54 | 66 |
| 91 | Trinidad and Tobago | 1.3 | 5 | 5,360 | 95 | 70 | 10 |
| 92 | Israel | 4.4 | 21 | 6,210 | — | 75 | 7 |
| 93 | Hong Kong | 5.7 | 1 | 6,910 | 90 | 76 | 3 |
| 94 | Singapore | 2.6 | 1 | 7,410 | 83 | 73 | 2 |
| 95 | Iran | 51.9 | 1,648 | — | 50 | 59 | 39 |
| 96 | Iraq | 17.6 | 435 | — | 30 | 63 | 42 |
| 97 | Romania | 23.0 | 238 | — | 98 | 71 | 29 |

**High-Income Oil Exporters**

| GNP Rank | Country | Population (millions) Mid-1988 | Area (thousands of square kilometers) | GNP/ Capita (dollar) 1986 | Adult Literacy (percent) 1980 | Life Expectancy at Birth (years) 1980 | Percentage of Labor Force in Agriculture 1980 |
|---|---|---|---|---|---|---|---|
| 98 | Saudi Arabia | 14.2 | 2,150 | 6,950 | 25 | 63 | 61 |
| 99 | Kuwait | 2.0 | 18 | 13,890 | 60 | 73 | 2 |
| 100 | United Arab Emirates | 1.5 | 84 | 14,680 | 56 | 69 | 5 |
| 101 | Libya | 4.0 | 1,760 | — | — | 61 | — |

**Industrial Market Economies**

| GNP Rank | Country | Population (millions) Mid-1988 | Area (thousands of square kilometers) | GNP/ Capita (dollar) 1986 | Adult Literacy (percent) 1980 | Life Expectancy at Birth (years) 1980 | Percentage of Labor Force in Agriculture 1980 |
|---|---|---|---|---|---|---|---|
| 102 | Spain | 39.0 | 505 | 4,860 | — | 76 | 14 |
| 103 | Ireland | 3.5 | 70 | 5,070 | 98 | 74 | 18 |
| 104 | New Zealand | 3.3 | 269 | 7,460 | 99 | 74 | 9 |
| 105 | Italy | 57.3 | 301 | 8,550 | 98 | 77 | 11 |
| 106 | United Kingdom | 57.1 | 245 | 8,870 | 99 | 75 | 2 |
| 107 | Belgium | 9.9 | 31 | 9,230 | 99 | 75 | 3 |
| 108 | Austria | 7.6 | 84 | 9,990 | 99 | 74 | 9 |
| 109 | Netherlands | 14.7 | 41 | 10,020 | 99 | 77 | 6 |
| 110 | France | 55.9 | 547 | 10,720 | 99 | 77 | 8 |
| 111 | Australia | 16.5 | 7,687 | 11,920 | 100 | 78 | 6 |
| 112 | West Germany | 61.2 | 249 | 12,080 | 99 | 75 | 4 |
| 113 | Finland | 4.9 | 337 | 12,160 | 100 | 75 | 11 |
| 114 | Denmark | 5.1 | 43 | 12,600 | 99 | 75 | 7 |
| 115 | Japan | 122.7 | 372 | 12,840 | 99 | 78 | 12 |
| 116 | Sweden | 8.4 | 450 | 13,160 | 99 | 77 | 5 |
| 117 | Canada | 26.1 | 9,976 | 14,120 | 99 | 76 | 5 |
| 118 | Norway | 4.2 | 324 | 15,400 | 99 | 77 | 7 |
| 119 | United States | 246.1 | 9,363 | 17,480 | 99 | 75 | 2 |
| 120 | Switzerland | 6.6 | 41 | 17,680 | 99 | 77 | 5 |

**Nonreporting Nonmembers**

| GNP Rank | Country | Population (millions) Mid-1988 | Area (thousands of square kilometers) | GNP/ Capita (dollar) 1986 | Adult Literacy (percent) 1980 | Life Expectancy at Birth (years) 1980 | Percentage of Labor Force in Agriculture 1980 |
|---|---|---|---|---|---|---|---|
| 121 | Albania | 3.1 | 29 | — | 70 | 72 | 61 |
| 122 | Angola | 8.2 | 1,247 | — | 15 | 42 | 59 |
| 123 | Bulgaria | 9.0 | 111 | — | 95 | 72 | 37 |

## Appendix Table 1.1   Basic Development Indicators (Cont.)

| GNP Rank | Country | Population (millions) Mid-1988 | Area (thousands of square kilometers) | GNP/ Capita (dollar) 1986 | Adult Literacy (percent) 1980 | Life Expectancy at Birth (years) 1980 | Percentage of Labor Force in Agriculture 1980 |
|---|---|---|---|---|---|---|---|
| 124 | Cuba | 10.4 | 115 | — | 99 | 75 | 23 |
| 125 | Czechoslavakia | 15.6 | 128 | — | 100 | 72 | 11 |
| 126 | East Germany | 16.6 | 108 | — | 99 | 73 | 10 |
| 127 | North Korea | 21.9 | 121 | — | — | 64 | 49 |
| 128 | Mongolia | 2.0 | 1,565 | — | 80 | 65 | 52 |
| 129 | USSR | 286.0 | 22,402 | — | 100 | 69 | 14 |
| 130 | Taiwan* | 19.8 | 33 | — | 89 | 73 | 20 |

*Sources:* World Bank, *World Bank Development Report 1983, 1984,* and *1988* (New York: Oxford University Press); Population Reference Bureau, Inc., "1988 World Population Data Sheet"; *The World Almanac and Book of Facts 1985* (New York: Newspaper Enterprise Association, Inc., 1984); *Information Please Almanac 1985* (New York: Houghton Mifflin Co., 1985).

*Note:* GNP rankings and income categorizations are based on those in the World Bank's *World Development Report 1988.* The World Bank has ranked a number of countries whose previous GNP figures were not available for publication.

*The World Bank's *World Development Report 1988* does not list Taiwan; figures here are taken from earlier reports.

## Appendix Table 1.2   Average Per Capita Food Supply, 1983–85

**CALORIE SUPPLY PER CAPITA**

| Economic Class and Region | Vegetable Products (cal/day) | (%) | Animal Products (cal/day) | (%) | Total (cal/day) | (%) |
|---|---|---|---|---|---|---|
| Developed Countries | 2364 | (105) | 1010 | (248) | 3374 | (127) |
| Developing Countries | 2222 | (98) | 205 | (50) | 2427 | (91) |
| WORLD | 2258 | (100) | 407 | (100) | 2665 | (100) |

**PROTEIN SUPPLY PER CAPITA**

| Economic Class and Region | Vegetable Products (g/day) | (%) | Animal Products (g/day) | (%) | Total (g/day) | (%) |
|---|---|---|---|---|---|---|
| Developed Countries | 42.4 | (93) | 54.7 | (244) | 97.1 | (142) |
| Developing Countries | 46.9 | (102) | 11.3 | (50) | 58.2 | (85) |
| WORLD | 45.8 | (100) | 22.4 | (100) | 68.2 | (100) |

*Source:* ERS/USDA, Agriculture and Trade Indicators Branch, January 1989.
*Note:* All percentages are based on world totals.

## Appendix Table 1.3   Growth of Total and Per Capita GNP for Various Time Periods

| | Compound Growth Rates (percent) | | | | | | | |
| | Total GNP | | | | Per Capital GNP | | | |
| Region | 1966–70 | 1971–75 | 1976–80 | 1981–85 | 1966–70 | 1971–75 | 1976–80 | 1981–85 |
|---|---|---|---|---|---|---|---|---|
| Developed Nations | 4.3 | 2.9 | 3.4 | 2.6 | 3.3 | 1.9 | 2.6 | 1.8 |
| Centrally Planned Nations | 4.7 | 3.6 | 2.1 | 1.6 | 2.5 | 1.6 | 0.7 | 0.5 |
| Developing Nations | 5.8 | 5.7 | 5.0 | 1.6 | 3.3 | 3.3 | 2.6 | −1.0 |
| WORLD | 4.4 | 3.4 | 3.8 | 2.4 | 2.3 | 1.4 | 2.0 | 0.6 |

*Source:* ERS/USDA, Agricultural and Trade Indicators Branch, January 1989.

## Appendix Table 1.4   Income Distribution in Selected Countries

| | | Percent of Income Received by | | |
| Country | Per Capita GNP in U.S. $ (1970 prices) | Lowest 40 percent | Highest 20 percent | Gini Concentrate Ratio* |
|---|---|---|---|---|
| **Developing Countries** | | | | |
| Pakistan(1963–64) | 94 | 6.5 | 45.5 | 0.365 |
| Tanzania(1967) | 94 | 5.0 | 57.0 | 0.458 |
| Sri Lanka(1969–70) | 109 | 6.0 | 46.0 | 0.370 |
| India(1963–64) | 110 | 5.0 | 52.0 | 0.418 |
| Kenya(1969) | 153 | 3.8 | 68.0 | 0.550 |
| Philippines(1965) | 224 | 3.9 | 55.4 | 0.465 |
| South Korea(1970) | 269 | 7.0 | 45.0 | 0.362 |
| Tunisia(1970) | 306 | 4.1 | 55.0 | 0.473 |
| Ivory Coast(1970) | 329 | 3.9 | 57.2 | 0.493 |
| Taiwan(1968) | 366 | 7.8 | 41.4 | 0.325 |
| Colombia(1970) | 388 | 3.5 | 59.4 | 0.507 |
| Malaysia(1970) | 401 | 3.4 | 55.9 | 0.475 |
| Brazil(1970) | 457 | 3.1 | 62.2 | 0.519 |
| Peru(1970) | 546 | 1.5 | 60.0 | 0.557 |
| Costa Rica(1971) | 617 | 5.4 | 50.6 | 0.419 |
| Mexico(1969) | 697 | 4.0 | 64.0 | 0.526 |
| Uruguay(1967) | 721 | 4.3 | 47.4 | 0.406 |
| Chile(1968) | 904 | 4.5 | 56.8 | 0.463 |
| **Developed Countries** | | | | |
| Japan(1968) | 1713 | 4.6 | 43.8 | 0.372 |
| France(1962) | 2303 | 1.9 | 53.7 | 0.481 |
| Norway(1963) | 2362 | 4.5 | 40.5 | 0.346 |
| United Kingdom(1968) | 2414 | 6.0 | 39.2 | 0.322 |
| New Zealand(1970–71) | 2502 | 4.4 | 41.0 | 0.346 |
| Australia(1967–68) | 2632 | 6.6 | 38.7 | 0.310 |
| West Germany(1970) | 3209 | 5.9 | 45.6 | 0.378 |
| Canada(1965) | 3510 | 6.4 | 40.2 | 0.322 |
| United States(1970) | 5244 | 6.7 | 38.8 | 0.315 |

## Appendix Table 1.4    Income Distribution in Selected Countries (Cont.)

| Country | Per Capita GNP in U.S. $ (1970 prices) | Percent of Income Received by | | Gini Concentrate Ratio* |
|---|---|---|---|---|
| | | Lowest 40 percent | Highest 20 percent | |
| **Socialist Countries** | | | | |
| Yugoslavia(1968) | 602 | 6.5 | 41.5 | 0.337 |
| Poland(1964) | 661 | 9.8 | 36.0 | 0.265 |
| Hungary(1967) | 873 | 8.5 | 33.5 | 0.249 |
| East Germany(1970) | 2046 | 10.4 | 30.7 | 0.213 |

*Source:* Montek S. Ahluwalia, "Inequality, Poverty, and Development," *Journal of Development Economics* 3 (1976): 340–341.

*Measure of income concentration used in economic analysis. A value of zero would mean total equality.

## Appendix Table 1.5    World Agricultural Demand Patterns in 2000 (in millions of metric tons)

| Region | Meat | Milk | Cereals | Oilseed | Fiber |
|---|---|---|---|---|---|
| North Africa/Middle East | 13.2 | 43.0 | 142 | 10 | 1.7 |
| Subsaharan Africa | 9.9 | 19.3 | 108 | 9 | 0.8 |
| European Community | 25.4 | 111.0 | 133 | 44 | 1.2 |
| Other Western Europe | 7.3 | 26.3 | 58 | 10 | 0.4 |
| USSR | 24.3 | 118.3 | 306 | 20 | 3.6 |
| Eastern Europe | 14.8 | 56.7 | 139 | 17 | 1.2 |
| South Asia | 4.1 | 72.7 | 291 | 17 | 6.4 |
| East Asia | 18.7 | 15.1 | 224 | 23 | 3.5 |
| China, Vietnam, Laos, Kampuchea (Cambodia), North Korea | 42.4 | 14.3 | 457 | 37 | 7.3 |
| Oceania | 3.2 | 8.8 | 16 | 2 | 0.4 |
| Latin America | 29.5 | 68.0 | 161 | 18 | 1.9 |
| North America | 33.9 | 79.1 | 254 | 43 | 1.5 |
| WORLD | 226.7 | 632.6 | 2289 | 250 | 29.9 |
| Percent of Growth from 1980 to 2000 | 64 | 36 | 46 | 62 | 37 |

*Source:* U.S. Department of Agriculture.

## Appendix Table 1.6 Growth of Agricultural Output, by Major Regions, 1950–85
### Compound Annual Growth (percent)

**TOTAL**

| Region | 1950–85 | 1950–60 | 1960–70 | 1970–80 | 1980–85 |
|---|---|---|---|---|---|
| Developed Countries | 2.4 | 2.4 | 1.9 | 1.8 | 4.0 |
| Centrally Planned Countries* | 2.6 | 3.8 | 1.7 | 2.1 | 0.7 |
| Developing Countries | 3.0 | 3.5 | 2.8 | 2.8 | 3.3 |
| Africa | 2.4 | 2.8 | 2.7 | 1.8 | 2.8 |
| Middle East | 3.8 | 5.3 | 2.9 | 3.3 | 3.7 |
| South Asia | 2.7 | 3.0 | 2.9 | 2.1 | 3.9 |
| East Asia | 3.5 | 3.4 | 4.5 | 4.3 | 0.7 |
| Latin America | 3.4 | 3.8 | 2.8 | 3.5 | 2.9 |
| WORLD | 2.5 | 3.1 | 2.4 | 2.4 | 2.8 |

**PER CAPITA**

| Region | 1950–85 | 1950–60 | 1960–70 | 1970–80 | 1980–85 |
|---|---|---|---|---|---|
| Developed Countries | 1.4 | 1.2 | 0.8 | 0.9 | 3.3 |
| Centrally Planned Countries* | 0.9 | 2.2 | 0.9 | 0.4 | –0.4 |
| Developing Countries | 0.6 | 1.3 | 0.3 | 0.3 | 0.7 |
| Africa | –0.1 | 0.6 | 0.2 | –0.9 | –0.2 |
| Middle East | 0.8 | 2.5 | 0.0 | 0.5 | 0.2 |
| South Asia | 0.6 | 1.1 | 0.6 | –0.2 | 1.4 |
| East Asia | 1.2 | 1.2 | 1.9 | 1.9 | –1.4 |
| Latin America | 0.6 | 1.0 | 0.0 | 0.9 | 0.5 |
| WORLD | 0.7 | 1.3 | 0.4 | 0.5 | 1.0 |

*Source:* World Bank and ERS/USDA, as cited in T. Kelley White, "The Global Food System and the Future U.S. Farm and Food Supply," ERS/USDA, 1984, 4; for 1980–85, ERS/USDA, Agriculture and Trade Indicators Branch, January 1989.

*Excludes China.

## Appendix Table 1.7 World Grain Yields*

| | 1961–65 | | 1979–80 | | 1986 | |
|---|---|---|---|---|---|---|
| Region | (kg/ha) | (%) | (kg/ha) | (%) | (kg/ha) | (%) |
| United States | 2736 | (187) | 4154 | (188) | 4706 | (182) |
| Other Developed Countries | 2017 | (138) | 2821 | (128) | 3262 | (126) |
| Eastern Europe and USSR | 1173 | (80) | 1712 | (78) | 2192 | (85) |
| Latin America | 1331 | (91) | 1838 | (83) | 2045 | (79) |
| North Africa and Middle East | 1075 | (74) | 1479 | (67) | 1563 | (60) |
| Subsaharan Africa | 849 | (58) | 1209 | (55) | 1067 | (41) |
| China | 1538 | (105) | 3029 | (137) | 3874 | (150) |
| Other Asian Countries | 1130 | (77) | 1687 | (76) | 1975 | (76) |
| WORLD | 1460 | (100) | 2209 | (100) | 2588 | (100) |

*Source:* ERS/USDA, Agriculture and Trade Indicators Branch, January 1989.

*Note:* All percentages are based on world totals.

*Includes wheat, rice, barley, maize, oats, millet, and sorghum.

## Appendix Table 1.8   Total and Irrigated Cropland, 1961–65, 1980, and 1985

| Region | Cropland (million hectares) | | | Irrigated Area (million hectares) | | | Irrigated Area as Percentage of Cropland | | |
|---|---|---|---|---|---|---|---|---|---|
| | 1961–65 | 1980 | 1985 | 1961–65 | 1980 | 1985 | 1960–65 | 1980 | 1985 |
| United States | 180 | 191 | 190 | 15 | 21 | 18 | 8 | 11 | 9 |
| Other Developed Countries* | 173 | 173 | 191 | 9 | 12 | 13 | 5 | 7 | 7 |
| Eastern Europe and USSR | 284 | 278 | 278 | 11 | 22 | 25 | 4 | 8 | 9 |
| Latin America | 116 | 192 | 179 | 8 | 14 | 15 | 7 | 7 | 8 |
| North Africa and Middle East | 81 | 87 | 108 | 14 | 18 | 22 | 17 | 21 | 20 |
| Subsaharan Africa** | 126 | 156 | 160 | 3 | 5 | 7 | 2 | 3 | 4 |
| China | 104 | 100 | 101 | 39 | 46 | 44 | 38 | 46 | 44 |
| Other Asian Countries*** | 253 | 265 | 267 | 50 | 70 | 76 | 20 | 26 | 28 |
| WORLD | 1317 | 1442 | 1474 | 149 | 208 | 220 | 11 | 14 | 15 |

*Source:* ERS/USDA, Agriculture and Trade Indicators Branch, January 1989.

*Canada, Western Europe, and Oceania; excludes Japan and South Africa.

**Includes South Africa.

***Includes Japan.

## Appendix Table 1.9   Consumption of Fertilizers* per Hectare of Cropland, ** 1961–65, 1979–80, and 1986

| Region | 1961–65 | | 1979–80 | | 1986 | |
|---|---|---|---|---|---|---|
| | (kg/ha) | (%) | (kg/ha) | (%) | (kg/ha) | (%) |
| United States | 45.6 | (163) | 112.7 | (141) | 93.0 | (107) |
| Other Developed Countries | 43.8 | (157) | 157.5 | (197) | 160.0 | (184) |
| Eastern Europe and USSR | 27.7 | (99) | 105.0 | (131) | 129.0 | (148) |
| Latin America | 11.2 | (40) | 46.0 | (57) | 41.0 | (47) |
| North Africa and Middle East | 6.2 | (22) | 42.8 | (53) | 54.8 | (63) |
| Subsaharan Africa | 1.8 | (6) | 9.7 | (12) | 13.7 | (16) |
| China | 12.2 | (44) | 152.7 | (191) | 164.2 | (189) |
| Other Asian Countries | 5.7 | (20) | 44.1 | (55) | 61.4 | (70) |
| WORLD | 27.9 | (100) | 80.1 | (100) | 87.1 | (100) |

*Source:* ERS/USDA, Agriculture and Trade Indicators Branch, January 1989.

*Note:* All percentages are based on world totals.

*Phosphorous, nitrogen, and potassium.

**Arable land and land in permanent crops in FAO land classification.

## Appendix Table 1.10   Estimates of the World's Arable Land Existing in 1970, 1980, 1985, and 1990 (Projected), and Potentials for Increase (in million hectares)

| Region | 1970 | 1980 | 1985 | 1990 (Projected) | Ultimate Potential |
|---|---|---|---|---|---|
| Developed Countries | 672.0 | 679.9 | 676.0 | 681.0 | 840 |
| Latin America | 145.5 | 171.8 | 178.6 | 185.9 | 580 |
| North and Mideast Africa | 106.1 | 106.8 | 108.0 | 109.0 | 260 |
| Subsaharan Africa | 145.1 | 156.1 | 159.4 | 162.0 | 300 |
| Asia and Pacific Islands | 339.7 | 349.9 | 354.5 | 357.5 | 520 |
| WORLD | 1,408.4 | 1,464.5 | 1,476.5 | 1,495.4 | 2,500 |

*Source:* FAO, *Production Yearbook, 1976 and 1986;* and Francis Urban, ERS/USDA, February 1989.

## Appendix Table 2.1   Agricultural Officers in the USAID Work Force, * 1980–88

| | | Agricultural Officers | | | | |
|---|---|---|---|---|---|---|
| | | Washington | | | | Percentage of Agency Total |
| Year | Agency Total | Civil Service | Foreign Service | Overseas | Total | |
| 1980 | 3636 | 15 | 43 | 174 | 232 | 6.4 |
| 1982 | 3347 | 17 | 39 | 194 | 250 | 7.5 |
| 1986 | 3197 | 17 | 39 | 174 | 230 | 7.2 |
| 1988 | 3650 | — | — | — | 246 | 6.7 |

*Source:* BIFAD, *Budget Recommendations: 1985* (Washington, D.C.: USAID, February 1984), 53; USAID Office of Personnel, 1989.

*Excludes overseas complement, positions requested from reserve, and International Development Intern positions.

### Appendix Table 2.2    All Countries Receiving U.S. Bilateral Foreign Assistance, by Region and Kind, 1946–87 ($millions)

| Region | Devel. Assist. | P.L. 480 | ESF | Other Economic Assist. | Military Assist. | Total Assist. |
|---|---|---|---|---|---|---|
| **Middle East and South Asia** | | | | | | |
| Afghanistan | 318.0 | 188.6 | 25.4 | 18.9 | 5.6 | 556.5 |
| Bahrain | 0.1 | — | 1.1 | 1.2 | — | 2.4 |
| Bangladesh | 1379.4 | 1114.8 | — | — | 2.3 | 2496.5 |
| Bhutan | — | 4.7 | — | — | — | 4.7 |
| Cyprus | 56.3 | 30.6 | 165.0 | 0.3 | — | 252.2 |
| Egypt | 130.2 | 3379.0 | 10238.6 | 11.2 | 9372.4 | 23131.4 |
| Greece | 777.4 | 238.8 | 348.9 | 536.8 | 6151.9 | 8053.8 |
| India | 4882.1 | 5854.6 | — | 346.7 | 147.5 | 11230.9 |
| Iran | 392.6 | 108.8 | 213.1 | 47.5 | 1404.8 | 2166.8 |
| Iraq | 18.8 | 25.8 | — | 0.9 | 50.0 | 95.5 |
| Israel | 582.9 | 593.8 | 12651.0 | 0.1 | 24026.8 | 37854.6 |
| Jordan | 292.3 | 200.7 | 1280.8 | 1.5 | 1482.7 | 3258.0 |
| Lebanon | 124.0 | 98.3 | 115.0 | 1.7 | 265.5 | 604.5 |
| Maldive Islands | — | 7.2 | — | — | 0.1 | 7.3 |
| Nepal | 215.6 | 138.7 | — | 37.1 | 2.9 | 394.3 |
| Oman | — | — | 104.5 | 4.0 | 199.7 | 308.2 |
| Pakistan | 2292.2 | 2491.1 | 1804.1 | 98.7 | 2227.5 | 8913.6 |
| Saudi Arabia | 27.4 | — | — | 4.4 | 292.4 | 324.2 |
| Sri Lanka | 411.6 | 544.7 | 7.2 | 3.8 | 6.7 | 974.0 |
| Syria | (206.7) | 137.5 | 426.6 | — | 0.1 | 357.5 |
| Turkey | 1416.0 | 427.9 | 2417.5 | 33.0 | 8969.7 | 13264.1 |
| North Yemen | 243.7 | 64.8 | 25.1 | 11.7 | 39.2 | 384.5 |
| South Yemen | — | 4.5 | — | — | — | 4.5 |
| Cento | 35.7 | — | 3.9 | * | — | 39.6 |
| Near East and South Asia Regional Spending | 196.1 | 347.3 | 108.0 | 6.1 | 0.1 | 657.6 |
| **Latin America** | | | | | | |
| Argentina | 114.6 | 0.1 | 19.9 | 46.3 | 263.6 | 444.5 |
| Bahamas | — | 0.3 | — | * | 0.1 | 0.4 |
| Barbados | — | 1.4 | — | 2.4 | 0.3 | 4.1 |
| Belize | 34.6 | 3.0 | 29.8 | 18.9 | 2.4 | 88.7 |
| Bermuda | — | — | — | — | — | — |
| Bolivia | 550.1 | 247.3 | 178.8 | 82.9 | 87.2 | 1146.3 |
| Brazil | 1349.7 | 591.8 | 79.9 | 176.5 | 640.0 | 2837.9 |
| Chile | 662.1 | 423.8 | — | 88.5 | 217.0 | 1391.4 |
| Colombia | 886.3 | 273.6 | 31.5 | 190.3 | 288.2 | 1669.9 |
| Costa Rica | 284.8 | 140.5 | 745.1 | 98.0 | 38.4 | 1306.8 |
| Cuba | 2.8 | 0.7 | — | 0.5 | 16.1 | 20.1 |
| Dominican Republic | 358.3 | 397.0 | 427.4 | 45.6 | 84.9 | 1313.2 |
| Ecuador | 314.2 | 109.3 | 65.9 | 168.8 | 147.1 | 805.3 |
| El Salvador | 636.9 | 359.9 | 1177.7 | 55.6 | 787.6 | 3017.7 |
| Grenada | 1.6 | — | 58.1 | 0.2 | 0.1 | 60.0 |
| Guatemala | 422.0 | 175.7 | 224.2 | 110.6 | 52.8 | 985.3 |
| Guyana | 84.5 | 21.3 | 9.6 | 1.7 | 0.1 | 117.2 |
| Haiti | 254.4 | 235.2 | 125.3 | 13.2 | 12.6 | 640.7 |
| Honduras | 509.8 | 136.2 | 482.9 | 62.2 | 388.3 | 1579.4 |
| Jamaica | 250.1 | 265.4 | 422.2 | 40.6 | 31.4 | 1009.7 |
| Mexico | 76.4 | 74.4 | 1.2 | 250.7 | 16.1 | 418.8 |
| Nicaragua | 220.7 | 45.0 | 62.7 | 51.5 | 32.4 | 412.3 |

## Appendix Table 2.2 All Countries Receiving U.S. Bilateral Foreign Assistance, by Region and Kind, 1946–87 ($millions) (Cont.)

| Region | Devel. Assist. | P.L. 480 | ESF | Other Economic Assist. | Military Assist. | Total Assist. |
|---|---|---|---|---|---|---|
| **Latin America (Cont.)** | | | | | | |
| Panama | 350.0 | 27.7 | 90.2 | 110.7 | 61.9 | 640.5 |
| Paraguay | 123.5 | 37.2 | — | 43.6 | 30.8 | 235.1 |
| Peru | 644.2 | 499.1 | 14.0 | 111.4 | 277.0 | 1545.7 |
| Suriname | 3.0 | 1.8 | 1.5 | 0.1 | 0.2 | 6.6 |
| Trinidad and Tobago | 9.2 | 1.2 | 29.7 | 0.8 | 0.2 | 41.1 |
| Uruguay | 79.1 | 41.7 | 26.5 | 18.2 | 90.3 | 255.8 |
| Venezuela | 71.7 | 29.4 | — | 101.7 | 152.8 | 355.6 |
| Regional Office Central America and Panama | 461.3 | — | 96.5 | 14.8 | — | 572.6 |
| Other West Indies– East Caribbean | 329.3 | 23.2 | 158.7 | 41.8 | 29.7 | 582.7 |
| Latin America Regional Spending | 661.1 | 7.4 | 29.5 | 214.6 | 10.4 | 923.0 |
| | | | | | | |
| **East Asia** | | | | | | |
| Brunei | — | — | — | — | — | — |
| Burma | 121.1 | 39.4 | 9.0 | 63.1 | 90.0 | 322.6 |
| China | — | 2.3 | —· | — | — | 2.3 |
| Hong Kong | — | 43.8 | — | — | — | 43.8 |
| Indochina Associated States | 2.0 | — | 823.6 | — | 731.5 | 1557.1 |
| Indonesia | 1606.8 | 1722.6 | 63.0 | 71.5 | 652.9 | 4116.8 |
| Japan | 21.8 | 145.5 | — | 2518.9 | 1239.7 | 3925.9 |
| Kampuchea (Cambodia) | 6.4 | 366.5 | 543.3 | — | 1280.3 | 2196.5 |
| South Korea | 710.2 | 2122.0 | 2332.0 | 898.3 | 8789.8 | 14852.3 |
| Laos | 101.4 | 26.2 | 774.0 | 2.5 | 1606.7 | 2510.8 |
| Malaysia | 20.0 | 17.9 | — | 54.1 | 193.5 | 285.5 |
| Philippines | 703.5 | 615.3 | 990.3 | 943.0 | 1508.7 | 4760.8 |
| Ryukyu Islands | — | 50.6 | — | 363.1 | — | 413.7 |
| Singapore | — | 2.8 | — | — | 19.4 | 22.2 |
| Thailand | 418.8 | 23.0 | 456.7 | 84.6 | 2239.9 | 3223.0 |
| Vietnam | 90.4 | 1475.5 | 5378.5 | 0.1 | 16416.1 | 23360.6 |
| Western Samoa | — | — | — | 16.8 | — | 16.8 |
| Taiwan | 638.9 | 343.1 | 727.4 | 502.3 | 4360.4 | 6572.1 |
| Asia Regional Spending | 337.3 | 5.2 | 199.4 | 31.1 | — | 573.0 |
| | | | | | | |
| **Africa** | | | | | | |
| Algeria | 2.5 | 199.7 | 1.3 | 0.1 | 0.2 | 203.8 |
| Angola | 0 | 29.8 | — | — | — | 29.8 |
| Benin (Dahomey) | 38.2 | 18.9 | — | 13.8 | 0.4 | 71.3 |
| Botswana | 38.9 | 91.9 | 93.7 | 25.0 | 30.5 | 280.0 |
| Burkina Faso | 114.6 | 145.8 | — | 19.1 | 0.8 | 280.3 |
| Burundi | 33.1 | 32.3 | — | 2.6 | 0.6 | 68.6 |
| Cameroon | 194.3 | 19.0 | 12.0 | 36.5 | 28.1 | 289.9 |
| Cape Verde | 36.4 | 37.5 | 1.0 | — | 0.2 | 75.1 |
| Central African Republic | 15.0 | 6.1 | — | 18.3 | 1.1 | 40.5 |
| Chad | 57.6 | 68.5 | 25.6 | 8.3 | 22.6 | 182.6 |
| Comoros | 2.7 | 4.1 | — | — | * | 6.8 |
| Congo | 9.4 | 11.5 | — | 0.1 | 0.1 | 21.1 |

## Appendix Table 2.2    All Countries Receiving U.S. Bilateral Foreign Assistance, by Region and Kind, 1946–87 ($millions) (Cont.)

| Region | Devel. Assist. | P.L. 480 | ESF | Other Economic Assist. | Military Assist. | Total Assist. |
|---|---|---|---|---|---|---|
| Djibouti | 4.9 | 9.3 | 17.9 | — | 9.9 | 42.0 |
| Entente States | 42.0 | — | — | — | — | 42.0 |
| Equatorial Guinea | 7.3 | 2.1 | — | — | 1.4 | 10.8 |
| Ethiopia | 257.5 | 283.8 | 3.3 | 34.8 | 280.2 | 859.6 |
| Gabon | 3.7 | 0.8 | — | 19.1 | 16.0 | 39.6 |
| Gambia, The | 35.1 | 25.3 | 6.0 | 10.9 | 0.2 | 77.5 |
| Ghana | 242.2 | 224.6 | — | 38.6 | 3.0 | 508.4 |
| Guinea | 51.7 | 152.0 | 32.4 | 5.2 | 9.0 | 250.3 |
| Guinea Bissau | 20.9 | 20.4 | — | — | 0.1 | 41.4 |
| Ivory Coast | 17.7 | 15.4 | 0.3 | 19.0 | 1.0 | 53.4 |
| Kenya | 333.6 | 186.6 | 136.1 | 59.8 | 248.5 | 964.6 |
| Lesotho | 93.9 | 105.7 | 5.5 | 18.9 | 0.1 | 224.1 |
| Liberia | 320.0 | 110.0 | 230.9 | 70.4 | 85.6 | 816.9 |
| Libya | 115.5 | 35.3 | 21.8 | 39.9 | 17.6 | 230.1 |
| Madagascar | 20.4 | 87.9 | 6.9 | — | 4.3 | 119.5 |
| Malawi | 127.4 | 10.1 | 25.6 | 16.7 | 3.5 | 183.3 |
| Mali | 170.7 | 93.4 | 21.5 | 18.7 | 4.2 | 308.5 |
| Mauritania | 67.5 | 70.6 | — | 13.2 | 0.4 | 151.7 |
| Mauritius | 3.7 | 36.3 | 17.9 | 0.9 | — | 58.8 |
| Morocco | 444.3 | 949.8 | 119.8 | 40.6 | 684.4 | 2238.9 |
| Mozambique | 13.1 | 156.1 | 41.5 | — | — | 210.7 |
| Niger | 186.9 | 76.8 | 21.8 | 35.2 | 20.7 | 341.4 |
| Nigeria | 260.1 | 67.0 | 73.0 | 29.4 | 2.0 | 431.5 |
| Rwanda | 58.9 | 42.4 | 13.1 | 1.0 | 1.9 | 117.3 |
| Sao Tome and Principe | 2.9 | 2.6 | — | — | 0.1 | 5.6 |
| Senegal | 206.9 | 136.1 | 69.6 | 32.2 | 23.7 | 468.5 |
| Seychelles | 2.2 | 3.2 | 12.3 | 1.9 | 0.1 | 19.7 |
| Sierra Leone | 29.7 | 72.0 | — | 51.5 | 0.3 | 153.5 |
| Somalia | 215.3 | 317.7 | 144.0 | 5.5 | 191.9 | 874.4 |
| South Africa | 7.9 | — | 23.0 | 1.3 | — | 32.2 |
| Sudan | 345.7 | 513.5 | 516.1 | 0.1 | 326.7 | 1702.1 |
| Swaziland | 71.3 | 8.7 | 12.9 | 19.1 | 0.2 | 112.2 |
| Tanzania | 244.1 | 182.2 | 20.5 | 19.4 | — | 466.2 |
| Togo | 38.3 | 37.3 | 7.9 | 34.2 | 0.4 | 118.1 |
| Tunisia | 410.8 | 564.5 | 81.6 | 27.4 | 668.2 | 1752.5 |
| Uganda | 88.3 | 25.1 | 3.0 | 3.8 | 0.3 | 120.5 |
| Zaire | 205.5 | 393.2 | 355.7 | 56.9 | 213.2 | 1224.5 |
| Zambia | 41.8 | 126.3 | 241.1 | 22.4 | — | 431.6 |
| Zimbabwe | 10.2 | 23.4 | 278.6 | — | 0.9 | 313.1 |
| Portuguese African Territories | 3.2 | 0.2 | — | — | — | 3.4 |
| Sahel Regional | 260.0 | 0.6 | — | — | — | 260.6 |
| East Africa Regional Development Office | 30.7 | 2.6 | — | — | — | 33.3 |
| South Africa Region Osarac | 33.6 | — | 145.9 | — | — | 179.5 |
| Africa Regional Spending | 818.9 | 1.2 | 10.4 | 12.3 | 8.9 | 851.7 |

## Appendix Table 2.2 All Countries Receiving U.S. Bilateral Foreign Assistance, by Region and Kind, 1946–87 ($millions) (Cont.)

| Region | Devel. Assist. | P.L. 480 | ESF | Other Economic Assist. | Military Assist. | Total Assist. |
|---|---|---|---|---|---|---|
| **Europe** | | | | | | |
| Albania | — | — | — | 20.4 | — | 20.4 |
| Austria | 726.1 | 81.0 | — | 328.1 | 122.0 | 1257.2 |
| Belgium and Luxembourg | 556.8 | 0.2 | — | 32.1 | 1275.2 | 1864.3 |
| Czechoslovakia | — | 2.0 | — | 191.0 | — | 193.0 |
| Denmark | 275.4 | 0.1 | — | 1.0 | 640.1 | 916.6 |
| Finland | — | 24.6 | — | 26.6 | 0.6 | 51.8 |
| France | 3113.8 | 17.7 | 76.5 | 709.1 | 4548.6 | 8465.7 |
| East Germany | — | 0.8 | — | — | — | 0.8 |
| West Germany | 1274.8 | 140.3 | — | 2428.4 | 939.4 | 4782.9 |
| West Berlin | 8.2 | — | 110.8 | 12.9 | — | 131.9 |
| Hungary | — | 14.4 | — | 18.3 | — | 32.7 |
| Iceland | 35.3 | 16.4 | 24.9 | 0.3 | 0.2 | 77.1 |
| Ireland | 127.6 | — | 85.0 | — | — | 212.6 |
| Italy | 1774.2 | 465.6 | 10.0 | 1171.0 | 2545.3 | 5966.1 |
| Malta | (0.1) | 9.3 | 74.7 | * | 0.5 | 84.4 |
| Netherlands | 991.6 | * | — | 36.0 | 1284.7 | 2312.3 |
| Norway | 274.9 | * | — | 25.0 | 943.9 | 1243.8 |
| Poland | 61.7 | 231.9 | 10.0 | 401.7 | — | 705.3 |
| Portugal | 134.6 | 319.5 | 709.3 | — | 1147.4 | 2310.8 |
| Romania | 12.3 | 10.1 | — | — | — | 22.4 |
| Spain | 93.1 | 381.7 | 605.0 | 0.3 | 3437.4 | 4517.5 |
| Sweden | 106.9 | — | — | 2.1 | — | 109.0 |
| Switzerland | — | — | — | — | — | — |
| United Kingdom | 3648.3 | 0.3 | 186.6 | 3836.9 | 1107.5 | 8779.6 |
| USSR | — | — | — | 186.4 | — | 186.4 |
| Yugoslavia | 109.9 | 854.8 | 434.7 | 335.7 | 723.4 | 2458.5 |
| European Regional Spending | 550.0 | 0.8 | — | 67.5 | — | 618.3 |
| | | | | | | |
| **Oceania and Others** | | | | | | |
| Australia | — | — | — | 8.0 | 115.6 | 123.6 |
| New Zealand | — | — | — | 4.3 | 4.3 | 8.6 |
| Pacific Islands, Trust Territories of | — | * | — | 824.2 | — | 824.2 |
| Papua New Guinea | — | 0.3 | — | 5.0 | 0.3 | 5.6 |
| Oceania Regional | 30.1 | 2.6 | 3.7 | 71.7 | 1.3 | 109.4 |
| Canada | — | — | — | 17.5 | 13.0 | 30.5 |
| | | | | | | |
| Interregional Activities | 17756.4 | 2908.2 | 640.5 | 25855.3 | 4432.9 | 51593.3 |
| | | | | | | |
| TOTAL* | 66,281 | 38,494 | 52,645 | 46,379 | 123,734 | 327,533 |

*Source:* USAID, *U.S. Overseas Grants and Loans* (Washington, D.C.: 1987)

*Columns do not add exactly to totals due to rounding.

[a]AID-administered assistance

[b]Assistance related to development administered by agencies other than AID.

### Appendix Table 2.3   U.S. Foreign Cooperative Program Obligations, Total and by Major Classification, 1968–89 (in current $, billions)

| | 1968–72 Average ($ bill) | 1973–77 Average ($ bill) | 1978–82 Average ($ bill) | 1984 ($ bill) | 1989 Appropriated ($ bill) | 1989 Appropriated (% tot) | 1989 Appropriated (% Gr Tot) |
|---|---|---|---|---|---|---|---|
| Economic Assistance | | | | | | | |
| Development assistance[a] | 1.4 | 1.5 | 1.9 | 1.9 | 2.4 | (26) | (16) |
| P.L. 480 | 1.2 | 1.2 | 1.4 | 1.1 | 1.5 | (16) | (10) |
| ESF | 0.5 | 1.2 | 2.2 | 2.9 | 3.3 | (35) | (23) |
| Other economic assistance[b] | 0.1 | 0.1 | 0.2 | 0.6 | 0.7 | (7) | (5) |
| Multilateral assistance | 0.5 | 0.9 | 1.6 | 1.8 | 1.5 | (16) | (10) |
| Total | 3.7 | 4.9 | 7.3 | 8.3 | 9.4 | (100) | (64) |
| Military Assistance | 3.5 | 3.4 | 3.7 | 6.5 | 5.4 | (100) | (36) |
| GRAND TOTAL | 7.2 | 8.3 | 11.0 | 14.8 | 14.8 | — | (100) |

*Sources:* USAID, *U.S. Overseas Loans and Grants* (Washington, D.C.:various years); USAID, *1983 Aid Presentation to Office of Management and Budget* (Washington, D.C.: October 1982); USAID, *Congressional Presentation, Fiscal Year 1984* and *Fiscal Year 1990* (Washington, D.C.:1983, reproduced from the Commission on Security and Economic Assistance, *A Report to the Secretary of State* (Carlucci Report), November 1983; BIFAD, staff memo, 26 September 1988.

[a]AID-administered assistance.

### Appendix Table 2.4   Distribution of U.S. Bilateral Foreign Assistance, by Type for Selected Periods, 1946–87 and 1984–87

| | 1946–87 Amount ($ billions) | 1946–87 Percentage of Total | 1984–87 Amount ($ billions) | 1984–87 Percentage of Total |
|---|---|---|---|---|
| Type of Assistance | | | | |
| Development assistance[a] | 66.3 | 20.2 | 10.4 | 16.0 |
| P.L. 480 | 38.5 | 11.7 | 6.8 | 10.5 |
| ESF | 52.6 | 16.1 | 17.2 | 26.5 |
| Other economic assistance[b] | 46.4 | 14.2 | 7.3 | 11.2 |
| Military assistance | 123.7 | 37.8 | 23.2 | 35.8 |
| Total | 327.5 | 100.0 | 64.9 | 100.0 |

*Source:* USAID, *U.S. Overseas Loans and Grants* (Washington, D.C.: 1987).

[a]USAID-administered assistance.

[b]Assistance related to development administered by agencies other than USAID.

## Appendix Table 2.5  Distribution of U.S. Bilateral Foreign Assistance, by Region, 1946–87 ($ billions)

| Region | Total Assistance | Distributed Between | | Distributed Between | |
|---|---|---|---|---|---|
| | | Loans | Grants | Economic | Military |
| Middle East and South Asia | 115.3 | 50.2 | 65.1 | 60.7 | 54.6 |
| % of total | 35 | 44 | 56 | 53 | 47 |
| East Asia | 68.8 | 11.8 | 57.0 | 29.6 | 39.2 |
| % of total | 21 | 17 | 83 | 43 | 57 |
| European Nations | 47.3 | 11.5 | 35.8 | 28.6 | 18.7 |
| % of total | 14 | 24 | 76 | 60 | 40 |
| Latin America | 24.4 | 11.0 | 13.4 | 20.6 | 3.8 |
| % of total | 8 | 45 | 55 | 84 | 16 |
| Africa | 19.0 | 5.9 | 13.1 | 16.1 | 2.9 |
| % of total | 6 | 31 | 69 | 85 | 15 |
| Oceania and Others | 1.1 | 0.2 | 0.9 | 1.0 | 0.1 |
| % of total | ** | 18 | 82 | 91 | 9 |
| Canada | * | * | * | * | * |
| % of total | ** | ** | ** | ** | ** |
| Interregional Activities | 51.6 | 0.3 | 51.3 | 47.2 | 4.4 |
| % of total | 15 | 1 | 99 | 91 | 9 |
| TOTAL | 327.5 | 90.9 | 236.6 | 203.8 | 123.7 |
| % of total | 100 | 28 | 72 | 62 | 38 |

*Source:* USAID, *U.S. Overseas Loans and Grants* (Washington, D.C.:1987).

*Less than $50 million.

**Less than 0.5 percent.

## Appendix Table 2.6  All Countries Receiving U.S. Bilateral Foreign Assistance, by GNP Rank and by Kind, 1984–87 ($ millions)

| GNP Rank | Country | Devel. Assist.[a] | P.L. 480 | ESF | Other Economic Assist.[b] | Military Assist. | Total Assist. |
|---|---|---|---|---|---|---|---|
| 1 | Ethiopia | 0.5 | 181.1 | 0.0 | 0.0 | 0.0 | 181.6 |
| | % of total | 0.2 | 99.8 | 0.0 | 0.0 | 0.0 | 100.0 |
| 2 | Bhutan | 0.0 | 2.1 | 0.0 | 0.0 | 0.0 | 2.1 |
| | % of total | 0.0 | 100.0 | 0.0 | 0.0 | 0.0 | 100.0 |
| 3 | Burkina Faso | 31.6 | 46.4 | 0.0 | 4.9 | 0.2 | 83.1 |
| | % of total | 37.7 | 56.1 | 0.0 | 5.9 | 0.3 | 100.0 |
| 4 | Nepal | 65.4 | 6.5 | 0.0 | 9.2 | 0.4 | 81.5 |
| | % of total | 80.0 | 8.0 | 0.0 | 11.3 | 0.7 | 100.0 |
| 5 | Bangladesh | 304.5 | 468.5 | 0.0 | 0.0 | 1.2 | 774.2 |
| | % of total | 39.3 | 60.5 | 0.0 | 0.0 | 0.2 | 100.0 |
| 6 | Malawi | 54.8 | 2.2 | 25.6 | 4.2 | 3.3 | 90.1 |
| | % of total | 60.8 | 2.4 | 28.4 | 4.7 | 3.7 | 100.0 |
| 7 | Zaire | 87.0 | 82.7 | 55.0 | 16.9 | 29.4 | 271.0 |
| | % of total | 32.1 | 30.5 | 20.3 | 6.3 | 10.8 | 100.0 |
| 8 | Mali | 50.4 | 38.8 | 18.0 | 8.9 | 0.7 | 116.8 |
| | % of total | 43.2 | 33.2 | 15.4 | 7.6 | 0.6 | 100.0 |

### Appendix Table 2.6    All Countries Receiving U.S. Bilateral Foreign Assistance, by GNP Rank and by Kind, 1984–87 ($ millions) (Cont.)

| GNP Rank | Country | Devel. Assist.[a] | P.L. 480 | ESF | Other Economic Assist. | Military Assist. | Total Assist. |
|---|---|---|---|---|---|---|---|
| 9 | Burma | 44.3 | 0.0 | 0.0 | 23.6 | 0.9 | 68.8 |
|  | % of total | 64.4 | 0.0 | 0.0 | 34.3 | 1.3 | 100.0 |
| 10 | Mozambique | 3.2 | 84.6 | 40.0 | 0.0 | 0.0 | 127.8 |
|  | % of total | 2.5 | 66.2 | 31.3 | 0.0 | 0.0 | 100.0 |
| 11 | Madagascar | 8.9 | 38.8 | 6.9 | 0.0 | 4.4 | 59.0 |
|  | % of total | 15.1 | 65.8 | 11.7 | 0.0 | 7.4 | 100.0 |
| 12 | Uganda | 39.6 | 7.8 | 0.0 | 0.0 | 0.2 | 47.6 |
|  | % of total | 83.1 | 16.4 | 0.0 | 0.0 | 0.5 | 100.0 |
| 13 | Burundi | 13.3 | 7.0 | 0.0 | 2.4 | 0.4 | 23.1 |
|  | % of total | 57.6 | 30.3 | 0.0 | 10.4 | 1.7 | 100.0 |
| 14 | Tanzania | 39.3 | 18.6 | 20.5 | 5.9 | 0.0 | 84.3 |
|  | % of total | 46.7 | 22.0 | 24.3 | 7.0 | 0.0 | 100.0 |
| 15 | Togo | 16.0 | 9.8 | 7.9 | 9.8 | 0.2 | 43.7 |
|  | % of total | 36.7 | 22.4 | 18.0 | 22.4 | 0.5 | 100.0 |
| 16 | Niger | 87.9 | 26.8 | 16.8 | 11.0 | 13.2 | 155.7 |
|  | % of total | 56.5 | 17.2 | 10.7 | 7.1 | 8.5 | 100.0 |
| 17 | Benin(Dahomey) | 0.8 | 5.8 | 0.0 | 5.3 | 0.3 | 12.2 |
|  | % of total | 6.6 | 47.5 | 0.0 | 43.4 | 2.5 | 100.0 |
| 18 | Somalia | 77.6 | 106.1 | 104.1 | 0.0 | 95.5 | 383.3 |
|  | % of total | 20.2 | 27.7 | 27.2 | 0.0 | 24.9 | 100.0 |
| 19 | Central African Rep. | 7.6 | 1.5 | 0.0 | 8.5 | 1.0 | 18.6 |
|  | % of total | 40.8 | 8.1 | 0.0 | 45.7 | 5.4 | 100.0 |
| 20 | India | 333.5 | 423.7 | 0.0 | 0.0 | 1.0 | 758.2 |
|  | % of total | 44.0 | 55.9 | 0.0 | 0.0 | 0.1 | 100.0 |
| 21 | Rwanda | 31.3 | 17.1 | 12.0 | 0.5 | 0.3 | 61.2 |
|  | % of total | 51.2 | 27.9 | 19.6 | 0.8 | 0.5 | 100.0 |
| 22 | Kenya | 97.4 | 70.2 | 75.4 | 17.2 | 77.5 | 337.7 |
|  | % of total | 28.9 | 20.8 | 22.3 | 5.1 | 22.9 | 100.0 |
| 23 | Zambia | 8.7 | 41.0 | 91.5 | 0.0 | 0.0 | 141.2 |
|  | % of total | 6.2 | 29.0 | 64.8 | 0.0 | 0.0 | 100.0 |
| 24 | Sierra Leone | 2.1 | 30.2 | 0.0 | 12.4 | 0.3 | 45.0 |
|  | % of total | 4.7 | 67.1 | 0.0 | 27.6 | 0.6 | 100.0 |
| 25 | Sudan | 144.1 | 330.7 | 244.0 | 0.1 | 115.9 | 834.8 |
|  | % of total | 14.6 | 43.3 | 28.6 | 0.0 | 13.5 | 100.0 |
| 26 | Haiti | 110.8 | 95.7 | 67.4 | 7.0 | 4.9 | 285.8 |
|  | % of total | 38.7 | 33.5 | 23.6 | 2.5 | 1.7 | 100.0 |
| 27 | Pakistan | 99.1 | 323.8 | 914.8 | 16.7 | 1252.3 | 2606.7 |
|  | % of total | 3.8 | 12.4 | 35.2 | 0.6 | 48.0 | 100.0 |
| 28 | Lesotho | 43.4 | 33.3 | 0.0 | 6.1 | 0.1 | 82.9 |
|  | % of total | 52.3 | 40.2 | 0.0 | 7.4 | 0.1 | 100.0 |
| 29 | Ghana | 9.5 | 83.8 | 0.0 | 5.9 | 0.9 | 100.1 |
|  | % of total | 9.5 | 83.7 | 0.0 | 5.9 | 0.9 | 100.0 |
| 30 | Sri Lanka | 131.4 | 133.8 | 0.0 | 2.2 | 0.6 | 268.0 |
|  | % of total | 49.0 | 49.9 | 0.0 | 0.9 | 0.2 | 100.0 |
| 31 | Mauritania | 24.0 | 20.0 | 0.0 | 6.6 | 0.4 | 51.0 |
|  | % of total | 47.1 | 39.2 | 0.0 | 12.9 | 0.8 | 100.0 |
| 32 | Senegal | 99.8 | 51.5 | 64.5 | 8.5 | 11.4 | 235.7 |
|  | % of total | 42.3 | 21.9 | 27.4 | 3.6 | 4.8 | 100.0 |

## Appendix Table 2.6    All Countries Receiving U.S. Bilateral Foreign Assistance, by GNP Rank and by Kind, 1984–87 ($ millions) (Cont.)

| GNP Rank | Country | Devel. Assist.[a] | P.L. 480 | ESF | Other Economic Assist. | Military Assist. | Total Assist. |
|---|---|---|---|---|---|---|---|
| 33 | Afghanistan | 3.4 | 11.5 | 0.0 | 0.0 | 0.0 | 14.9 |
|  | % of total | 22.8 | 77.2 | 0.0 | 0.0 | 0.0 | 100.0 |
| 34 | Chad | 30.1 | 30.4 | 22.8 | 0.3 | 22.6 | 106.2 |
|  | % of total | 28.3 | 28.6 | 21.5 | 0.3 | 21.3 | 100.0 |
| 35 | Guinea | 11.3 | 28.2 | 10.0 | 0.8 | 8.0 | 58.3 |
|  | % of total | 19.4 | 48.4 | 17.2 | 1.3 | 13.7 | 100.0 |
| 36 | Kampuchea (Cambodia) | 0.0 | 6.2 | 0.0 | 0.0 | 0.0 | 6.2 |
|  | % of total | 0.0 | 100.0 | 0.0 | 0.0 | 0.0 | 100.0 |
| 37 | Laos | 0.0 | 1.5 | 0.0 | 0.0 | 0.0 | 1.5 |
|  | % of total | 0.0 | 100.0 | 0.0 | 0.0 | 0.0 | 100.0 |
| 38 | Liberia | 57.9 | 44.7 | 121.7 | 12.4 | 33.1 | 269.8 |
|  | % of total | 21.5 | 16.6 | 45.1 | 4.5 | 12.3 | 100.0 |
| 39 | Indonesia | 300.1 | 157.1 | 0.0 | 0.0 | 114.7 | 571.9 |
|  | % of total | 52.5 | 27.5 | 0.0 | 0.0 | 20.0 | 100.0 |
| 40 | North Yemen | 104.7 | 45.0 | 0.0 | 3.8 | 16.9 | 170.4 |
|  | % of total | 61.4 | 26.5 | 0.0 | 2.2 | 9.9 | 100.0 |
| 41 | Philippines | 145.9 | 150.9 | 725.4 | 19.4 | 301.6 | 1343.2 |
|  | % of total | 10.9 | 11.2 | 54.0 | 1.4 | 22.5 | 100.0 |
| 42 | Morocco | 80.7 | 234.2 | 48.6 | 9.3 | 201.3 | 574.1 |
|  | % of total | 14.1 | 40.7 | 8.5 | 1.6 | 35.1 | 100.0 |
| 43 | Bolivia | 123.1 | 120.4 | 14.7 | 23.0 | 6.2 | 287.4 |
|  | % of total | 42.8 | 41.9 | 5.1 | 8.0 | 2.2 | 100.0 |
| 44 | Zimbabwe | 4.2 | 16.4 | 96.1 | 0.0 | 0.8 | 117.5 |
|  | % of total | 3.6 | 14.0 | 81.8 | 0.0 | 0.6 | 100.0 |
| 45 | Nigeria | 22.9 | 0.0 | 0.0 | 0.0 | 0.2 | 23.1 |
|  | % of total | 99.1 | 0.0 | 0.0 | 0.0 | 0.9 | 100.0 |
| 46 | Dominican Rep. | 107.8 | 120.4 | 169.2 | 10.8 | 23.0 | 431.2 |
|  | % of total | 25.0 | 27.9 | 39.3 | 2.5 | 5.3 | 100.0 |
| 47 | Papua New Guinea | 0.0 | 0.0 | 0.0 | 3.7 | 0.2 | 3.9 |
|  | % of total | 0.0 | 0.0 | 0.0 | 94.9 | 5.1 | 100.0 |
| 48 | Ivory Coast | 4.1 | 0.2 | 0.0 | 0.0 | 0.7 | 5.0 |
|  | % of total | 82.0 | 4.0 | 0.0 | 0.0 | 14.0 | 100.0 |
| 49 | Honduras | 173.4 | 77.3 | 388.5 | 19.2 | 267.1 | 925.5 |
|  | % of total | 18.7 | 8.3 | 42.0 | 2.1 | 28.9 | 100.0 |
| 50 | Egypt | 0.0 | 897.9 | 3806.9 | 0.0 | 5091.0 | 9795.8 |
|  | % of total | 0.0 | 9.2 | 38.8 | 0.0 | 52.0 | 100.0 |
| 51 | Nicaragua | 0.0 | 0.0 | 0.0 | 0.1 | 0.0 | 0.1 |
|  | % of total | 0.0 | 0.0 | 0.0 | 100.0 | 0.0 | 100.0 |
| 52 | Thailand | 102.6 | 0.0 | 27.1 | 26.4 | 343.3 | 499.4 |
|  | % of total | 20.5 | 0.0 | 5.4 | 5.3 | 68.8 | 100.0 |
| 53 | El Salvador | 351.6 | 215.1 | 868.6 | ** | 566.2 | 2001.5 |
|  | % of total | 17.6 | 10.7 | 43.4 | * | 28.3 | 100.0 |
| 54 | Botswana | 13.1 | 33.4 | 27.4 | 9.5 | 24.1 | 107.5 |
|  | % of total | 12.2 | 31.1 | 25.5 | 8.8 | 22.4 | 100.0 |
| 55 | Jamaica | 111.0 | 138.4 | 220.5 | 14.7 | 23.2 | 507.8 |
|  | % of total | 21.8 | 27.3 | 43.4 | 2.9 | 4.6 | 100.0 |

**Appendix Table 2.6   All Countries Receiving U.S. Bilateral
Foreign Assistance, by GNP Rank and by Kind,
1984–87 ($ millions)
(Cont.)**

| GNP Rank | Country | Devel. Assist.[a] | P.L. 480 | ESF | Other Economic Assist. | Military Assist. | Total Assist. |
|---|---|---|---|---|---|---|---|
| 56 | Cameroon | 92.7 | 5.1 | 9.0 | 12.2 | 11.2 | 130.2 |
| | % of total | 71.2 | 3.9 | 6.9 | 9.4 | 8.6 | 100.0 |
| 57 | Guatemala | 142.7 | 96.6 | 180.8 | 11.6 | 11.4 | 443.1 |
| | % of total | 32.2 | 21.8 | 40.8 | 2.6 | 2.6 | 100.0 |
| 58 | Congo | 3.9 | 0.4 | 0.0 | 0.0 | ** | 4.3 |
| | % of total | 90.7 | 9.3 | 0.0 | 0.0 | * | 100.0 |
| 59 | Paraguay | 3.3 | 0.3 | 0.0 | 9.0 | 0.4 | 13.0 |
| | % of total | 25.4 | 2.3 | 0.0 | 69.3 | 3.0 | 100.0 |
| 60 | Peru | 191.7 | 144.2 | 12.3 | 17.6 | 20.1 | 385.9 |
| | % of total | 49.6 | 37.4 | 3.2 | 4.6 | 5.2 | 100.0 |
| 61 | Turkey | 2.4 | 0.0 | 533.1 | 2.6 | 2533.9 | 3072.0 |
| | % of total | 0.1 | 0.0 | 17.3 | 0.1 | 82.5 | 100.0 |
| 62 | Tunisia | 4.8 | 65.4 | 61.3 | 6.9 | 277.8 | 416.2 |
| | % of total | 1.2 | 15.7 | 14.7 | 1.7 | 66.7 | 100.0 |
| 63 | Ecuador | 98.9 | 28.1 | 43.9 | 15.9 | 22.4 | 209.2 |
| | % of total | 47.3 | 13.4 | 21.0 | 7.6 | 10.7 | 100.0 |
| 64 | Mauritius | 2.6 | 1.3 | 13.9 | 0.0 | 0.0 | 17.8 |
| | % of total | 14.6 | 7.3 | 78.1 | 0.0 | 0.0 | 100.0 |
| 65 | Colombia | 0.0 | 0.0 | 0.0 | 43.0 | 35.5 | 78.5 |
| | % of total | 0.0 | 0.0 | 0.0 | 54.8 | 45.2 | 100.0 |
| 66 | Chile | 0.0 | 0.0 | 0.0 | 5.2 | 0.0 | 5.2 |
| | % of total | 0.0 | 0.0 | 0.0 | 100.0 | 0.0 | 100.0 |
| 67 | Costa Rica | 72.9 | 81.7 | 568.1 | 11.3 | 24.6 | 758.6 |
| | % of total | 9.6 | 10.8 | 74.9 | 1.5 | 3.2 | 100.0 |
| 68 | Jordan | 0.1 | 0.0 | 326.4 | 0.0 | 333.6 | 660.1 |
| | % of total | 0.0 | 0.0 | 49.5 | 0.0 | 50.5 | 100.0 |
| 69 | Lebanon | 1.6 | 11.6 | 75.2 | 0.0 | 17.3 | 105.7 |
| | % of total | 1.5 | 11.0 | 71.1 | 0.0 | 16.4 | 100.0 |
| 70 | Brazil | 0.0 | 2.1 | 0.0 | 4.8 | 0.0 | 6.9 |
| | % of total | 0.0 | 30.4 | 0.0 | 69.6 | 0.0 | 100.0 |
| 71 | Malaysia | 0.0 | 0.0 | 0.0 | 0.1 | 19.3 | 19.4 |
| | % of total | 0.0 | 0.0 | 0.0 | 0.5 | 99.5 | 100.0 |
| 72 | South Africa | 7.9 | 0.0 | 23.0 | 0.0 | 0.0 | 30.9 |
| | % of total | 25.6 | 0.0 | 74.4 | 0.0 | 0.0 | 100.0 |
| 73 | Mexico | 0.0 | 3.7 | 0.0 | 45.2 | 0.9 | 49.8 |
| | % of total | 0.0 | 7.4 | 0.0 | 90.8 | 1.8 | 100.0 |
| 74 | Uruguay | 0.0 | 0.0 | 26.6 | 0.6 | 1.0 | 28.2 |
| | % of total | 0.0 | 0.0 | 94.4 | 2.1 | 3.5 | 100.0 |
| 75 | Poland | 0.0 | 39.1 | 5.0 | 0.0 | 0.0 | 44.1 |
| | % of total | 0.0 | 88.7 | 11.3 | 0.0 | 0.0 | 100.0 |
| 76 | Portugal | 0.0 | 0.0 | 261.4 | 0.0 | 430.9 | 692.3 |
| | % of total | 0.0 | 0.0 | 37.8 | 0.0 | 62.2 | 100.0 |
| 77 | Yugoslavia | 0.0 | 0.0 | 0.0 | 0.0 | 0.4 | 0.4 |
| | % of total | 0.0 | 0.0 | 0.0 | 0.0 | 100.0 | 100.0 |
| 78 | Panama | 67.2 | 1.5 | 63.2 | 0.1 | 35.8 | 167.8 |
| | % of total | 40.0 | 0.9 | 37.7 | 0.1 | 21.3 | 100.0 |
| 79 | Argentina | 0.0 | 0.0 | 0.0 | 2.5 | 0.0 | 2.5 |
| | % of total | 0.0 | 0.0 | 0.0 | 100.0 | 0.0 | 100.0 |

## Appendix Table 2.6 All Countries Receiving U.S. Bilateral Foreign Assistance, by GNP Rank and by Kind, 1984–87 ($ millions) (Cont.)

| GNP Rank | Country | Devel. Assist.[a] | P.L. 480 | ESF | Other Economic Assist. | Military Assist. | Total Assist. |
|---|---|---|---|---|---|---|---|
| 80 | South Korea | 0.0 | 0.0 | 0.0 | 0.0 | 630.2 | 630.2 |
| | % of total | 0.0 | 0.0 | 0.0 | 0.0 | 100.0 | 100.0 |
| 81 | Algeria | 0.0 | 0.3 | 0.0 | 0.0 | 0.2 | 0.5 |
| | % of total | 0.0 | 60.0 | 0.0 | 0.0 | 40.0 | 100.0 |
| 82 | Venezuela | 0.0 | 0.0 | 0.0 | 1.3 | 0.4 | 1.7 |
| | % of total | 0.0 | 0.0 | 0.0 | 76.4 | 23.6 | 100.0 |
| 83 | Gabon | 0.0 | 0.0 | 0.0 | 7.2 | 3.4 | 10.6 |
| | % of total | 0.0 | 0.0 | 0.0 | 67.9 | 32.1 | 100.0 |
| 84 | Greece | 0.0 | 0.0 | 0.0 | 0.0 | 1779.0 | 1779.0 |
| | % of total | 0.0 | 0.0 | 0.0 | 0.0 | 100.0 | 100.0 |
| 85 | Oman | (0.1) | 0.0 | 69.6 | 0.0 | 89.4 | 158.9 |
| | % of total | 0.0 | 0.0 | 43.7 | 0.0 | 56.3 | 100.0 |
| 86 | Trinidad and Tobago | 0.0 | 0.0 | 0.0 | 0.0 | 0.2 | 0.2 |
| | % of total | 0.0 | 0.0 | 0.0 | 0.0 | 100.0 | 100.0 |
| 87 | Israel | 0.0 | 0.0 | 5958.5 | 0.0 | 6622.6 | 12581.1 |
| | % of total | 0.0 | 0.0 | 47.4 | . 0.0 | 52.6 | 100.0 |
| 88 | Singapore | 0.0 | 0.0 | 0.0 | 0.0 | 0.2 | 0.2 |
| | % of total | 0.0 | 0.0 | 0.0 | 0.0 | 100.0 | 100.0 |
| 89 | Spain | 0.0 | 0.0 | 40.5 | 0.0 | 1299.1 | 1339.6 |
| | % of total | 0.0 | 0.0 | 3.0 | 0.0 | 97.0 | 100.0 |
| 90 | Ireland | 0.0 | 0.0 | 85.0 | 0.0 | 0.0 | 85.0 |
| | % of total | 0.0 | 0.0 | 100.0 | 0.0 | 0.0 | 100.0 |
| 91 | Italy | 1.8 | 0.0 | 10.0 | 0.0 | 0.0 | 11.8 |
| | % of total | 15.3 | 0.0 | 84.7 | 0.0 | 0.0 | 100.0 |
| 92 | Austria | 0.0 | 0.0 | 0.0 | 0.0 | 0.3 | 0.3 |
| | % of total | 0.0 | 0.0 | 0.0 | 0.0 | 100.0 | 100.0 |
| 93 | Finland | 0.0 | 0.0 | 0.0 | 0.0 | 0.2 | 0.2 |
| | % of total | 0.0 | 0.0 | 0.0 | 0.0 | 100.0 | 100.0 |
| | **Countries without GNP Rank:** | | | | | | |
| | Angola | 0.0 | 13.7 | 0.0 | 0.0 | 0.0 | 13.7 |
| | % of total | 0.0 | 100.0 | 0.0 | 0.0 | 0.0 | 100.0 |
| | Bahamas | 0.0 | 0.0 | 0.0 | ** | 0.1 | 0.1 |
| | % of total | 0.0 | 0.0 | 0.0 | * | 100.0 | 100.0 |
| | Barbados | 0.0 | 0.0 | 0.0 | 0.1 | 0.2 | 0.3 |
| | % of total | 0.0 | 0.0 | 0.0 | 33.3 | 66.7 | 100.0 |
| | Belize | 26.9 | 0.0 | 21.9 | 9.6 | 2.3 | 60.7 |
| | % of total | 44.3 | 0.0 | 36.1 | 15.8 | 3.8 | 100.0 |
| | Cape Verde | 9.8 | 13.2 | 0.0 | 0.0 | 0.2 | 23.2 |
| | % of total | 42.2 | 56.9 | 0.0 | 0.0 | 0.9 | 100.0 |
| | Comoros | 2.7 | 2.3 | 0.0 | 0.0 | ** | 5.0 |
| | % of total | 54.0 | 46.0 | 0.0 | 0.0 | * | 100.0 |
| | Cyprus | 0.0 | 0.0 | 59.4 | 0.0 | 0.0 | 59.4 |
| | % of total | 0.0 | 0.0 | 100.0 | 0.0 | 0.0 | 100.0 |
| | Djibouti | 0.3 | 2.8 | 11.9 | 0.0 | 8.1 | 23.1 |
| | % of total | 1.3 | 12.1 | 51.5 | 0.0 | 35.1 | 100.0 |

**Appendix Table 2.6    All Countries Receiving U.S. Bilateral
Foreign Assistance, by GNP Rank and by Kind,
1984–87 ($ millions)
(Cont.)**

| Country | Devel. Assist.[a] | P.L. 480 | ESF | Other Economic Assist. | Military Assist. | Total Assist. |
|---|---|---|---|---|---|---|
| Equatorial Guinea | 4.3 | 1.8 | 0.0 | 0.0 | 1.4 | 7.5 |
| % of total | 57.3 | 24.0 | 0.0 | 0.0 | 18.7 | 100.0 |
| Gambia, The | 17.5 | 11.3 | 6.0 | 4.0 | 0.3 | 39.1 |
| % of total | 44.8 | 28.9 | 15.3 | 10.2 | 0.8 | 100.0 |
| Grenada | 1.6 | 0.0 | 58.1 | 0.1 | 0.2 | 60.0 |
| % of total | 2.7 | 0.0 | 96.8 | 0.2 | 0.3 | 100.0 |
| Guinea–Bissau | 8.6 | 5.3 | 0.0 | 0.0 | ** | 13.9 |
| % of total | 61.9 | 38.9 | 0.0 | 0.0 | * | 100.0 |
| Guyana | 0.0 | 9.8 | 0.0 | ** | 0.0 | 9.8 |
| % of total | 0.0 | 100.0 | 0.0 | * | 0.0 | 100.0 |
| Iceland | 0.0 | 0.0 | 0.0 | 0.0 | ** | ** |
| % of total | 0.0 | 0.0 | 0.0 | 0.0 | * | 100.0 |
| Maldive Islands | 0.0 | 2.8 | 0.0 | 0.0 | ** | 2.8 |
| % of total | 0.0 | 100.0 | 0.0 | 0.0 | * | 100.0 |
| Ryukyu Islands | 0.0 | 0.0 | 0.0 | ** | 0.0 | ** |
| % of total | 0.0 | 0.0 | 0.0 | * | 0.0 | 100.0 |
| Sao Tome and Principe | 1.1 | 1.9 | 0.0 | 0.0 | ** | 3.0 |
| % of total | 36.7 | 63.3 | 0.0 | 0.0 | * | 100.0 |
| Seychelle | 0.4 | 0.9 | 8.3 | 1.0 | ** | 10.6 |
| % of total | 3.8 | 8.5 | 78.3 | 9.4 | * | 100.0 |
| Suriname | 0.0 | 0.0 | 0.0 | 0.0 | ** | ** |
| % of total | 0.0 | 0.0 | 0.0 | 0.0 | * | 100.0 |
| Swaziland | 33.1 | 1.3 | 0.6 | 5.7 | 0.3 | 41.0 |
| % of total | 80.7 | 3.2 | 1.5 | 13.9 | 0.7 | 100.0 |
| Western Samoa | 0.0 | 0.0 | 0.0 | 4.3 | 0.0 | 4.3 |
| % of total | 0.0 | 0.0 | 0.0 | 100.0 | 0.0 | 100.0 |
| **Regional:** | | | | | | |
| Middle East and South Asia | 10.1 | 7.7 | 32.1 | 1.4 | ** | 51.3 |
| % of total | 20.0 | 15.0 | 62.6 | 2.4 | * | 100.0 |
| Latin America | 358.4 | ** | 208.6 | 56.7 | 35.8 | 659.5 |
| % of total | 54.4 | * | 31.6 | 8.6 | 5.4 | 100.0 |
| Asia | 78.9 | 0.0 | 76.1 | 1.0 | 0.0 | 156.0 |
| % of total | 50.6 | 0 | 7.3 | 0.0 | 2.3 | 100.0 |
| Africa | 350.7 | 0 | 28.3 | 0.0 | 8.9 | 387.9 |
| % of total | 90.4 | 0.0 | 7.3 | 0.0 | 2.3 | 100.0 |
| Europe | 0.0 | 0.0 | 0.0 | 0.0 | 0.0 | 0.0 |
| % of total | 0.0 | 0.0 | 0.0 | 0.0 | 0.0 | 100.0 |
| Oceania and Others | 19.7 | 0.3 | 3.7 | 23.5 | 1.2 | 48.4 |
| % of total | 40.7 | 0.6 | 7.6 | 48.6 | 2.5 | 100.0 |
| Total Regional | 817.8 | 8.0 | 348.8 | 82.6 | 45.9 | 1303.1 |
| % of total | 62.8 | 0.6 | 26.8 | 6.3 | 3.5 | 100.0 |
| **Interregional Activities** | 4965.5 | 1106.0 | 25.9 | 6602.3 | 306.7 | 13006.4 |
| % of total | 38.2 | 8.5 | 0.2 | 50.7 | 2.4 | 100.0 |
| TOTAL | 10399.7 | 6781.6 | 17219.6 | 7254.0 | 23228.5 | 64883.4 |
| % of total | 16.0 | 10.5 | 26.5 | 11.2 | 35.8 | 100.0 |

*Source:* USAID, *U.S. Overseas Loans and Grants* (Washington, D.C.:1987); World
Bank, *World Development Report 1988.*

[a]AID-administered assistance; [b]Assistance related to development administered
by agencies other than AID; *Less than 0.1; **Less than 50,000.

## Appendix Table 2.7    U.S. Bilateral Aid: Changes in Regional Focus, 1969–86 ($ millions)

| | Nixon 1969–72 | Nixon 1973–74 | Ford 1975–76 | Carter 1977–80 | Reagan 1981–84 | Reagan 1985–86 |
|---|---|---|---|---|---|---|
| **Development Assistance** | | | | | | |
| Middle East and South Asia[b] | 764 | 507 | 795 | 590 | 629 | 658 |
| Egypt and Israel | 47 | 38 | 186 | 244 | 275 | 226 |
| East Asia | 710 | 748 | 350 | 363 | 249 | 272 |
| Central America | 73 | 82 | 123 | 96 | 199 | 364 |
| Other Latin America | 421 | 309 | 300 | 316 | 399 | 513 |
| Africa | 288 | 279 | 311 | 517 | 730 | 1,035 |
| Europe | 16 | 4 | 10 | 57 | 49 | 9 |
| Oceania | 52 | 68 | 70 | 33 | 7 | 13 |
| **Security Assistance**[a] | | | | | | |
| Middle East and South Asia[b] | 394 | 395 | 431 | 726 | 1,466 | 2,090 |
| Egypt and Israel | 253 | 1,449 | 1,665 | 3,685 | 4,204 | 5,764 |
| East Asia | 3,537 | 3,491 | 983 | 364 | 425 | 648 |
| Central America | 7 | 8 | 14 | 13 | 383 | 766 |
| Other Latin America | 58 | 106 | 135 | 41 | 159 | 302 |
| Africa | 54 | 33 | 89 | 202 | 555 | 611 |
| Europe | 43 | 63 | 39 | 288 | 393 | 626 |
| Oceania | 1 | 0 | 0 | 0 | 0 | 2 |

*Source:* USAID, *U.S. Overseas Loans and Grants,* various issues, as cited in John W. Sewell, Stuart K. Tucker, et al., *Growth, Exports, and Jobs in a Changing World Economy: Agenda 1988,* Overseas Development Council (New Brunswick, N.J.: Transaction Books, 1988).

*Note:* Years are fiscal years. The transition quarter between FY76 and FY77 is not included.

[a]Security assistance includes all military assistance programs and the ESF.

[b]Excludes Israel and Egypt.

## Appendix Table 2.8    Loans, Grants, and Repayments of U.S. Bilateral Foreign Assistance, 1946–87 ($ millions)

| 1988 GNP Rank | Country | Total Loans and Grants | Total Loans | Principal Repayments |
|---|---|---|---|---|
| 1 | Ethiopia | 859.6 | 179.3 | 84.0 |
| 2 | Bhutan | 4.7 | 0.0 | 0.0 |
| 3 | Burkina Faso | 280.3 | 0.0 | 0.0 |
| 4 | Nepal | 394.3 | 2.9 | 2.0 |
| 5 | Bangladesh | 2496.5 | 984.3 | 68.0 |
| 6 | Malawi | 183.3 | 36.4 | 5.0 |
| 7 | Zaire | 1224.5 | 590.8 | 102.0 |
| 8 | Mali | 308.5 | 6.4 | 1.0 |
| 9 | Burma | 322.6 | 57.2 | 36.0 |
| 10 | Mozambique | 210.7 | 49.2 | 0.0 |

## Appendix Table 2.8    Loans, Grants, and Repayments of U.S. Bilateral Foreign Assistance, 1946–87 ($ millions) (Cont.)

| 1988 GNP Rank | Country | Total Loans and Grants | Total Loans | Principal Repayments |
|---|---|---|---|---|
| 11 | Madagascar | 119.5 | 60.3 | 3.0 |
| 12 | Uganda | 120.5 | 12.0 | 3.0 |
| 13 | Burundi | 68.6 | 0.0 | 0.0 |
| 14 | Tanzania | 466.2 | 140.4 | 10.0 |
| 15 | Togo | 118.1 | 0.0 | 0.0 |
| 16 | Niger | 341.4 | 9.0 | 4.0 |
| 17 | Benin (Dahomey) | 71.3 | 23.0 | 1.0 |
| 18 | Somalia | 874.4 | 233.9 | 57.0 |
| 19 | Central African Republic | 40.5 | 0.0 | 0.0 |
| 20 | India | 11230.9 | 7211.8 | 4042.0 |
| 21 | Rwanda | 117.3 | 1.5 | 2.0 |
| 22 | China | 2.3 | 0.0 | 0.0 |
| 23 | Kenya | 964.6 | 395.2 | 180.0 |
| 24 | Zambia | 431.6 | 282.0 | 23.0 |
| 25 | Sierra Leone | 153.5 | 40.4 | 4.0 |
| 26 | Sudan | 1702.1 | 510.9 | 77.0 |
| 27 | Haiti | 640.7 | 112.3 | 9.0 |
| 28 | Pakistan | 8913.6 | 5240.0 | 1658.0 |
| 29 | Lesotho | 224.1 | 0.0 | 0.0 |
| 30 | Ghana | 508.4 | 275.6 | 94.0 |
| 31 | Sri Lanka | 974.0 | 721.8 | 79.0 |
| 32 | Mauritania | 151.7 | 1.4 | 1.0 |
| 33 | Senegal | 468.5 | 28.9 | 1.0 |
| 34 | Afghanistan | 556.5 | 116.3 | 25.0 |
| 35 | Chad | 182.6 | 0.0 | 0.0 |
| 36 | Guinea | 250.3 | 140.2 | 30.0 |
| 37 | Kampuchea | 2196.5 | 289.3 | 79.0 |
| 38 | Laos | 2510.8 | * | 0.0 |
| 39 | Vietnam | 23360.6 | 563.4 | 459.0 |
| 40 | Liberia | 816.9 | 242.3 | 46.0 |
| 41 | South Yemen | 4.5 | 0.0 | 0.0 |
| 42 | Indonesia | 4116.8 | 2958.8 | 883.0 |
| 43 | North Yemen | 384.5 | 60.4 | 15.0 |
| 44 | Philippines | 4760.8 | 1064.4 | 560.0 |
| 45 | Morocco | 2238.9 | 1296.5 | 528.0 |
| 46 | Bolivia | 1146.3 | 480.2 | 125.0 |
| 47 | Zimbabwe | 313.1 | 12.3 | 0.0 |
| 48 | Nigeria | 431.5 | 83.9 | 22.0 |
| 49 | Dominican Republic | 1313.2 | 716.0 | 155.0 |
| 50 | Papua New Guinea | 5.6 | 0.0 | 0.0 |
| 51 | Ivory Coast | 53.4 | 14.6 | 8.0 |
| 52 | Honduras | 1579.4 | 491.7 | 89.0 |
| 53 | Egypt | 23131.4 | 10139.4 | 5157.0 |
| 54 | Nicaragua | 412.3 | 257.0 | 33.0 |
| 55 | Thailand | 3223.0 | 844.0 | 637.0 |
| 56 | El Salvador | 3017.7 | 721.2 | 143.0 |
| 57 | Botswana | 280.0 | 41.2 | 19.0 |
| 58 | Jamaica | 1009.7 | 687.0 | 41.0 |
| 59 | Cameroon | 289.9 | 111.1 | 29.0 |

## Appendix Table 2.8 Loans, Grants, and Repayments of U.S. Bilateral Foreign Assistance, 1946–87 ($ millions) (Cont.)

| 1988 GNP Rank | Country | Total Loans and Grants | Total Loans | Principal Repayments |
|---|---|---|---|---|
| 60 | Guatemala | 985.3 | 347.8 | 54.0 |
| 61 | Congo | 21.1 | 1.9 | 0 |
| 62 | Paraguay | 235.1 | 87.1 | 47.0 |
| 63 | Peru | 1545.7 | 830.7 | 271.0 |
| 64 | Turkey | 13264.1 | 5563.3 | 3670.0 |
| 65 | Tunisia | 1752.5 | 973.2 | 638.0 |
| 66 | Ecuador | 805.3 | 311.0 | 144.0 |
| 67 | Mauritius | 58.8 | 17.4 | 4.0 |
| 68 | Colombia | 1669.9 | 1092.5 | 506.0 |
| 69 | Chile | 1391.4 | 908.0 | 497.0 |
| 70 | Costa Rica | 1306.8 | 510.1 | 39.0 |
| 71 | Jordan | 3258.0 | 1201.7 | 856.0 |
| 72 | Syria | 357.5 | 274.7 | 34.0 |
| 73 | Lebanon | 604.5 | 276.8 | 267.0 |
| 74 | Brazil | 2837.9 | 1753.0 | 686.0 |
| 75 | Malaysia | 285.5 | 202.4 | 200.0 |
| 76 | South Africa | 32.2 | 1.3 | 1.0 |
| 77 | Mexico | 418.8 | 123.6 | 95.0 |
| 78 | Uruguay | 255.8 | 124.1 | 76.0 |
| 79 | Hungary | 32.7 | 15.9 | 16.0 |
| 80 | Poland | 705.3 | 160.3 | 93.0 |
| 81 | Portugal | 2310.8 | 926.6 | 669.0 |
| 82 | Yugoslavia | 2458.5 | 548.0 | 528.0 |
| 83 | Panama | 640.5 | 285.8 | 82.0 |
| 84 | Argentina | 444.5 | 338.6 | 298.0 |
| 85 | South Korea | 14852.3 | 3852.0 | 2464.0 |
| 86 | Algeria | 203.8 | 11.6 | 12.0 |
| 87 | Venezuela | 355.6 | 252.5 | 253.0 |
| 88 | Gabon | 39.6 | 15.2 | 15.0 |
| 89 | Greece | 8053.8 | 3850.8 | 3760.0 |
| 90 | Oman | 308.2 | 268.6 | 199.0 |
| 91 | Trinidad and Tobago | 41.1 | 0 | 0 |
| 92 | Israel | 37854.6 | 13214.1 | 11395.0 |
| 93 | Hong Kong | 43.8 | 0 | 0 |
| 94 | Singapore | 22.2 | 17.2 | 17.0 |
| 95 | Iran | 2166.8 | 794.2 | 727.0 |
| 96 | Iraq | 95.5 | 14.4 | 15.0 |
| 97 | Romania | 22.4 | 0 | 0 |
| 98 | Saudia Arabia | 324.2 | 258.5 | 258.0 |
| 99 | Libya | 230.1 | 7.0 | 7.0 |
| 100 | Spain | 4517.5 | 2695.5 | 2242.0 |
| 101 | Ireland | 212.6 | 109.3 | 109.0 |
| 102 | New Zealand | 8.6 | 5.8 | 5.0 |
| 103 | Italy | 5966.1 | 401.4 | 401.0 |
| 104 | United Kingdom | 8779.6 | 4213.3 | 2456.0 |
| 105 | Belgium/ Luxembourg | 1864.3 | 103.6 | 104.0 |
| 106 | Austria | 1257.2 | 52.9 | 40 0 |
| 107 | Netherlands | 2312.3 | 188.8 | 189.0 |
| 108 | France | 8465.7 | 705.9 | 705.0 |

## Appendix Table 2.8   Loans, Grants, and Repayments of U.S. Bilateral Foreign Assistance, 1946–87 ($ millions) (Cont.)

| 1988 GNP Rank | Country | Total Loans and Grants | Total Loans | Principal Repayments |
|---|---|---|---|---|
| 109 | Australia | 123.6 | 123.4 | 124.0 |
| 110 | West Germany | 4782.9 | 1036.2 | 1036.0 |
| 111 | Finland | 51.8 | 47.2 | 39.0 |
| 112 | Denmark | 916.6 | 28.9 | 29.0 |
| 113 | Japan | 3925.9 | 939.4 | 940.0 |
| 114 | Sweden | 109.0 | 22.0 | 22.0 |
| 115 | Canada | 30.5 | 17.5 | 18.0 |
| 116 | Norway | 1243.8 | 61.5 | 61.0 |

**FOREIGN ASSISTANCE PROVIDED BUT NO GNP FIGURES WERE AVAILABLE FOR FOLLOWING COUNTRIES**

| | | | | |
|---|---|---|---|---|
| | Albania | 20.4 | 0 | 0 |
| | Angola | 29.8 | 0 | 0 |
| | Bahamas | 0.4 | 0 | 0 |
| | Bahrain | 2.4 | 0 | 0 |
| | Barbados | 4.1 | 0 | 0 |
| | Belize | 88.7 | 26.5 | 0 |
| | Cape Verde | 75.1 | 0 | 0 |
| | Centro | 39.6 | 0 | 0 |
| | Comoros | 6.8 | 0 | 0 |
| | Cuba | 20.1 | 0 | 0 |
| | Cyprus | 252.2 | 0.8 | 1.0 |
| | Czechoslovakia | 193.0 | 7.6 | 3.0 |
| | Djibouti | 42.0 | 0 | 0 |
| | Entente States | 42.0 | 37.4 | 1.0 |
| | Equatorial Guinea | 10.8 | 0 | 0 |
| | Gambia, The | 77.5 | 0 | 0 |
| | East Germany | 0.8 | 0 | 0 |
| | Grenada | 60.0 | 0 | 0 |
| | Guinea–Bissau | 41.4 | 0 | 0 |
| | Guyana | 117.2 | 79.9 | 6.0 |
| | Iceland | 77.1 | 41.2 | 41.0 |
| | Indochina Associate States | 1557.1 | 0 | 0 |
| | Maldive Islands | 7.3 | 7.2 | 0 |
| | Malta | 84.4 | 5.0 | 0 |
| | Pacific Islands | 824.2 | 0.9 | 1.0 |
| | Portuguese Africa Territories | 3.4 | 0 | 0 |
| | Ryukyu Islands | 413.7 | 19.1 | 16.0 |
| | Sao Tome and Principe | 5.6 | 0 | 0 |
| | Seychelles | 19.7 | 0 | 0 |
| | Suriname | 6.6 | 1.0 | 1.0 |
| | Swaziland | 112.2 | 11.8 | 0 |
| | Taiwan | 6572.1 | 948.8 | 812.0 |
| | USSR | 186.4 | 0 | 0 |
| | West Berlin | 131.9 | 0 | 0 |
| | Western Samoa | 16.8 | 0 | 0 |

**Regional Spending**

| | | | | |
|---|---|---|---|---|
| | Middle East and South Asia | 657.6 | 0 | 0 |
| | Latin America | 923.0 | 20.0 | 1.0 |
| | ROCAP (Regional Office Central America and Panama) | 572.6 | 291.4 | 76.0 |

### Appendix Table 2.8   Loans, Grants, and Repayments of U.S. Bilateral Foreign Assistance, 1946–87 ($ millions) (Cont.)

| Country | Total Loans and Grants | Total Loans | Principal Repayments |
|---|---|---|---|
| West Indies and Eastern Caribbean | 582.7 | 193.9 | 5.0 |
| Asia | 573.0 | 4.5 | 0 |
| Africa | 851.7 | 3.3 | 1.0 |
| Sahel | 260.6 | 0 | 0 |
| Regional (East Africa) | 33.3 | 2.6 | 2.0 |
| Regional (South Africa) | 179.5 | 17.3 | 0 |
| Europe | 618.3 | 169.8 | 169.0 |
| Oceania | 109.4 | 1.8 | 0 |
| Interregional Spending | 51593.3 | 303.7 | 187.0 |
| TOTAL COUNTRIES AND REGIONS | 327,533 | 90,918 | 54,365 |

*Source:* USAID, *U.S. Overseas Loans and Grants* (Washington, D.C.: 1987); World Bank, *World Development Report 1988.*

*Note:* In this source, financial assistance for Luxembourg is combined with that for Belgium, GNP rank 105.       *Less than $50,000

### Appendix Table 2.9   Private Voluntary Contributions from 18 DAC Nations, 1975 and 1985 (constant 1985 dollars)

| Nation | Total Contribution ($ millions) | | Average Contribution Per Capita | |
|---|---|---|---|---|
| | 1975 | 1985 | 1975 | 1985 |
| Norway | 16 | 52 | 3.90 | 12.54 |
| Sweden | 57 | 78 | 6.98 | 9.34 |
| Switzerland | 47 | 54 | 7.39 | 8.27 |
| West Germany | 303 | 424 | 4.89 | 6.95 |
| Netherlands | 35 | 98 | 2.54 | 6.77 |
| Canada | 98 | 171 | 4.30 | 6.74 |
| United States | 1,186 | 1,513 | 5.55 | 6.32 |
| Ireland | NA | 22 | NA | 6.18 |
| Australia | 50 | 52 | 3.62 | 3.30 |
| Denmark | 9 | 16 | 1.81 | 3.13 |
| United Kingdom | 79 | 169 | 1.40 | 2.98 |
| Finland | 3 | 13 | 0.69 | 2.65 |
| New Zealand | 9 | 8 | 3.06 | 2.46 |
| Austria | 16 | 18 | 2.17 | 2.38 |
| France | 22 | 65 | 0.43 | 1.18 |
| Japan | 15 | 101 | 0.13 | 0.84 |
| Belgium | –30 | 4 | –3.01 | 0.41 |
| Italy | 4 | 8 | 0.08 | 0.14 |
| DAC Total | 1,919 | 2,866 | 2.95 | 4.13 |

*Sources:* Adapted from John W. Sewell, Stuart K. Tucker, et al., *Growth, Exports, and Jobs in a Changing World Economy; Agenda 1988,* Overseas Development Council (New Brunswick, N.J.: Transaction Books, 1988).

## Appendix Table 2.10    USAID Program and Budget Process

Some steps in this process:

■ At regular intervals, each in-country mission drafts a Country Development Strategy Statement (CDSS), which analyzes the country's economic situation and development programs, and describes USAID goals and strategy.

■ In the *Annual Budget Submission* (ABS), the mission lists projects in order of priority, with funding required, and includes descriptions of proposed new projects.

■ USAID regional and central bureaus review the ABS and recommend bureau programs and levels to the Bureau for Program and Policy Coordination (PPC).

■ PPC drafts a proposed USAID program and funding levels.

■ The USAID administrator decides differences between PPC and bureaus.

■ The State Department reviews USAID program and funding levels.

■ State and USAID submit their views (if different) to the Office of Management and Budget (OMB) in the White House.

■ OMB reviews USAID program and funding levels.

■ The president submits the budget for the entire U.S. government to Congress.

■ USAID submits a justification (Congressional Presentation) of its program and budget to Congress, and testifies in hearings.

■ EITHER Congress passes a bill that determines the amount of funds available for obligation in the budget year,
       OR

■ Congress fails to complete action and passes a "continuing resolution" allowing for funding of existing (but no new) programs at the previous year's level.

About 16 months will have elapsed from the time a mission includes a proposed project in an ABS to the beginning of the initial year for which Congress has approved funding. Typically, several months of consultation between the mission and the government of the country where it is working will precede preparation of the ABS.

Note that new projects originate as proposals from USAID in-country missions (unless they are worldwide or regional in scope), and their final approval depends on their consistency with the program approved by Congress.

Following project approval, USAID solicits proposals for carrying out the project. USAID and the host nation select the contractor and negotiate an agreement, and implementation begins.

*Source:* John C. Rothberg, "U.S. Foreign Assistance, A.I.D. and BIFAD—An Introduction," BIFAD Staff Paper, 1984 (Mimeographed), 12–13.

## Appendix Table 3.1   Major Primary Commodity Exports of Developing Countries, 1981–83

Developing Country Exports

| | ($ bil) | % of world exports of commodity | Major Developing Country Suppliers, (1981–83) (Percentage of world exports of commodity) |
|---|---|---|---|
| Petroleum | 216.5 | 81.0 | Saudia Arabia 27, Mexico 6, United Arab Emirates 6, Iran 6 |
| Sugar | 8.5 | 69.1 | Cuba 37, Brazil 6, Philippines 4, Thailand 4 |
| Coffee | 8.3 | 91.6 | Brazil 20, Colombia 16, Ivory Coast 5, El Salvador 5 |
| Copper | 5.1 | 63.8 | Chile 22, Zambia 12, Zaire 7, Peru 5 |
| Timber | 4.6 | 27.8 | Malaysia 11, Indonesia 4, Ivory Coast 2, Philippines 2 |
| Iron Ore | 3.2 | 46.8 | Brazil 25, India 5, Liberia 4, Venezuela 3 |
| Rubber | 3.0 | 98.3 | Malaysia 47, Indonesia 25, Thailand 15, Sri Lanka 4 |
| Cotton | 2.9 | 43.4 | Egypt 7, Pakistan 6, Turkey 4, Mexico 3 |
| Rice | 2.5 | 55.0 | Thailand 23, Pakistan 9, China 6, India 5 |
| Tobacco | 2.3 | 51.3 | Brazil 10, Turkey 7, Zimbabwe 6, India 5 |
| Maize | 2.0 | 19.2 | Argentina 9, Thailand 4, Yugoslavia 1, Zimbabwe 1 |
| Tin | 1.9 | 74.7 | Malaysia 29, Indonesia 13, Thailand 13, Bolivia 10 |
| Cocoa | 1.9 | 92.1 | Ivory Coast 26, Ghana 16, Nigeria 12, Brazil 12 |
| Tea | 1.5 | 84.6 | India 27, Sri Lanka 18, China 13, Kenya 9 |
| Palm oil | 1.4 | 81.6 | Malaysia 70, Indonesia 7, Ivory Coast 2, Papua New Guinea 1 |
| Beef | 1.3 | 16.7 | Argentina 5, Uruguay 3, Brazil 2, Yugoslavia 1 |
| Bananas | 1.2 | 86.7 | Costa Rica 17, Honduras 14, Ecuador 14, Colombia 10 |
| Wheat and meslin | 1.2 | 6.9 | Argentina 6, Turkey *, Uruguay *, Yugoslavia * |
| Phosphate rock | 1.1 | 62.9 | Morocco 34, Jordan 9, Togo 5, Senegal 3 |

*Source:* World Bank, *Commodity Trade and Price Trends* (1986 edition), tables 7 and 8, as cited in John W. Sewell, Stuart K. Tucker, et al., *Growth, Exports, and Jobs in a Changing Economy: Agenda 1988,* Overseas Development Council (New Brunswick, N.J.: Transaction Books, 1988), 220.

*Less than 0.5 percent.

## Appendix Table 3.2    U.S. Imports from Developing Countries, by Import Group, 1975–86

| Class of Imports | Total U.S. Imports ($ billions) | | | Developing Countries' Share of U.S. Imports[a] (percentages) | | |
|---|---|---|---|---|---|---|
| | 1975 | 1981 | 1986[b] | 1975 | 1981 | 1986 |
| IMPORTS:[c] | | | | | | |
| Food, feeds, and beverages | 10.5 | 19.7 | 24.2 | 59.0 | 56.5 | 55.5 |
| Fuels | 28.4 | 85.1 | 38.5 | 79.5 | 79.7 | 67.5 |
| Other industrial supplies | 24.1 | 55.6 | 63.4 | 24.6 | 25.4 | 24.5 |
| Capital goods | 10.1 | 35.5 | 76.3 | 18.6 | 24.7 | 25.3 |
| Automotive goods | 12.8 | 31.0 | 78.6 | 2.1 | 3.3 | 7.8 |
| Consumer goods | 14.7 | 40.6 | 78.4 | 43.1 | 51.4 | 54.1 |
| Other | 2.8 | 5.8 | 10.6 | 23.7 | 24.4 | 20.8 |
| **Total** | **103.4** | **273.4** | **370.0** | **42.4** | **45.8** | **33.8** |

*Sources:* Bureau of the Census, *Highlights of U.S. Export and Import Trade* (Washington, D.C.: U.S. GPO, 1975), tables E–7 and I–8C; (1981), tables E–7 and I–13; and (1986), tables B–18 and C–20, as cited in John W. Sewell, Stuart K. Tucker, et al., *Growth, Exports, and Jobs in a Changing World Economy: Agenda 1988,* Overseas Development Council (New Brunswick, N.J.: Transaction Books, 1988), 216.

[a]Israel is included; Oceania, Turkey, Portugal, and developing centrally planned economies in Europe are omitted from developing countries' share; [b]Total imports understated due to discrepancy in published data; [c]Imports are c.i.f. values except for 1986 imports, which are customs values.

## Appendix Table 3.3    U.S. Exports to Developing Countries, by Export Group, 1975–86

| Class of Exports | Total U.S. Exports ($ billions) | | | Developing Countries' Share of U.S. Exports[a] (Percentages) | | |
|---|---|---|---|---|---|---|
| | 1975 | 1981 | 1986[b] | 1975 | 1981 | 1986 |
| EXPORTS:[c] | | | | | | |
| Food, feeds, and beverages | 19.1 | 37.9 | 22.2 | 35.0 | 41.2 | 40.1 |
| Fuels | 4.8 | 10.7 | 8.2 | 15.3 | 19.5 | 30.5 |
| Other industrial supplies | 25.4 | 57.0 | 49.3 | 39.3 | 40.4 | 37.8 |
| Capital goods | 35.4 | 80.2 | 76.6 | 43.0 | 45.1 | 38.2 |
| Automotive goods | 10.1 | 18.0 | 22.1 | 27.4 | 33.7 | 17.7 |
| Consumer goods | 6.5 | 15.8 | 14.1 | 35.6 | 44.3 | 35.6 |
| Other | 6.4 | 14.1 | 20.5 | 53.3 | 42.9 | 22.9 |
| **Total** | **107.7** | **233.7** | **212.9** | **38.2** | **41.1** | **34.2** |

*Sources:* Bureau of the Census, *Highlights of U.S. Export and Import Trade* (Washington, D.C.: U.S. GPO, 1975), tables E–7 and I–8C; (1981), tables E–7 and I–13; and (1986), tables B–18 and C–20, as cited in John W. Sewell, Stuart K. Tucker, et al., *Growth, Exports, and Jobs in a Changing World Economy: Agenda 1988,* Overseas Development Council (New Brunswick, N.J.: Transaction Books, 1988).

[a]Israel is included; Oceania, Turkey, Portugal, and developing centrally planned economies in Europe are omitted from developing countries' share; [b]Total exports understated due to discrepancy in published data; [c]Exports are f.a.s. values.

## Appendix Table 3.4   Ten Largest Developing Country Markets for U.S. Exports, 1975–87

| Country | 1975 U.S. Exports ($ billions) | 1975 Share of U.S. Exports to All Developing Countries (%) | 1984 U.S. Exports ($ billions) | 1984 Share of U.S. Exports to All Developing Countries (%) | 1987 U.S. Exports ($ billions) | 1987 Share of U.S. Exports to All Developing Countries (%) |
|---|---|---|---|---|---|---|
| Mexico | 5.1 | 12.4 | 12.0 | 16.1 | 14.6 | 18.0 |
| South Korea | 1.8 | 4.4 | 6.0 | 8.1 | 8.1 | 10.0 |
| Taiwan | 1.7 | 4.1 | 5.0 | 6.7 | 7.4 | 9.1 |
| Singapore | 1.0 | 2.4 | 3.7 | 5.0 | 4.1 | 5.1 |
| Hong Kong | 0.8 | 1.9 | 3.1 | 4.2 | 4.0 | 4.9 |
| Brazil | 3.1 | 7.5 | 2.6 | 3.5 | 4.0 | 4.9 |
| Venezuela | 2.2 | 5.4 | 3.4 | 4.6 | 3.6 | 4.4 |
| China | 0.3 | 0.7 | 3.0 | 4.0 | 3.5 | 4.3 |
| Saudi Arabia | 1.5 | 3.7 | 5.6 | 7.5 | 3.4 | 4.2 |
| Egypt | — | — | — | — | 2.2 | 2.7 |
| South Africa | 1.3 | 3.2 | 2.2 | 2.9 | — | — |
| **Total (10 countries)** | **18.8** | **45.7** | **46.6** | **62.6** | **54.9** | **67.6** |
| **Total U.S. Exports** | **107.7** | | **217.9**[a] | | **252.9** | |
| All Developing Countries | 41.1 | | 74.4 | | 81.2 | |
| (% of total exports) | | 38.2 | | 34.1 | | 32.1 |
| Developed Countries[b] | 66.9 | | 143.6 | | 165.4 | |
| (% of total exports) | | 62.1 | | 65.9 | | 65.4 |

*Sources:* Overseas Development Council table based on Bureau of the Census, *Highlights of U.S. Export and Import Trade* (Washington, D.C.: U.S. GPO 1975), table E–3 and (1981), table E–3, as cited in John P. Lewis and Valeriana Kallab, eds., *U.S. Foreign Policy and the Third World: Agenda 1983* (Washington, D.C.: Overseas Development Council, 1983), 179; Bureau of the Census, *Highlights of U.S. Export and Import Trade,* Rept. FT990/December 1984 (Washington, D.C.: U.S. GPO, 1985), table B–5, as cited in John W. Sewell, Stuart K. Tucker, et al., *Growth, Exports, and Jobs in a Changing World Economy: Agenda 1988,* Overseas Development Council (New Brunswick, N.J.: Transaction Books, 1988).

*Notes:* Countries are ranked according to 1987 percentage shares of U.S. exports to developing countries. Data include developing, centrally planned economies. Total U.S. export figures include trade with unidentified countries. All figures are f.a.s. (free alongside ship) transaction values.

[a]Includes Communist areas in Europe and Asia.

[b]Does not include Communist areas in Europe and Asia.

## Appendix Table 3.5   U.S. Trade with "Very Poor" and "Poor" Countries, 1987* ($ millions)

| | Very Poor | | | | Poor | | |
|---|---|---|---|---|---|---|---|
| Country | Total Transactions | Exports | Imports | Country | Total Transactions | Exports | Imports |
| China | 10,407.8 | 3,497.3 | 6,910.5 | Indonesia | 4,486.3 | 767.3 | 3,719.0 |
| India | 4,188.8 | 1,463.4 | 2,725.4 | Nigeria | 4,061.8 | 295.1 | 3,766.7 |
| Pakistan | 1,171.4 | 733.2 | 438.2 | Thailand | 3,931.5 | 1,544.4 | 2,387.1 |
| Haiti | 869.1 | 459.0 | 410.1 | Philippines | 3,844.4 | 1,363.3 | 2,481.1 |
| Bangladesh | 612.3 | 193.1 | 419.2 | Colombia | 3,825.9 | 1,411.5 | 2,414.4 |
| Sri Lanka | 541.0 | 77.2 | 463.8 | Egypt | 2,706.6 | 2,210.3 | 496.3 |
| Zaire | 424.3 | 103.5 | 320.8 | Turkey | 2,379.6 | 1,482.5 | 897.1 |
| Ghana | 374.2 | 114.6 | 259.6 | Dominican Rep. | 2,359.2 | 1,142.2 | 1,217.0 |
| Ethiopia | 214.3 | 136.4 | 77.9 | Ecuador | 2,011.0 | 620.7 | 1,390.3 |
| Sudan | 175.4 | 152.2 | 23.2 | Chile | 1,900.7 | 796.2 | 1,104.5 |
| Kenya | 160.2 | 75.0 | 85.2 | Peru | 1,628.8 | 814.1 | 814.7 |
| Guinea | 156.1 | 35.3 | 120.8 | Costa Rica | 1,331.3 | 581.2 | 750.1 |
| Uganda | 104.1 | 18.7 | 85.4 | Jamaica | 1,023.8 | 601.4 | 422.4 |
| Zambia | 98.8 | 47.5 | 51.3 | Guatemala | 1,022.2 | 480.3 | 541.9 |
| Nepal | 94.2 | 56.6 | 37.6 | Honduras | 982.5 | 417.8 | 564.7 |
| Madagascar | 91.4 | 18.3 | 73.1 | El Salvador | 689.9 | 389.8 | 300.1 |
| Mozambique | 80.4 | 50.3 | 30.1 | Cameroon | 490.1 | 47.2 | 442.9 |
| Senegal | 56.6 | 49.2 | 7.4 | Ivory Coast | 486.7 | 82.2 | 404.5 |
| Tanzania | 49.1 | 34.8 | 14.3 | Congo | 466.0 | 9.3 | 456.7 |
| Somalia | 47.4 | 43.2 | 4.2 | Morocco | 437.0 | 382.8 | 54.2 |
| Sierra Leone | 47.4 | 26.3 | 21.1 | Jordan | 376.5 | 365.0 | 11.5 |
| Mauritania | 46.1 | 26.1 | 20.0 | Bolivia | 253.6 | 140.3 | 113.3 |
| Togo | 45.5 | 19.6 | 25.9 | Paraguay | 207.1 | 183.2 | 23.9 |
| Benin (Dahomey) | 33.8 | 18.0 | 15.8 | Tunisia | 192.0 | 119.2 | 72.8 |
| Malawi | 32.0 | 4.9 | 27.1 | Mauritius | 180.0 | 26.1 | 153.9 |
| Burma | 20.4 | 7.8 | 12.6 | Liberia | 170.6 | 70.1 | 100.5 |
| Rwanda | 16.0 | 4.3 | 11.7 | Syria | 159.6 | 93.2 | 66.4 |
| Mali | 15.1 | 10.2 | 4.9 | Zimbabwe | 149.9 | 75.4 | 74.5 |
| Chad | 14.1 | 14.1 | 0.0 | Lebanon | 130.9 | 96.6 | 34.3 |
| Lesotho | 12.2 | 6.9 | 5.3 | North Yemen | 121.0 | 116.5 | 4.5 |
| Niger | 11.2 | 3.7 | 7.5 | Papua New Guinea | 74.9 | 50.9 | 24.0 |
| Burkina Faso | 10.7 | 10.3 | 0.4 | Botswana | 36.0 | 28.9 | 7.1 |
| Burundi | 6.7 | 1.7 | 5.0 | South Yemen | 15.8 | 14.4 | 1.4 |
| Cen. African Rep. | 6.6 | 1.7 | 4.9 | Nicaragua | 4.8 | 3.5 | 1.3 |
| Laos | 1.4 | 0.3 | 1.1 | | | | |
| Total Very Poor Countries | 20,236.1 | 7,514.7 | 12,721.4 | Total Poor Countries | 42,138.0 | 16,822.9 | 25,315.1 |
| TOTAL U.S. | 676,948.1 | 252,865.8 | 424,082.3 | TOTAL U.S. | 676,948.1 | 252,865.8 | 424,082.3 |
| Proportion Very Poor Countries (percent) | 3.0 | 3.0 | 3.0 | Proportion Poor Countries (percent) | 6.2 | 6.7 | 6.0 |

*Source:* Bureau of the Census, *Highlights of U.S. Export and Import Trade* (Washington, D.C.: U.S. GPO, 1988), tables B–22 and C–26.

*"Very Poor" and "Poor" countries are defined according to figures on appendix table 1.1: those classified as very poor have 1986 per capita GNPs of up to $460; those classified as poor have 1986 per capita GNPs of $460–1,600.

## Appendix Table 3.6 U.S. World Market Share for Selected Cereal Crops for Various Years (by percent)

| Crop | 1969–71 Market Share | 1981–82 Market Share | 1986–87 Market Share |
|---|---|---|---|
| Wheat | 53 | 59 | 31 |
| Coarse grains | 76 | 74 | 57 |
| Soybeans | 73 | 71 | 47 |
| Cotton | 22 | 32 | 29 |
| Rice | 17 | 21 | 18 |

*Source:* Larry Lev, Michael T. Weber, and H.C. Bittenbender, *Michigan Agriculture and Its Linkages to Developing Nations* (East Lansing: Institute of International Agriculture, Michigan State University, March 1984), 38; USDA, *1988 Agricultural Chartbook*, Handbook no. 673, 14–19.

## Appendix Table 3.7 Value of U.S. Agricultural Exports, 1975–87

| Year | Total Value ($bil) | To Developing Countries ($bil) | Share to Developing Countries (percent) | To Centrally Planned Countries ($bil) | Share to Centrally Planned Countries (percent) | To More Developed Countries ($bil) | Share To More Developed Countries (percent) |
|---|---|---|---|---|---|---|---|
| 1975 | 21.9 | 7.5 | 34.3 | 1.8 | 8.2 | 12.6 | 57.5 |
| 1976 | 23.0 | 6.8 | 29.6 | 2.4 | 10.4 | 13.8 | 60.0 |
| 1977 | 23.6 | 7.4 | 31.4 | 1.7 | 7.2 | 14.5 | 61.4 |
| 1978 | 29.4 | 9.7 | 33.0 | 3.4 | 11.6 | 16.3 | 55.4 |
| 1979 | 34.7 | 10.8 | 31.1 | 5.8 | 16.7 | 18.1 | 52.2 |
| 1980 | 41.2 | 14.6 | 35.4 | 5.4 | 13.1 | 21.2 | 51.5 |
| 1981 | 43.3 | 16.0 | 37.0 | 5.3 | 12.2 | 22.0 | 50.8 |
| 1982 | 36.6 | 12.9 | 35.2 | 4.2 | 11.5 | 19.5 | 53.3 |
| 1983 | 36.1 | 14.4 | 39.9 | 2.9 | 8.0 | 18.8 | 52.1 |
| 1984 | 37.8 | 15.0 | 39.7 | 4.2 | 11.1 | 18.6 | 49.2 |
| 1985 | 29.0 | 12.0 | 41.4 | 2.6 | 9.0 | 14.4 | 49.6 |
| 1986 | 26.2 | 10.8 | 41.2 | 1.2 | 4.6 | 14.2 | 54.2 |
| 1987* | 28.6 | 11.6 | 40.6 | 1.7 | 5.9 | 15.3 | 53.5 |

*Source:* USDA, Foreign Agriculture Trade of the United States, various issues.

*ERS/USDA, Agricultural and Trade Indicators Branch, March 1989, personal correspondence.